A Glossary of Islamic Terms

Aisha Bewley

Ta-Ha Publishers
1 Wynne Road
London SW9 0BB

Published in Rabi Al-Awwal 1419 AH/July 1998 CE by

Ta-Ha Publishers Ltd.
1 Wynne Road
London SW9 0BB
website: http://www.taha.co.uk/
email: sales@taha.co.uk

Typesetting by Bookwork, Norwich
email: ABewley@compuserve.com

British Library Cataloguing in Publication Data
A catalogue record for this book is available from the British Library.

ISBN 1 897940 72 6 (paper)
ISBN 1 897940 78 5 (case)

Printed and Bound by Deluxe Printers, London.
website: http://www.de-luxe.com
email: printers@de-luxe.com

Table of Contents

بسم الله الرحمن الرحيم

Preface

The inspiration for this book came about largely as the result of the necessity of having to compile glossaries for a number of books. This resulted in the gradual growth of a basic glossary over the course of time. Eventually it seemed sensible to compile a glossary which would be more or less comprehensive. Of course, given the nature of language, a completely comprehensive glossary is impossible, and there will inevitably be some oversights and omissions. If there are some glaring omissions, that is entirely my fault and perhaps could be rectified in future editions, Allah willing.

At the inspired suggestion of Hajj Idris Mears, rather than simply arranging the book as an alphabetical dictionary, I have divided the book into various key topics. This will enable the reader to approach the book in two ways. First there is an alphabetical index at the back of the book by which a particular word can be located, rather in the way one uses a thesaurus. But if someone is interested in a particular field, such as *ḥadīth* or philosophy, then he or she can go straight to that section and find the relevant material all in one place. This will also enable others to have an overall view of the topic and perhaps glimpse the depths of Islamic knowledge. Occasionally a word will be repeated in several sections for this reason. Sometimes, of course, the definition will vary slightly because of a particular usage which pertains to an individual field.

The sections which deal with specific topics also mention some major figures and books related to the topics being dealt with. Again, this is by no means comprehensive, so if the reader finds that some notable individual or book is omitted, that is probably due to my oversight and is by no means intended to denigrate that person or book.

I hope that this will prove useful to all those engaged in studying the vast corpus of Islamic knowledge and perhaps inspire some to look into areas of knowledge which they have not yet had the opportunity to study.

Finally, my thanks are due to Hajj Ahmad Thomson for his help in proofreading the text as well as offering many valuable suggestions.

Aisha Bewley
Spring, 1418/1998

Transliteration

ء = ’		ض = ḍ	
ا = a		ط = ṭ	
ب = b		ظ = ẓ	
ت = t		ع = ‘	
ث = th		غ = gh	
ج = j		ف = f	
ح = ḥ		ق = q	
خ = kh		ك = k	
د = d		ل = l	
ذ = dh		م = m	
ر = r		ن = n	
ز = z		ه = h	
س = s		و = w	
ش = sh		ى = y	
ص = ṣ		ة = t	

short vowels:

ـَ = a

ـِ = i

ـُ = u

General and Historical Terms

It has been related that the Prophet said, may Allah bless him and grant him peace, "Dust be upon the face of the person who does not bless me when I am mentioned in his presence." (Muslim)

Since this is primarily a reference book, it would be impractical to ask Allah's blessings and peace on the Prophet Muḥammad and on his family and Companions every time they are mentioned in the text. Accordingly this general supplication is made here and now: may the blessings and peace of Allah be upon the Prophet Muḥammad and his family and Companions until the Last Day. Amin.

It has been related that the Prophet said, may Allah bless him and grant him peace, "If anyone blesses me in a book or letter, the angels continue to ask forgiveness for him as long as my name is on it." (at-Tabarani)

General Terms

'abā: a sleeveless garment resembling a mantle, open in the front.

Aḍḥa: see *'Īd al-Aḍḥa.*

adhān: the call to prayer.

adīb: littérateur, writer, essayist. It denotes someone who is characterised by *adab*, meaning either someone well-disciplined, or, more frequently, someone skilled in literary accomplishments.

'ahd: covenant, compact, pact or contract. *Dhū 'ahd* denotes someone who has a contract with the Muslims (i.e. a *dhimmī*). *"Wilāya 'ahd"* means succession to the khalifate by virtue of a covenant with the preceding khalif.

ahl: House, family, kin.

Ahl al-Bayt: "the People of the House," the family of the Prophet.

Ahl adh-dhimma: "People of the Pact", protected non-Muslim subjects. (See *dhimma*).

Ahl al-Ḥadīth: a term used to denote the conservative traditionalists, especially at the time of the Mu'tazilite/Ash'arite conflict during the 'Abbasid era.

Ahl al-Kitāb: "the People of the Book", principally the Jews and Christians whose religions are based on the Divine Books revealed to Mūsā and 'Īsā; a term also used to refer to any other group who claim to be following a Book revealed prior to the Qur'ān.

ahl al-ḥall wa'l-'aqd: "the people of loosing and binding," i.e. the *'ulamā'* (scholars), leaders and army commanders who make binding decisions for the community.

Ahl al-Ḥarb: "the people of war", non-Muslims living beyond the Muslim frontier.

Ahl al-Madīna: the people of Madina, particularly the first three generations: the Companions, the Ṭābi'ūn, and the Ṭābi'ū't-Ṭābi'īn.

Ahl aṣ-Ṣūfiyya: the people of *taṣawwuf* or Sufism.

a'imma: the plural of *imām*.

'ajamī: a non-Arab, often in reference to Persians.

'ajwa: an excellent quality of date.

Ākhira: the Next World, what is on the other side of death, the Hereafter, the dimension of existence after this world.

'ālim (plural *'ulamā'*)**:** a man of knowledge, a scholar, especially in the sciences of Islam.

ama: a female slave. Thus the female version of "'Abdullah" is "Amatullāh".

amān: guarantee of safety, safe-conduct.

Āmīn: "Ameen", a compound of verb and noun meaning "Answer our prayer" or "So be it".

amīr: the one who commands, the source of authority in a situation; a military commander.

'amma: common, public, general.

amr (plural *awāmir, umūr*)**:** command, matter, affair.

al-amr bi'l-ma'rūf wa'n-nahy 'an al-munkar: promotion of good and prevention of evil. This is a duty for all Muslims which is prescribed in the Qur'ān.

'anaza: a spear-headed stick, longer than a staff and shorter than a spear. The Prophet used one for a *sutra* in the prayer.

anbiyā': the plural of *nabī.*

'aql: intellect, the faculty of reason.

arak: a tree from which *siwak* (tooth brush) is made.

arḍ: the earth. The opposite is *samāwāt*, "the heavens".

arkān: (the plural of *rukn*), used for the five indispensable pillars of Islam which are: the *shahāda*, the *ṣalāt*, the *zakāt*, the fast of Ramaḍān and the *Ḥajj.*

'Āshūrā': the 10th day of Muḥarram, the first month of the Muslim lunar calendar. It is considered a highly desirable day to fast.

al-Asmā' al-Ḥusnā: the Most Beautiful Names, meaning the Ninety-nine Names of Allah.

'Aṣr: the mid-afternoon prayer. It is also the name of *Sūra* 103 of the Qur'ān.

'aṭā': something which is given; a gift; a soldier's stipend.

'awāmir: certain snakes living in houses which are actually jinn. It is the plural of *'āmir.*

'awra: the private parts, the parts of the person which it is indecent to expose in public. For a man, it is what is between the navel and the knee, and for a free woman, all except the face and hands.

āya(t): a verse of the Qur'ān. It literally means "sign" and also refers to the signs that one sees in Creation. (Sometimes written as *āya*, which is a more faithful representation of the Arabic.) The plural is *āyāt.*

Ayatollah: "Sign of Allah", a honorific title of high-ranking Shi'ite religious authorities.

bādiya: desert or semi-arid environment.

badr (plural *budūr*)**:** the full moon.

Banū'l-Aṣfar: a term used for the Byzantines/Romans. Asfar is meant to be a name for "Rūm" (Roman) or Rum, the son of Esau. Some state that the Roman emperors were called the 'sons of Sufar' and that the Israelites say that this is Sophar, son of Eliphaz son of Esau. It may mean the Edomites.

Banū Isrā'īl: the tribe of Israel, the children or descendants of Israel or Ya'qūb.

baraka: blessing, any good which is bestowed by Allah, and especially that which increases, a subtle beneficient spiritual energy which can flow through things or people.

Barqa: Cyrenaica in modern Libya.

basmala: the expression "In the name of Allah, the All-Merciful, the All-Compassionate".

ba'th: the quickening or bringing the dead back to life at the end of the world. *Ba'th* also means sending forth with a Message.

batūl: ascetic and chaste, detached from worldly things and devoted to Allah. It is a title used for both Fāṭima (the Prophet's daughter) and Maryam.

bay'a: literally it means the striking together of the hands of two contracting parties to ratify a contract; hence the act of swearing allegiance.

Bayram: Turkish name for *'īd.*

Bayt al-Ḥaram: "the Sacred House", the Ka'ba.

bedug: a drum used in Indonesia to call people to the prayer in forested areas where the voice does not carry.

al-Burda: lit. "the Cloak" , meaning the mantle of the Prophet, the name of a popular poem written in praise of the Prophet by al-Būṣirī.

busr: partially ripe dates.

Calendar, Muslim: a lunar calendar whose months are: Muḥarram, Ṣafar, Rabī' al-Awwal, Rabī' ath-Thānī, Jumādā al-Ulā, Jumādā al-Ākhira, Rajab, Sha'bān, Ramaḍān, Shawwāl, Dhū'l-Qa'da, Dhū'l-Ḥijja. The lunar year is approximately eleven days shorter than the solar year.

daff: tambourine.

Dajjāl: the false Messiah whose appearance marks the imminent end of the world. The root in Arabic means "to deceive, cheat, take in".

dakka (sometimes *dikka*)**:** a platform to which a staircase leads in the mosque.

ḍamma: the Arabic vowel *u*.

da'wa: inviting or calling people to worship Allah by following the Messenger of Allah.

Deen: see *Dīn*.

dhabīḥa (plural *dhabā'iḥ*)**:** an animal slaughtered for food.

dhanb (plural *dhunūb*)**:** wrong action, sin.

dhimma: obligation or contract, in particular a treaty of protection for non-Muslims living in Muslim territory.

dhimmī: a non-Muslim living under the protection of Muslim rule on payment of the *jizya*.

Dhū'l-Ḥijja: the twelfth month of the Muslim lunar calendar in which the *Ḥajj* takes place.

dhū maḥram: a male, whom a woman can never marry because of close relationship (e.g. a brother, a father, an uncle etc.); or her own husband.

Dhū'l-Qa'da: the eleventh month of the Muslim lunar calendar.

Dhuhr: see *Ẓuhr*.

Dīn: often written *Deen*, the life-transaction, lit. the debt between two parties, in this usage between the Creator and created. The plural is *adyān*.

du'ā': making supplication to Allah.

dulūk ash-shams: early afternoon, the sun's declining from the meridian.

Ḍuḥa: forenoon, in particular the voluntary morning prayer.

Eid: see *'Īd.*

fājir (plural *fujjār* or *fajara*)**:** a reprobate; someone who behaves immorally or sinfully; someone who disobeys the commands of Allah and commits immoral actions.

Fajr: dawn, daybreak. There is the "false dawn" which rises without spreading out, and the"true dawn" in which the light rises and spreads. It also means the dawn prayer. Among the Mālikīs, it designates the two *sunna rak'ats* before the obligatory *Ṣubḥ* prayer while others use *Fajr* and *Ṣubḥ* interchangeably.

falāḥ: success, prosperity, the lasting attainment of that which one desires.

faqīh (plural *fuqahā'*)**:** a man learned in the knowledge of *fiqh* who by virtue of his knowledge can give a legal judgement.

farḍ (plural *farā'iḍ*)**:** obligatory, an obligatory act of worship or practice of the *Dīn* as defined by the *Sharī'a.*

fatḥa: the Arabic vowel *a.*

Fātiḥa: "the Opener," the first *sūra* of the Qur'an.

fatwā (plural *fatāwā*)**:** an authoritative statement on a point of law.

fez: crimson brimless head-covering worn in the later Ottoman Empire and in some successor-states, outlawed in Turkey by Kemal Atatūrk.

fiqh: the science of the application of the *Sharī'a.* A practitioner or expert in *fiqh* is called a *faqīh.*

Firdaws: Paradise, one of the highest parts of the Garden.

fitna (plural *fitan*)**:** civil strife, sedition, schism, trial, temptation.

Fiṭr: see *'Īd al-Fiṭr.*

fiṭra: the first nature, the natural, primal condition of mankind in harmony with nature.

Follower: see *Ṭābi'ūn.*

furūsiya: excellent horsemanship.

fuṣḥā: classical Arabic; pure, eloquent Arabic.

ghāzī: someone taking part in a *ghazwa* or military expedition against unbelievers.

ghazwa (plural *ghazawāt*)**:** raid, a military expedition, especially a desert raid.

ghulām: a young man, often a slave.

ghusl: full ritual bath.

ḥadd (plural *ḥudūd*)**:** Allah's boundary limits for the lawful and unlawful. The *ḥadd* punishments are specific fixed penalties laid down by Allah for specified crimes.

ḥadīth: reported speech of the Prophet.

ḥadīth qudsī: those words of Allah on the tongue of His Prophet which are not part of the Revelation of the Qur'an.

Ḥajar al-Aswad: the Black Stone in the Ka'ba.

ḥājib: a chamberlain, door-keeper.

Ḥajj: the annual pilgrimage to Makka which is one of the five pillars of Islam.

ḥalāl: lawful in the *Sharī'a.*

ḥalaqa: a circle of people gathered for the purpose of study.

ḥalīf (plural *ḥulafā'*)**:** confederate, ally.

ḥammām: bath-house.

ḥanīf (pl. *hunafâ'*)**:** one who possesses the true religion innately.

al-Ḥanīfīya: the religion of Ibrāhīm, the primordial religion of *tawḥīd* and sincerity to Allah.

ḥanūt: an aromatic compound of camphor, reed perfume and red and white sandalwood used for perfuming shrouds.

ḥarām: unlawful in the *Sharī'a.*

ḥarba: a short spear, javelin.

ḥarīm: the harem, something forbidden to those who do not have permission to enter, particularly women's apartments; it is also used to denote parts of land withdrawn from cultivation because they are needed to gain access to other land or property.

ḥasanāt: good deeds, acts of obedience to Allah. The opposite is *sayyi'āt*. The singular is *ḥasana.*

ḥāshiya: gloss, supercommentary on a text. *Ḥāshiya* means "margin", and this commentary was written in the margins of a book.

Ḥawḍ: the watering-place or Basin of the Prophet in the Next World, whose drink will refresh those who have crossed the *Sirāṭ* before entering the Garden.

ḥays: dates mixed with butter, sometimes with *sawīq* added.

hidāya: guidance.

hijā': satire.

ḥijāb: a partition which separates two things; a curtain; in modern times used to describe a form of women's dress.

Ḥijāz: the region along the western seaboard of Arabia in which Makka, Madina, Jeddah and Ta'if are situated.

Hijra: emigration in the way of Allah. Islamic dating begins with the *Hijra* of the Prophet Muḥammad from Makka to Madina in 622 CE.

hilāl: new moon; crescent moon.

ḥilm: forbearance, self-restraint.

ḥizb: a part of people; a set portion of the Qur'ān for recitation; a sixtieth of the Qur'ān.

hudā: guidance.

ḥudūd: the plural of *ḥadd.*

ḥunafā': the plural of *ḥanīf.*

ḥurr: free.

ḥurriya: freedom.

ḥurūf: letters (singular *ḥarf*).

'ibāda: act of worship.

Iblīs: the personal name of the Devil. He is also called Shayṭān or the "enemy of Allah".

ibn as-sabīl: traveller, wayfarer. It literally means "son of the road".

'Īd al-Aḍḥa: the *Ḥajj* festival which takes places on the 10th of the month of Dhū'l-Ḥijja.

'Īd al-Fiṭr: the festival at the end of the fast of Ramaḍān on the 1st of the month of Shawwāl.

idhkhīr: a kind of sweet rush well-known for its good smell and found in the Ḥijāz.

idhn: permission.

'ifrīt: a powerful sort of jinn; a demon or imp.

ifṭār: breaking the fast.

iḥsān: absolute sincerity to Allah in oneself: it is to worship Allah as though you were seeing Him because He sees you.

ijāza: a certification, by a teacher that a particular student was qualified to teach a particular subject or to transmit a specific book or collection of traditions.

ijmā‘: consensus, particularly the consensus of the people of knowledge among the Muslims on matters of *fiqh*.

ijtihād: to struggle, to exercise personal judgement in legal matters.

ikhlāṣ: sincerity, pure unadulterated genuineness.

ikhwa: brothers. The singular is *akh*. Another plural which is often used is *ikhwān*.

Imām: (1) Muslim religious or political leader; (2) one of the succession of Muslim leaders, beginning with ‘Alī, regarded as legitimate by the Shi‘a; (3) leader of Muslim congregational worship. The plural is *a'imma*.

‘imāma (plural *‘amā'im*)**:** turban.

īmān: belief, faith, acceptance of Allah and His Messenger. Belief consists of believing in Allah, His angels, His Books, His Messengers, the Last Day, the Garden and the Fire, and that everything, both good and bad, is by the decree of Allah.

‘Ishā': the night prayer.

Iskandar: Alexander the Great.

Islām: submission to the will of Allah, the way of life embodied by all the Prophets, given its final form in the guidance brought by the Prophet Muḥammad, may Allah bless him and grant him peace. The five pillars of Islam are: the affirmation of the *shahāda*, performing the prayer or *ṣalāt*, paying the *zakāt*, fasting the month of Ramaḍān, and performing the *Ḥajj* once in a lifetime if you are able to do so.

Isrā': the Night Journey of the Prophet to Jerusalem, which took place on 27 Rajab.

istikhāra: a prayer performed by someone who has not made up his mind in the hopes of being inspired to make a wise decision.

izār: a piece of cloth used as a waist-wrapper both by men and women.

jabarīya: "compulsion", tyranny.

jadīdī: modern, modernist.

Jahannam: Hell.

Jāhilīya: the Time of Ignorance before the coming of Islam.

Jaḥīm: Hellfire.

jalbāb: a long loose fitting garment worn by the Arabs.

jalīs (plural *julasā'*)**:** a companion with whom one sits.

jamā'a: the main body of the Muslim Community; also designates the group prayer.

jāmi' (plural *jawāmi'*)**:** Friday mosque, a mosque where *Jumu'a* is held; sometimes used for any mosque.

janāza: also written as *jināza*: the dead person, the funeral bier; the funeral prayer.

Janna: the Garden, Paradise.

jāriya: female slave.

jawāmi' al-kalim: It is said of the Prophet that he spoke *"jawāmi' al-kalim"*, meaning comprehensive but concise language, language which conveys many meanings in few words.

Jibrīl: or Jibrā'īl, the angel Gabriel who brought the revelation of the Qur'ān to the Prophet Muḥammad, may Allah bless him and grant him peace.

jihād: struggle, particularly fighting in the way of Allah to establish Islam.

jinn: inhabitants of the heavens and the earth made of smokeless fire who are usually invisible.

jizya: a protection tax payable by non-Muslims as a tribute to a Muslim ruler, traditionally 4 dinars or 40 dirhams per year.

jubba: a cloak.

julasā': colleagues. The singular is *jalīs*.

Jumādā al-Ākhira: the sixth month of the Muslim lunar calendar.

Jumādā al-Ulā: the fifth month of the Muslim lunar calendar.

Jumu'a: the day of gathering, Friday, and particularly the *Jumu'a* prayer which is performed instead of *Ẓuhr* by those who attend it. Friday only acquired this name with the coming of Islam. Before that it was known as *al-'Arūba*.

jund: army, band, group, wing of the army. It also denotes a military district. For instance, the five districts or *ajnād* of Greater Syria were Damascus, Ḥims, Qinnasrīn, Jordan, and Palestine.

kāfir (plural *kāfirūn* or *kuffār*)**:** a person who rejects Allah and His Messenger. The opposite is believer or *mu'min.*

kalīma: literally the "word" = the *shahāda.*

kasra: the Arabic vowel *i.*

katm: a plant used for dyeing hair.

khalif: (the Arabic is *khalīfa,* plural *khulafā'*); Caliph. Someone who stands in for someone else, in this case the leader of the Muslim community, although it is sometimes used for the deputy of someone in a higher position of authority.

khalūq: a kind of thick yellowy perfume used by women.

khamīṣa: A black woollen square blanket with borders at each end.

khamr: wine; and by extension any intoxicant which affects a person's faculty of thought and his ability to perform the prayer properly.

khāṣṣa: special, elite, private; closest friends.

khaṭīb: a speaker or orator; the one who delivers the *khuṭba.*

khāzin (plural *khazana*)**:** a treasurer, storekeeper, guard.

al-Khiḍr: or al-Khāḍir, "the green one," whose journey with Mūsā is mentioned in the Qur'ān 18:60-82. He may or may not be a Prophet, and appears often to people.

khil'a: robe of honour which is bestowed.

khilāfa: the caliphate or khalifate, governance by means of a khalif.

khimār: a veil or *yashmaq* which covers the head and lower part of the face but leaves the eyes exposed.

khuff: leather socks.

khumra: a small mat just sufficient for the face and the hands (on prostrating during prayers).

khums: the fifth taken from the booty which is given to the ruler for distribution.

khusūf: lunar eclipse.

khuṭba: a speech, and in particular a standing speech given by the Imam before the *Jumu'a* prayer and after the two *'Īd* prayers.

kināya: an allusive form of speech which does not clearly disclose the speaker's intention.

kiswa: the huge embroidered black and gold cloth that drapes the Ka'ba.

Kitāb: book, particularly the Book of Allah, the Qur'ān.

kitābī: Jew or Christian, one of the People of the Book.

kitmān: concealment of information.

kuḥl: kohl, antimony powder used both as decoration and a medicine for the eyes.

kuffār: plural of *kāfir*.

kūfiya: white or colored headcloth worn by men in Arabia and parts of the Fertile Crescent.

kufr: disbelief, to cover up the truth, to reject Allah and refuse to believe that Muḥammad is His Messenger.

kunya: a respectful but intimate way of addressing people as "the father of so-and-so" or "the mother of so-and-so."

kusūf: solar eclipse.

laḥd: a grave, about five feet deep in which a niche is dug for the body into the side facing *qibla* so that the body is protected by the overhang.

lawḥ: board, slate, wooden tablet used for writing, especially in schools.

Al-Lawḥ al-Maḥfūẓ: the Preserved Tablet in the Unseen which is also referred to as the *Umm al-Kitāb*, the place of recording what will be; the repository of Destiny.

Laylat al-Barā'a: the night preceding the 15th of Sha'bān (and hence also *Niṣf Sha'bān* or Middle of Sha'bān), the Night of Quittancy, also called *Shabi Barāt* in India and Iran. In a *ḥadīth*, it says that Allah descends to the lowest heaven on that night and calls on people to grant them forgiveness.

madhhab: a school of law founded on the opinion of a *faqīh*. The four main schools now are Ḥanafi, Mālikī, Shāfi'ī and Ḥanbalī. There are also *madhhabs* which have ceased to exist: the Awzā'ī, Ẓāhirī, Jarīrī (from Ibn Jarīr aṭ-Ṭabarī) and the *madhhab* of Sufyān ath-Thawrī. The Shi'a also designate their *fiqh* as the Imāmī or 'Ja'farī *madhhab'* after Ja'far aṣ-Ṣādiq. Among the Shi'a, there are also the Akḥbarīs and the Uṣūlīs.

madrasa (plural *madāris*)**:** a traditional place of study and learning.

maghfira: forgiveness.

Maghrib: the sunset prayer. The Maghrib also designates the Muslim territories in the northwest of Africa and is the Arabic name for Morocco.

maḥkama: court of justice, tribunal.

maḥram: a male relative with whom marriage is forbidden. (See *dhū maḥram*).

mā'ida: table; the name of *Sūra* 5 of the Qur'ān.

majlis (plural *majālis*)**:** sitting, session, gathering of notables in a Bedouin tent, audience of a shaykh, assembly, ruling council, parliament.

makrūh: abominable, reprehensible but not unlawful in the *Sharī'a*.

malā': council, senate.

malik: king.

manāqib: virtues, glorious deeds, feats; a type of biography.

manāra: minaret.

mandūb: commendable, recommended.

maqṣūra: a stall or compartment erected in the mosque for the ruler, usually near the *miḥrāb*.

māristān: hospital.

marthiya: elegy, funeral oration, dirge.

ma'rūf: well-known, generally accepted, beneficial, courtesy.

mashāyikh: shaykhs. A plural of *shaykh*.

mashhad: martyrium; a place where a martyr died or is buried; a religious shrine celebrating such a person or his tomb.

mashruba: an attic room; a roofed vestibule.

mashūra: consulting with experts.

al-Masīḥ ad-Dajjāl: the anti-Messiah. *"Dajjāl"* means a liar and great deceiver.

masīḥī (plural *masīḥiyyūn*)**:** Christian.

masjid (plural *masājid*)**:** mosque, lit. a place of *sajda* or prostration.

Masjid-al-Aqṣā: the great mosque in Jerusalem.

Masjid al-Jamā'a: central mosque.

masnūn: *sunna*, referring to an act which the Prophet's early community performed regularly.

ma'ṣūm: infallible or protected from committing wrong actions.

ma'ūda: in pre-Islamic times, the unwanted female child who was buried alive. The practice was forbidden in the Qur'ān in 81:8.

maw'iẓa: sermon, admonition.

mawlid: or *mawlūd*, a time, place and celebration of the birth of anyone, especially that of the Prophet, who was born on the 12th Rabī' al-Awwal/30th August 570 CE.

mawt: death.

maysir: game of chance, gambling. It is unlawful in Islam.

miḥrāb: the prayer niche, a recess in a mosque indicating the direction of *qibla*.

Mihrajān: Magian festival at the autumn equinox.

mikhṣara: staff or whip held in the hand with which a speaker makes gestures; a ruler's rod.

minbar: steps on which the Imam stands to deliver the *khutba*, or sermon, on Friday.

mīr: from the Arabic *amīr*, a title of respect used in India and Iran for descendants of the Prophet.

Mi'rāj: the ascension of the Prophet Muḥammad from Jerusalem to the seven heavens which took place on the 27th of the month of Rajab.

mirbaḍ: a place where dates are dried.

miskīn (plural *masākīn*)**:** very poor, wretched, indigent, those who do not have anything and have to resort to begging to be able to live.

miswāk: another term for the *siwāk*.

mīthāq: solemn covenant, treaty, compact.

mīzān: balance, scale – symbol of harmony in creation and also the scales of the Final Reckoning.

mu'addib: schoolmaster.

mu'adhdhin: someone who calls the *adhān* or call to prayer.

mu'allim: teacher, master of a craft.

mubārak: blessed by Allah, imbued with *baraka*.

mubashshirāt: lit. "good news", good dreams.

muftī: someone qualified to give a legal opinion or *fatwā*.

Muḥarram: the first month of the Muslim lunar year.

mujaddid: rennovater, renewer.

mujāhid (plural *mujāhidūn*)**:** a person who takes part in *jihād.*

mujazziz: a *qā'if*, a learned man who reads foot and hand marks.

mu'jiza: an evidentiary miracle given to a Prophet to prove his prophethood.

mukhābarāt: secret police.

mūlay: lit. "my master", from *mawlā*, a title used in Morocco for *sharifs*, descendants of the Prophet.

mu'min (plural *mu'minūn*)**:** a believer, someone who possesses *īmān*, who trusts in Allah.

munāfiq (plural *munāfiqūn*)**:** a hypocrite, someone who outwardly professes Islam on the tongue, but inwardly rejects Allah and His Messenger.

munawarra: "the radiant", "the illuminated", used to describe Madina.

muqātila: soldiers, fighters.

musaḍ'afīn: weak and oppressed people.

muṣallā: place for praying. *'Īd* prayers are normally held outside the mosque at a *muṣallā.*

muṣḥaf (plural *maṣaḥif*)**:** a copy of the Quran.

mushrik (plural *mushrikūn*)**:** someone who commits *shirk.*

muslim: someone who follows the way of Islam, not abandoning what is obligatory, keeping within the bounds set by Allah, and following the *Sunna* as much as possible.

mutaṭāwi'a: those who enforce obedience, vigilantes who enforce the prayer and beat people for moral laxity.

muttaqūn: pious and righteous persons who fear Allah much (abstain from all kinds of sins and evil deeds which He has forbidden) and love Allah much (perform all kinds of good deeds which He has ordained).

muwaḥḥid: unifier.

nabī (plural *anbiyā'*)**:** a Prophet.

nabīdh: a drink made by soaking grapes, raisins, dates, etc, in water without allowing them to ferment to the point of becoming intoxicating. If it does become intoxicating, it is still called *nabīdh.*

nafīla (plural *nawāfil*)**:** supererogatory or voluntary act of worship.

naḥw: grammar.

nahy: prohibition.

namāz: Persian word for prayer.

naql: transmission.

Nār: the Fire, Hell.

nās: mankind. Also the name of *Sūra* 114 of the Qur'ān.

nasab: lineage, descent.

Naṣārā: (singular *naṣrānī*) "Nazarenes", Christians. In modern times the term *'masīḥī'* is usually used for a Christian.

nawādir: anecdotes.

Nawrūz: Persian New Year, a Magian festival at the spring equinox.

nikāḥ: marriage.

niqāb: veil which covers the entire face, including the eyes.

nisā': women. Also the name of *Sūra* 4 of the Qur'ān.

niyya: intention.

nubūwa: prophethood.

nūr (plural *anwār*)**:** light.

pasha: a title of high rank, like a mayor.

payambar: a Persian/Turkish word meaning Prophet.

purdah: a Persian/Urdu word for the seclusion of women.

qabr (plural *qubūr*)**:** grave.

qāḍī (plural *quḍā*)**:** a judge, qualified to judge all matters in accordance with the *Sharī'a* and to dispense and enforce legal punishments.

qāḍī al-quḍāt: the chief qāḍī in charge of all other qāḍīs.

qaḍīb: staff, rod.

qā'idūn: literally, "those sitting down", people who remain inactive and do not actively fight.

qā'if: physiognomist.

qal'a: citadel, fortress.

qalam: pen.

qalansuwa: tall cone-shaped hat worn in Abbasid times by important people with a turban wrapped around it. This is the *qalansuwa* *tawīla* or *danniya*. The short *qalansuwa* was shaped like a skull-cap or fez with a turban wrapped around it.

qalīb: a well.

qamar: the moon. (*Badr* denotes the full moon and *hilāl* the crescent moon.)

qamīṣ: tunic (from Latin *camisa*).

qaṣīda: ode, poem.

qaṣr (plural *quṣūr*)**:** stronghold.

qattāt: a person who conveys information from someone to another with the intention of causing harm and enmity between them.

qibla: the direction faced in the prayer which is towards the Ka'ba in Makka. The first *qibla* had been Jerusalem and so the early Muslims had prayed towards two *qiblas*, a quality which is sometimes used to describe the fact that they became Muslim early on.

qirām: thin figured woollen curtain.

qiyām bi'l-layl: standing in prayer during the night.

al-Qiyāma: the arising of people at the Resurrection.

Qubba aṣ-Ṣakhra: Dome of the Rock in Jerusalem.

quḍā: the plural of *qāḍī*.

al-Quds: Jerusalem.

Qur'ān: the Holy Book, the Living Miracle, revealed from Allah as a guidance to mankind via the angel Jibrīl to the Prophet Muḥammad, may Allah bless him and grant him peace. The Revelation began in 610 and continued until shortly before the death of the Prophet in 11/632.

qurbān: sacrifice.

ra'āyā: "flock", meaning citizens, subjects.

Rabb: Lord, master. *Rabbi'l-'Ālamīn* means "the Lord of the worlds", the Lord in the Seen and the Unseen and at all levels of existence.

Rabī' al-Awwal: the third month of the Muslim calendar.

Rabī' ath-Thānī: the fourth month of the Muslim calendar.

rāhib: a monk.

Rajab: the seventh month of the Muslim lunar calendar.

rajaz: "trembling", a type of poetry with a particular metre which is easy on the ear and easily provokes emotions.

rak'a(t): a unit of the prayer consisting of a series of standings, bowing, prostrations and sittings.

Ramaḍān: the month of fasting, the ninth month in the Muslim lunar calendar.

raqā'iq: emotive stories or *ḥadīths* which provoke feelings and emotions.

rasūl (plural *rusul*)**:** a 'Messenger,' a Prophet who has been given a revealed Book by Allah. Every Messenger is a Prophet, but not every Prophet is a Messenger.

Rasūlu'llāh: the Messenger of Allah.

Rawḍa: lit. Meadow, the area of the Prophet's mosque between his grave and minbar, based on what the Prophet said: "What is between my house and my minbar is one of the meadows of the Garden."

ridā': a piece of cloth (sheet etc.) worn around the upper part of the body.

risāla: message, also a treatise or letter.

roza: the Persian word for *ṣawm*, fasting.

rūḥ (plural *arwāḥ*)**:** the soul, vital spirit.

rukn (plural *arkān*)**:** essential ingredient; pillar.

al-rukn al-yamānī: the Yemeni corner of the Ka'ba, facing south towards Yemen.

ruqya: Divine Speech recited as a means of curing disease. (It is a kind of treatment, i.e. to recite *Sūrat al-Fātiḥa* or any other *sūra* of the Qur'ān and then blow one's breath with saliva over a sick person's body-part).

rusul: the plural of *rasūl*.

ru'ya: vision, dream.

sa'dān: thorny plant suitable for grazing animals.

ṣadaqa: charitable giving in the Cause of Allah.

Ṣafar: the second month of the Muslim lunar calendar.

Ṣaḥāba: the Companions of the Prophet Muhammad, may Allah bless him and grant him peace. If a Muslim has seen the Prophet, or talked to him, at least once when the Prophet was alive, he is called *Ṣaḥābī*. The plural form of *Ṣaḥābī* is *Ṣaḥāba* or *Aṣḥāb*. The word

Ṣaḥāba al-Kirām includes all those great people each of whom has seen the Prophet at least once.

Ṣaḥābī: a Muslim who saw the Prophet at least once; a Companion.

ṣaḥib (plural *aṣḥāb*)**:** lit. companion, also a graduate student in a *madrasa.*

Ṣaḥīfa (plural *ṣuḥuf*)**:** portion of writing, page, a book revealed to a Prophet.

saḥūr: or *suḥūr*, the early morning meal taken before first light when fasting.

sajjāda: prayer rug.

Salaf: the early generations of the Muslims.

Salafī: derived from *Salaf*, used to describe the early generations of the Muslims, and adopted by a modern group of Muslims led by al-Afghānī and Muḥammad 'Abduh at the turn of the century.

ṣalā(t): the prayer, particularly the five daily obligatory prayers. One of the pillars of Islam.

ṣāliḥ (plural *ṣāliḥūn*)**:** righteous, a spiritually developed person, someone who is in the right place at the right time doing the right thing.

samā' (plural *samāwāt*)**:** Heaven. The opposite is *arḍ*, earth.

saqīfa: a roofed porch where the Muslims in Madīna met after the death of the Prophet to chose their first *khalīfa.*

sarīya: a small army-unit sent by the Prophet on *jihād*, without his participation in it.

sawīq: a mush made of wheat or barley (also with sugar and dates).

ṣawm: or *siyām*, fasting from food, drink and sexual intercourse from dawn to sunset, particularly for the month of Ramaḍān which is one of the pillars of Islam.

ṣawm ad-dahr: uninterrupted fasting.

sayyid: a descendant of the Prophet; also master.

Sayyid al-Anbiyā' wa'l-Mursalīn: "the Master of the Prophets and the Messengers", Muhammad, may Allah bless him and grant him peace.

Sha'bān: the eighth month of the Muslim lunar calendar.

shahāda: bearing witness, particularly bearing witness that there is no god but Allah and that Muḥammad is the Messenger of Allah. It is one of the pillars of Islam. It is also used for legal testimony in a court of law. It also means martyrdom.

shāhid (plural *shuhūd*): a witness, someone who testifies.

shahīd (plural *shuhadā'*): a martyr who dies fighting in the Cause of Allah.

Shamā'il: "good qualities", especially the characteristics of the Prophet.

shaqq: a simple grave, about five feet deep.

sharḥ: commentary.

Sharī'a: lit. road, the legal modality of a people based on the Revelation of their Prophet. The final *Sharī'a* is that of Islam.

sharīf: a descendant of the Prophet, may Allah bless him and grant him peace, through Fāṭima and 'Alī.

Shawwāl: the tenth month of the Muslim lunar calendar.

shaykh (plural *shuyūkh*)**:** someone who is over fifty, or the patriarch of the tribe or family, a title of respect.

Shaykh al-Islām: a title of respect dating from the time of the Būyids.

shayṭān (plural *shayāṭin*)**:** a devil, particularly Iblīs, one of the *jinn*.

Shi'a: lit. a party or faction, specifically the party who claim that 'Alī should have succeeded the Prophet as the first khalif and that the leadership of the Muslims rightfully belongs to his descendant.

shirk: the unforgiveable wrong action of worshipping something or someone other than Allah or associating something or someone as a partner with Him.

shuhadā': the plural of *shahīd.*

shuhūd: the plural of *shāhid.*

shūra: consultation. Also the title of *Sūra* 42 of the Qur'ān.

shurṭa: urban police.

shurūq: sunrise, when the sun is fully over the horizon.

shuyūkh: plural of shaykh.

siḥr: magic.

sirāṭ al-mustaqīm: "the straight path" of Islam, which leads to the Garden.

siwāk: a small stick, usually from the arak tree, whose tip is softened and used for cleaning the teeth.

Ṣubḥ: the dawn prayer.

Ṣuffa: a verandah attached to the Prophet's Mosque where the poor Muslims used to sleep.

ṣuḥuf: pages or manuscripts.

suḥūr: see *saḥūr*.

sukūn: stillness; a diacritic mark which means no vowel sound after a consonant.

ṣulḥ: reconciliation, or comprehensive peace settlement.

sulṭān: an abstract noun meaning power, especially that of government. It has come to designate a king or ruler who governs by virtue of his power.

sunan: plural of *sunna*; also collections of *ḥadīths*.

Sunna: the customary practice of a person or group of people. It has come to refer almost exclusively to the practice of the Messenger of Allah and to the first generation of Muslims.

Sunnī: the main body of Muslims, the *Ahl as-Sunna wa'l-Jamā'a*, who recognise and accept the *Khulafā' ar-Rāshidūn*, the first four khalifs.

ṭā'a: obedience to Allah. (The opposite is *ma'ṣiya*, disobedience.)

ta'addī: violation of trust.

Ṭabaqāt: chronicles, biographies arranged according to generations.

Tābi'ūn: the Followers, the second generation of the early Muslims who did not meet the Prophet Muḥammad, may Allah bless him and grant him peace, but who learned the *Dīn* of Islam from his Companions.

Tābi'ū't-Tābi'īn: "Followers of the Followers", the generation after the Tābi'ūn who did not meet any of the Companions.

tafsīr: commentary and explanation of the meanings of the Qur'ān.

ṭāghūt: covers a wide range of meanings: It means anything worshipped other than the Real God (Allah), i.e. all the false deities. It may be Shayṭān, devils, idols, stones, sun, stars, angels, human beings e.g. Jesus or other Messengers of Allah, who were falsely worshipped and taken as objects of worship.

tahajjud: voluntary prayers performed at night between *'Ishā'* and *Fajr*.

ṭahāra: purification, purity.

tahnīk: the Islamic customary process of chewing a piece of date and putting a part of its juice in a newborn child's mouth and calling the *adhān* softly in the child's ears, etc.

taḥrīf: distortion, modification of an original text; what has happened to the original teachings of Mūsā and 'Īsā.

takfīr: to declare that someone is a *kāfir* or unbeliever.

ṭalāq: divorce.

talqīn: instruction. This is the term used for instructing the dead in what to say in the grave, when questioned by Munkar and Nakīr.

tamattu': a form of *ḥajj*.

tanwīn: nunnation (gramm.)

tanzīl: "sending down", revelation.

taqīya: concealment of one's views to escape persecution.

taqwā: awe or fear of Allah, which inspires a person to be on guard against wrong action and eager for actions which please Him.

ta'rīkh: era, chronology, history.

tarjumān: translator.

taṣawwuf: Sufism.

tashdīd: doubled consonant.

taṭawwu': voluntary; supererogatory.

ta'ṭīl: negation, the concept of denying Allah all attributes.

tawassul: to seek the assistance of a person of virtue in praying to Allah.

tawba: returning to correct action after error, turning away from wrong action to Allah and asking His forgiveness.

tawfīq: success given by Allah.

tawḥīd: the doctrine of Divine Unity.

tayammum: purification for prayer with clean dust, earth, or stone, when water for *ghusl* or *wuḍū'* is either unavailable or would be detrimental to health.

ṭaylasān: a hooded stole. It was especially worn by the *qāḍīs* and *fuqahā'*, hence *qāḍīs* were sometimes known as the *arbāb aṭ-ṭayālisa*, 'the people of the stoles'.

ta'zīya: Shi'ite performance of 'mourning' for the death of Ḥusayn.

thā'r: blood revenge.

tharīd: a dish of bread, meat and broth, reported to be a favourite dish of the Prophet.

thawāb: reward. Muslims will be rewarded in the Hereafter for all their pious actions which they have done in the world. The rewards which Muslims will be given in the Hereafter are called *thawāb*.

thayyiba: a woman who has been married.

ṭibb: medicine.

ṭu'ām: foodstuffs.

'ulamā': plural of *'ālim*; scholars.

ulū'l-amr: those in command and those with authority.

'ulūm: plural of *'ilm*.

umanā': those who are faithful and trustworthy, the plural of *amīn*.

Umm al-Mu'minīn: lit. "Mother of the Believers", an honorary title given to the wives of the Prophet.

Umm al-Qur'ān: "Mother of the Qur'ān", the opening *sūra* of the Qur'ān which is called *al-Fātiḥa*. Also said to be its source in the Unseen.

umm walad: a slavegirl who has born her master's child. She cannot be sold and becomes free upon her master's death. The child is free from birth.

Umma: the body of Muslims as one distinct Community.

ummī (plural *ummīyūn*)**:** unlettered, untaught.

'umra: the lesser pilgrimage to the Ka'ba in Makka performed at any time of the year.

uṣūl: (singular *aṣl*): fundamentals; essentials.

uṣūl ad-Dīn: meaning *'ilm uṣūl ad-Dīn*, the science of the fundamental principles of the *Dīn* as distinct from other belief systems; the science of the tenets of belief. It can also be designated as *"al-fiqh al-akbar"*, "the greatest understanding".

waḥy: Revelation.

wājib: a necessary part of the *Sharī'a*.

walā': the tie of clientage established between a freed slave and the person who frees him, whereby the freed slave becomes integrated into the family of that person. (See *mawlā*.)

walīma: a feast accompanying a wedding.

wars: a kind of yellow dye and perfume.

wasīla: something which makes something else take place. The High Place with Allah reserved for the Prophet on the Last Day.

waswās: the whispering which is done by Shayṭān when he tries to make people deviate.

wiṣāl: fasting for more than one day continuously.

wuḍū': ritual washing to be pure for the prayer.

Yahūdī: a Jew.

yasīr: slight, insignificant, immaterial.

yatīm: orphan.

ẓālim: a person who is unjust and oppressive, a tyrant.

Ẓuhr: the midday prayer.

ẓulm: injustice, iniquity, tyranny.

Units of Weight and Measurement

awāq: plural of *ūqīyya*, a measurement of silver equivalent to forty dirhams or 123 gms of silver.

awsāq: plural of *wasq*, a measure of volume equal to sixty *sa'ṣ*.

barīd (plural *burūd*)**:** a postal stage of twelve miles, state communication and transport system, loan word from *veredus* (L.) via *beredos* (Gr.)

dāniq (plural *dawāniq*)**:** a coin equal to one sixth of a dirham.

dhirā' (plural *adhru'*)**:** a cubit varying from 45 cm to 66.5 cm.

dīnār (plural *danānīr*)**:** a gold coin 4.4 gm in weight.

dirham (plural *darāhim*)**:** a silver coin 3.08 gm in weight.

fals (plural *fulūs*)**:** a small copper coin, used as small change, but with no intrinsic value.

faraq (plural *furqān*)**:** a kind of large pot used as a measure in Madina, containing about three *ṣā's* of water.

farsakh (plural *farāsikh*)**:** a measurement of length, about three miles/five km.

irdabb or *ardabb* (plural *arādib*)**:** ardeb, a dry measure of about five and a half bushels.

jarīb (plural *ajriba*)**:** a grain measure of capacity of either 16, 26, or 29.5 litres; also a unit of area equal to ten *qaṣaba* squared, or 3,600 square cubits, which varied according to the length of the cubit.

mithqāl (plural *mathāqīl*)**:** "miskal", the weight of one dinar, the equivalent of 72 grains of barley (equals 4.4 grams). It may be somewhat less or more. [10 dirhams weigh 7 *mithqāls*.]

mudd (plural *amdād* or *midād*)**:** a measure of volume, approximately a double-handed scoop.

qafīz (plural *aqfiza*)**:** "cafiz", a measure of grain consisting of twelve *ṣā's;* also a unit of area equal to 360 square cubits.

qaṣaba (plural *qaṣabāt*)**:** a measure of 6 cubits.

qinṭār (plural *qanāṭīr*)**:** "kantar", a relatively large weight-measure for food-grains, etc., e.g. wheat, maize, oat, barley, approx. 45 kgs.

qīrāṭ (plural *qarārīṭ*)**:** a measure of weight with various meanings, either a twelfth of a dirham or a huge weight like that of Mount Uhud.

qisṭ (plural *aqsāṭ*)**:** a measure of grain, a bushel.

riṭl (plural *arṭāl*)**:** "rotl", a measure of weight, approximately one pound.

ṣā' (plural *aṣwā'* or *aṣwu'*)**:** a measure of volume equal to four *mudds*, a *mudd* being a double-handed scoop.

shibr (plural *ashbār*)**:** a handspan, unit of length.

'ūqīya: (plural *awāq*)**:** a measure of silver, equal to forty dirhams or 123 gms of silver.

wasq (plural *awsāq*)**:** a measure of volume equal to sixty *sa's*.

Arabic Expressions

'alayhi's-salām: "peace be upon him", a formula used after the name of a Prophet.

Allāhu akbar: the Arabic expression meaning "Allah is greater." Also called the *takbīr*.

Allāhu a'lam: an Arabic expression meaning "Allah knows best".

amma ba'd: an expression used for separating an introductory from the main topics in a speech; the introductory being usually concerned with Allah's praises and glorification. Literally it means "whatever comes after."

astaghfiru'llāh: the Arabic expression meaning "I ask forgiveness of Allah".

a'ūdhu billāhi min ash-shayṭān ar-rajīm: the Arabic expression meaning "I seek protection in Allah from the accursed Shaytan." One says this before beginning to recite the Qur'an.

'azza wa jall: a formula used after mentioning the name of Allah meaning "Mighty and Majestic is He".

barākallāh fīk: an expression which means: "May the blessings of Allah (be upon you)." When a Muslim wants to thank another person, he uses different statements to express his thanks, appreciation, and gratitude. One of them is to say "*Barākallāh.*"

bismi'llāh ar-Raḥmān ar-Raḥīm: the *basmala*: "In the name of Allah, the All-Merciful, the All-Compassionate".

fī amāni'llāh: valedictory phrase meaning "in Allah's protection."

fī sabīlillāh: the Arabic expression meaning "In the Way of Allah", "for the Cause of Allah".

al-ḥamdu lillāh wa shukru lillāh: the Arabic expression which means "Praise belongs to Allah and thanks to Allah."

ḥasbala: the Arabic expression, *"Ḥasbuna'llāh wa ni'ma'l-wakīl,"* meaning "Allah is enough for us and an excellent Guardian."

Ḥasbunā'llāh wa ni'ma'l-wakīl: the Arabic expression meaning "Allah is enough for us and an excellent Guardian."

ḥawqala: the Arabic expression, *"lā ḥawla wa lā quwwata illā billāh"* which means "There is no power nor strength save by Allah."

Innā lillāhi wa innā ilayhi rāji'ūn: This is something which a Muslim expresses when he is afflicted by a misfortune, the meaning of which is "We are from Allah and to Him we are returning." It is taken from an *āyat* of the Qur'an (2:156).

inshā'llāh: the Arabic expression meaning "If Allah wills".

istighfār: to ask the forgiveness of Allah, especially by saying, *"Astaghfiru'llāh"*, "I seek the forgiveness of Allah."

istithnā': exception, saying "*In shā'llāh,*" "If Allah wills."

jalla jalāluh: the formula said after the name of Allah meaning "Great is His Majesty."

jazāka'llāhu khayran: This is a statement of thanks and appreciation to be said to the person who does a favour. Instead of saying "thanks" (*Shukran*), this phrase is used. It means: "May Allah reward you for the good."

karrama'llāhu wajhahu: "May Allah honour him", a formula used when 'Alī ibn Abī Ṭālib is mentioned.

Labbayk: "At your service", the *talbīya* or call of the pilgrim to his Lord in the *Ḥajj.*

lā ḥawla wa lā quwwata illa billāh: The meaning of this expression is: "There is no power and no strength save in Allah." This is said by a Muslim when he is struck by a calamity, or is taken over by a situation beyond his control.

li-wajhi'llāh: literally, "for the Face of Allah," meaning in order to obtain the pleasure of Allah, purely for Allah Himself.

ma's-salāma: "with peace", a formula for ending letters.

māshā'llāh: a phrase meaning literally, "What Allah wishes," and it indicates a good omen.

mawlānā: "our master", a term of respect.

rabbanā wa laka'l-ḥamd: "Our Lord, praise is Yours," said after rising from *rukū'* after saying *"sami' Allāhu liman ḥamidah"* (unless he is the imam of the prayer).

raḍiya'llāhu 'anhā: the formula "May Allah be pleased with her", used after a female Companion.

raḍiya'llāhu 'anhu: This is an expression to be used by Muslims whenever a name of a Companion of the Prophet Muḥammad is mentioned or used in writing. It means: "May Allah be pleased with him."

raḍiya'llāhu 'anhum: the formula "May Allah be pleased with them", used after a group of Companions.

raḥimahu'llāh: the formula "May Allah have mercy on him"

as-salāmu 'alaykum: "Peace be upon you," the greeting of the Muslims.

ṣallā'llāhu 'alayhi wa sallam: "may Allah bless him and grant him peace", the formula spoken after mentioning the Prophet Muhammad.

sami' Allāhu liman ḥamidah: "Allah heard him who sent his praises to Him," said by someone praying when he rises from *rukū'* (unless he is following an Imām in the prayer).

sayyidunā: "our master", a term of respect.

subḥānallāh: "Glorified is Allah." To honour Allah and make Him free from all (unsuitable evil things) that are ascribed to Him, (or "Glorified be Allah").

subḥānahu wa ta'ālā: "Glorified is He and exalted," an expression that Muslims use when the name of Allah is pronounced or written.

ta'ālā: "Exalted is He", an expression used after the name of Allah is mentioned.

ta'awwudh: saying "I seek refuge with Allah..." (*a'ūdhu billāhi min ash-shayṭān ar-rajīm*).

tabāraka'llāh: the formula "Blessed is Allah".

taḥmīd: saying the expression *"al-ḥamdu lillāh"*, "Praise belongs to Allah".

takbīr: saying "*Allāhu Akbar*," "Allah is greater".

talbīya: saying *"Labbayk"* ("At Your service") during the *Ḥajj*.

tamjīd: glorifying Allah.

tarḍīya: saying one of the expressions which begin "*raḍiya'llahu...*"

tasbīh: glorification, saying *"Subḥānallāh"*, "Glory be to Allah".

tashmīt: Uttering a prayer for the sneezer which takes the form, *"yarḥamuk Allāh"*, "may Allah have mercy on you."

wajhu'llāh: "the Face of Allah", meaning for the sake of Allah, irrespective of any reward in this life, purely for Allah.

Historical Terms

Abbasids: the dynasty of khalifs who ruled from 132/750 to 656/1258 and had their capital in Baghdad. They based their claim to power on their descent from al-'Abbās, the uncle of the Prophet, may Allah bless him and grant him peace. During their reign, Islamic arts, literature, and culture blossomed and flourished. The location of the capital in Baghdad had a major impact on Islam, transforming it from a distinctly Mediterranean religion to one with more eastern elements.

abnā': literally "sons", a term applied to members of the Abbasid household and by extension to the Khurāsānī and other *mawālī* who became adoptive members, The first generation of Khorasanis were called *abnā' ad-da'wa* or *abnā' ad-dawla*, which might be translated as "Sons of the Revolution". They enjoyed great prestige. In Baghdad, they wore turbans and garments with a border to distinguish them. Aṭ-Ṭabarī says that they numbered about 20,000.

Abraha: the Christian viceroy of the Negus who ruled Yemen in the sixth century and marched against Makka in 570, the year of the birth of the Prophet with the intention of destroying the Ka'ba. The year in which this happened is known as the "Year of the Elephant" since he had several elephants in his army. The army was destroyed by stones dropped by flocks of birds. This event is described in the Qur'an in *Sūra* 105: "*Do you not see what your Lord did with the Companions of the Elephant? Did He not bring all their schemes to nothing, unleashing upon them flock after flock of birds, bombarding them with stones of hard-baked clay, making them like stripped wheat-stalks eaten bare?*"

Abū Bakr: the first khalif after the Messenger of Allah, born either two years or six years after the Year of the Elephant (51 years before the *Hijra*). He was the best of the Companions, renowned for his sincerity, and the Prophet's closest friend. He died in 13/634 at the age of 63 and was buried beside the Messenger of Allah, may Allah bless him and grant him peace.

Abū'l-Ḥusayn, Banū: the Kalbite governors of Sicily at the end of the tenth and beginning of the eleventh century. They supported the Fāṭimids.

Abū Muslim: 'Abdu'r-Raḥmān ibn Muslim al-Khurāsānī, the mysterious individual who led the Abbasid rebellion in Khorasan in 128/746. He was murdered by the Abbasids in 132/750.

'Adnān: a descendant of Ismā'īl and ancestor of the northern Arabs. Qaḥṭān was the ancestor of the southern Arabs.

Aftasids: Muslim Berber dynasty that ruled one of the party kingdoms (*ṭā'ifas*) at Badajoz in western Spain (1022-94) in the period of disunity after the demise of the Umayyad caliphate of Cordoba.

agha: a title of honour among the Turks.

Agha Khan: modern leader of Ismā'īlī Shi'ite Muslims.

Aghlabids: a dynasty also called the Banū al-Aghlab, an Arab Muslim dynasty that ruled Ifriqīya (Tunisia and eastern Algeria) from 800 to 909, nominally subject to the 'Abbasid caliphs of Baghdad but in fact independent with their capital in Qayrawān.

ahl al-ayyām: the people who took part in the early battles along the Euphrates; those who did not revolt during the Ridda.

Ahl al-Kisā': "People of the Cloak". In 10 AH, a delegation of the Christians of Najrān came to the Prophet. On the basis of the Qur'anic *āyats*, 3:59-61, they met and the Prophet threw his cloak over 'Alī, Fāṭima, Ḥasan and Ḥusayn.

Ahl aṣ-Ṣuffa: the People of the Bench, the poor and needy among the Companions of the Prophet who lived on a verandah (*ṣuffa*) next to the house of the Prophet and the mosque in Madina. Also called *Aṣḥāb aṣ-Ṣuffa* or sometimes *Aḍyāf al-Islām* ("the guests of Islam").

Aḥzāb: the confederates: the term used for Quraysh and their allies at the Battle of the Trench.

ajnād: armies; administrative districts in greater Syria; the plural of *jund.*

akhbār: relatively short accounts usually introduced by an *isnād*. This is the earliest form of Islamic history.

Akhbārī: a school among the Shi'a who recognise four sources of Law: Qur'ān, *ḥadīth*, *'aql* and *ijmā'*. Opposed to the Uṣūlīs.

'Alawites: partisans of 'Alī ibn Abī Ṭālib.

'Alawī: offshoot of Shi'ite Islam prevalent in part of northern Syria; today, about 10% of the Syrian population, but Hafiz al-Asad, president since 1970, is an Alawite, so their importance outweighs their numbers. They are well-represented in the Syrian military.

'Alī ibn Abi Ṭālib: the fourth of the early khalifs, the cousin and son-in-law of the Prophet by marriage to his daughter, Fāṭima, and renowned for his bravery and wisdom. He is regarded by Shi'a Muslims as the first Imām after Muḥammad. He was murdered by a Khārijite in 40/661 and is buried at Najaf, Iraq.

'āmil: provincial governor (*walī* is also used to designate this post).

amīr (plural *umarā'*)**:** general, ruler, governor, prince.

'Amwas: a major plague in Syria in 18/639 which killed many of the Companions.

Anṣār: the "Helpers", the people of Madina who welcomed and aided the Prophet and the Muhājirūn.

al-'Aqaba: lit. the steep slope, a mountain pass to the north of Makka just off the caravan route to Madina, where the Prophet met with the first Muslims from Yathrīb (Madina) in two successive years. On the first occasion, they pledged to follow the Messenger, and on the second or Great Pledge of 'Aqaba, to defend him and his Companions as they would their own wives and children.

'aqīda (plural *'aqā'id*)**:** creed, dogma or tenet of faith firmly based on how things are, distinct from the testimony of faith (*shahāda*).

'Aqīq: a valley about seven kilometres west of Madina.

al-Aqṣā: important Jerusalem mosque, nearby which is the Dome of the Rock, whose golden dome covers the place where the Prophet left to ascend to heaven during the *Mi'rāj*.

'Arafa: a plain fifteen miles to the east of Makka on which stands the Jabal ar-Raḥma, the Mount of Mercy. One of the essential rites of *ḥajj* is to stand on 'Arafa on the 9th of *Dhū'l-Ḥijja*.

arḍ: "land", administrative territory.

'arḍ: presentation, a military review.

'arīf (plural *'urafā'*)**:** "one who knows", an overseer, an official in charge of a military division in early Baṣra and Kūfa.

'aṣabīya: tribal and group solidarity.

asāwira: heavy mailed cavalry, loanword from Middle Persian *usvārān*. *Uswār* is the singular in Arabic.

al-'Ashara al-Mubashshara: the ten Companions promised the Garden, which varies somewhat, but the usual order is: Abū Bakr, 'Umar, 'Uthmān, 'Alī, Ṭalha, az-Zubayr, 'Abdu'r-Raḥmān ibn 'Awf, Sa'd ibn Abī Waqqāṣ, Sa'īd ibn Zayd, and Abū 'Ubayda ibn al-Jarrāḥ.

Ash'arite: someone who adheres to the theological and philosophical position of Abū'l-Ḥasan al-Ash'arī (d. 324/936). The main features of this school are the negation of cause and effect as everything is caused by Allah, and the discontinuity between Allah and His creation. (Compare with *Māturīdite*).

'ashīra (plural *'ashā'ir*)**:** kinsfolk, clan, those descended from the same ancestor; the smallest subdivision of a tribe. A synonym for *qabīla*.

ashrāf: tribal leaders and notables.

'Askar al-Mahdī: military camp of al-Mahdī, the west bank in Baghdad which the khalif al-Manṣūr developed for his supporters.

Assassin: member of a militant group of Ismā'īlī Shi'ites who fought against the Seljuks and other Sunnī rulers between 1092 and 1256. The word "assassin" comes from *"ḥashashīn,"* that is, "hashish users," since it was reputed that the Assassins got high on hashish before going into action.

Awā'il: a literary genre which dealt with "firsts", "the first person to do this or that."

'Awālī'l-Madīna: the outskirts of Madina at a distance of four or more miles.

'awāṣim: strongholds; the inner line fortresses between military marches.

Aws: along with Khazraj, one of the two major tribes in Madina.

ayyām: (literally 'days'), tribal lore; battle days.

Ayyām al-'Arab: record of guerilla wars between Arab tribes, inter-tribal hostilities.

'ayyār (plural *'ayyārūn*)**:** Arabic for "vagabond" or "scoundrel", any member of a class of warriors common to Iraq and Iran in the ninth-twelfth centuries, often associated in *futuwwa* organizations.

al-Azhar: a Muslim mosque-university in Cairo of enormous prestige. It was founded by the Fatimids in 358/969.

Bāb-i 'Alī: the Sublime Porte, the office of the Ottoman Grand Vizier.

Badr: a place near the coast, about 95 miles to the south of Madina where, in 2 AH in the first battle fought by the newly established Muslim community, the 313 outnumbered Muslims led by the Messenger of Allah overwhelmingly defeated 1000 Makkan idolaters. Someone who took part in the Battle of Badr is called a *Badrī*.

Bakkā'ūn: the Weepers. These were the people that could not accompany the Prophet on his campaign to Tabūk because they lacked the resources to do so. They started to weep when they could not go.

al-Balāṭ: a paved area of Madina between the Mosque and the Market.

Banū: lit. sons, a tribe or clan. The Umayyads are the Banū Umayya and the Abbasids are the Banū'l-'Abbās. The Banū Isrā'īl are the tribe of Isrā'īl, also known as Ya'qūb son of Isḥāq.

Banū Ṭughsh: the Ikhshidids.

al-Baqī': the cemetery of the people of Madina where many of the family of the Prophet and his Companions are buried.

Barghawāṭa: a Berber confederation belonging to the Masmūda group, which dominated the Atlantic coast of Morocco between Salé and Safi from the eighth to the twelfth century. They practised a special religion which appears to have been a Berber distortion of Islam with Shi'ite infiltrations and a Khārijite moral austerity.

barīd: the post and information service.

Barmakids: also called Barmecides, from the Arabic *al-Barāmika*, or *al-Barmak*, a priestly family of Iranian origin from Balkh who achieved prominence in the eighth century as scribes and viziers to the early 'Abbasid caliphs. Their ancestor was a *barmak*, a title borne by the high priest in the Buddhist temple of Nawbahar.

al-Bayḍā': a place 60 kilometres south of Madina on the route to Madina, near Dhū'l-Ḥulayfa.

Bayt al-Māl: the "house of wealth," the treasury of the Muslims where income from *zakāt* and other sources is gathered for redistribution.

Bayt al-Maqdīs: the Pure House, a name of Jerusalem, referring to the Temple of Sulayman.

bey: a Turkic title for a chief. Today it is a term of respect.

Beylerbey: bey of beys, title of a provincial governor.

bid'a: innovation, changing the original teaching of the Prophet, something introduced into Islam after the formative period.

birdhawn: destrier, the heavy Persian warhorse.

Bi'tha: the beginning of the Prophet's mission, his call to Prophethood in 610.

Bu'āth: a battle between Aws and Khazraj two years before the *Hijra*.

Burāq: the mount on which the Prophet made the *Isrā'*.

Buwayhids: or Būyids, a Shi'ite Persian dynasty who controlled the Abbasid khalifate from 945 – 1055.

buyūtāt: outstanding or leading families.

Camel, Battle of: one of the major incidents of the first Civil War (*Fitna*) in which the forces of 'Alī defeated the forces of 'Ā'isha, Ṭalha, and az-Zubayr in a battle fought outside Baṣra in 36/656.

dā'ī: Shi'ite propagandist, recruiting officer.

Dār al-Ḥarb: the Abode of Conflict, the domain of the unbelievers.

Dār al-Hijra: the abode of those who emigrated in the Cause of Allah from Makka to Madina, i.e. Madina itself.

dār al-imāra: "house of government"; the Islamic administrative compound in cities such as Baṣra and Kūfa. The buildings included the governor's residence, prison and treasury, and housed the administrative departments.

Dār al-Islām: territory of Islam.

Dār Nidwa: the assembly of chiefs of Quraysh in Kūfa.

dār ar-rizq: "house of provisions", a military depot established to supply the Muslim army.

dār aṣ-ṣinā'a: shipyard, the source of the word "arsenal".

Dār aṣ-Ṣulḥ: or *Dār al-'Ahd*, territory not under Muslim law nor at war with the Muslims.

daskarat: (from *dastkart*), plural *dasākir*, originally landed estate often with a fortified mansion; frontier posts.

Da'wat al-Ḥaqq: "proclaiming the Truth," the duty of every Muslim.

Dayr al-Jamājim: a battle in Iraq in 82/701 which ended the rebellion of Ibn al-Ash'ath.

devshirme: Ottoman system of taking Christian boys, converting them to Islam, and training them for military or administrative service.

Dhāt al-Jaysh: a place about twelve miles from Madina.

Dhāt an-Niṭāqayn: a nickname for Asmā', the daughter of Abū Bakr. It literally means "a woman with two belts". She was called that by the Prophet because she tore her belt in two to tie up the provisions for the *Hijra* of the Prophet and Abū Bakr.

Dhū'l-Ḥulayfa: the *mīqāt* of the people of Madina, now called Bayar 'Alī.

Dhū Nūrayn: a title of 'Uthmān, the third khalif, because he married two daughters of the Prophet: Umm Kulthum and Ruqayya. It means "he who has two lights".

Dhū Qār: a short-lived victory of the Arab tribes over a Sasanid army around the turn of the seventh century.

Dhū Ṭuwa: a well known well, now within Makka, but in earlier times outside of it.

dihqān (plural *dahāqin*)**:** landlord, member of the land owning gentry in pre-Islamic Persia.

dīwān (plural *dawāwīn*)**:** originally the register of soldiers and pensions under 'Umar. Then it became a sort of governmental department – a *dīwān* for the collection of taxes, a *dīwān* for the writing of documents. So, administration in general. There were three registers: one for those were were able to fight but needed weapons (*dīwān al-muqātila*), one for stipends (*dīwān al-'aṭā'*) and the muster roll (*dīwān al-'arḍ*). It also means collected works of a poet.

dīwān al-khātam: department of the seal.

dīwān al-mustaghallāt: the department in charge of income from state property under the early Marwānids at Damascus.

dīwān at-tawqī': the chancery office or board of correspondence.

dīwān zimām: the registry department.

ḍiyā': landed estate.

Duldul: the mule of the Prophet which was a gift from the Muqawqis.

effendi: title in Ottoman system for a religious or civil authority. Replaced by bey today.

Fadak: a small, rich oasis in the north of the Ḥijāz which had been the property of the Jews of Banū Murra and Banū Sa'd ibn Bakr. They offered to surrender it to the Prophet provided they could keep half of the produce.

al-Fārūq: a name for the second khalif, 'Umar ibn al-Khaṭṭāb. It means a man who makes a distinction between truth and falsehood or between cases.

Fāṭima: the youngest daughter of the Prophet and Khadīja. She married 'Alī who became the fourth Rightly Guided Khalif. She died a few months after the Prophet in 11/632.

Fāṭimids: an Ismā'īlī Shi'ite dynasty which ruled in North Africa for three centuries until 1171. They are also called the Banū 'Ubayd.

Fijār War: "The War of Trangression", which took place because of a violation in the sacred months. It was between Quraysh and Kināna against Hawāzin. It was followed by the *Ḥilf al-Fuḍūl.*

firmān: royal rescript, Ottoman or Persian.

fitna: inter-Muslim conflict, civil war.

Fusṭāṭ: Egyptian garrison town in early Islamic times; later an administrative center, located near modern Cairo.

futūḥ: "conquests", accounts of conquest campaigns, a type of historical writing which was an extension of the *maghāzī.*

al-Ghāba: (literally "the forest") a well-known place near Madina.

Ghadīr al-Khumm: the pond of Khumm, an oasis between Makka and Madina where the Prophet stopped on his return from the Farewell *Ḥajj* and made a prayer for 'Alī. The Shi'a interpret this as being 'Alī's appointment as the Prophet's successor.

ghālī (plural *ghulāt*)**:** one who exaggerates or goes beyond bounds in reverence for 'Alī.

ghārāt: raids.

ghiyār: a token, like the *zunnār* (waist-band) worn by non-Muslim subjects.

Ḥabasha: Abyssinia.

Ḥafṣa bint 'Umar ibn al-Khaṭṭāb: one of the wives of the Prophet. She was married to Khunays ibn Ḥudhayfa before she married the Prophet. He was present at Badr and then died in Madina. She married the Prophet after the Battle of Uhud. She died in Madina in 45/665 at the age of about 60.

ḥājib: door keeper or chamberlain.

hama: a superstitious belief of the Arabs of the *Jāhilīya*. It was that the unavenged spirit of a slain person took the form of a night bird.

Ḥamza: an uncle of the Prophet who became a Muslim and was martyred at the battle of Uhud.

ḥaras: the bodyguard of an Islamic ruler or governor.

al-Ḥarra: a stony tract of black volcanic rock east of Madina where a terrible battle took place in 63 AH (26 August 683) between the forces of Yazīd I and ‘Abdullāh ibn az-Zubayr which ended in Madina being sacked and plundered.

Ḥarūrīya: the first Khārijites or schismatics who separated themselves from ‘Alī and based themselves at Ḥarūrā', a town two miles from Kūfa.

Hāshimite: someone descended from the family of Hāshim, the great grandfather of the Prophet.

ḥawārī: apostle in the Christian usage; a disciple.

Hawāzin: one of the large Arab tribes.

al-Ḥijr: “the rocky tract” a town in Arabia about 150 miles north of Madina, where the people of Thamūd lived.

Ḥilf al-Fuḍūl: “the Alliance of Virtue”, a pact in which the Prophet took part twenty years before the Revelation. Those who made this covenant – the houses of Hāshim, Zuhra and Taym – pledged that they would forever stand on the side of the victim of injustice.

ḥimā: a place of pasturage and water prohibited to the public. It was used for animals paid as *zakāt* and mounts used for *jihād*.

Ḥirā’: a mountain two miles north of Makka where the Prophet used to go into retreat in a cave before the Revelation came to him. It is now called Jabal an-Nūr or the Mount of Light.

Hirāql: Heraclius.

Homage of ar-Riḍwān: a pledge which the Muslims took to avenge ‘Uthmān when they thought that Quraysh had murdered him at al-Ḥudaybiyya in 6/628.

Hubal: pre-Islamic idol, god of the moon.

Al-Ḥudaybiya: a well-known place ten miles from Makka on the way to Jidda where the Homage of ar-Riḍwān took place.

Ḥunayn: a valley between Makka and Ṭā'if where the battle took place between the Prophet and Quraysh pagans in 8/630.

ḥurrās: watchmen or the night watch in cities, or sentries who guarded walls and gates.

Ibādiyya: the remnants of the Khārijite rebellion in the second civil war between the Umayyads and 'Abdullāh ibn az-Zubayr.

Ifriqīya: North Africa, particularly what is now Tunisia.

Ikhwān: "brethren", the plural of *akh* ("brother"). In Arabia, members of a religious and military brotherhood that figured prominently in the unification of the Arabian Peninsula under Ibn Sa'ūd (1912 - 30).

'ilj: a person of low social status; the plural *'ulūj* means riffraff.

Īlyā': a name for Jerusalem.

intifadā: an Arabic term literally meaning "a throwing off"; Palestinian uprising against Israeli occupation that began spontaneously in late 1987.

iqṭā': land grant.

jabābira: "tyrants", how the Abbasids referred to the Umayyads.

Jabal an-Nūr: see *Ḥirā'*.

Jabal Thawr: the cave near Makka in which the Prophet and Abū Bakr hid at the start of their *Hijra* to Madina.

janissary: Christian conscript foot-soldier in the Ottoman army, converted to Islam and trained to use firearms.

Jazīra: Mesopotamia or north-eastern Syria.

Ji'rāna: a place near Makka, where the Messenger of Allah distributed the booty from the Battle of Ḥunayn and from where he went into *iḥrām* to perform *'umra*.

al-Juḥfa: the *mīqāt* of the people of Syria and Europe.

kāhin (plural *kahana* or *kuhhān*)**:** a soothsayer in pagan times.

kapudanpasha: the Beylerbey of the sea, or admiral. Barbarossa was the kapudanpasha in 1531.

kātib: an administrative secretary; scribe.

Khadīja: the Prophet's first wife and his first follower. She was a moderately wealthy widow who hired Muḥammad to manage the caravan business left to her by her first husband. Five years later, when Muḥammad was twenty-five and Khadīja was forty, she proposed marriage to him. They had a happy marriage with several children, including four daughters, Zaynab, Ruqayya, Umm Kulthūm and Fāṭima. During her lifetime, the Prophet took no other wives. She died in 619.

al-Khandaq: the Ditch. In 5/627, the Makkans, assisted by the Jewish tribe of Banū Nadr and the Arab tribes of Banū Ghaṭafān and Banū Asad, marched on Madina with an army of ten thousand soldiers. The Prophet ordered a ditch to be dug on the unprotected side of Madina and manned constantly. The Makkans were forced to undertake a siege which failed.

Kharijites: or *Khawārij*, the earliest sect who separated themselves from the body of the Muslims and declared war on all those who disagreed with them, stating that a wrong action turns a Muslim into an unbeliever.

Khawārij: Kharijites.

Khaybar: Jewish colony to the north of Madina which was laid siege to and captured by the Muslims in the seventh year after the Hijra because of the Jews' continual treachery.

Khazraj: along with Aws, one of the two major tribes in Madina.

khedive: "Viceroy," title of Egypt's ruler (1867 – 1914).

Khulafā' ar-Rāshidūn: "the Rightly-guided Khalifs", especially the first four khalifs: Abū Bakr, 'Umar, 'Uthmān and 'Alī. Sometimes 'Umar ibn 'Abdu'l-'Azīz is referred to as the fifth of the Rāshidūn.

Khurāsān: Persian province east of the Caspian Sea; a centre of many dissident movements in early Islamic history.

Kisrā: Khosrau, a generic term for the emperor of Persia; also a silver coin of that name which the Muslims used for a period before minting Islamic coins.

Kūfa: a place in Iraq, near Najaf, that was the chief military garrison and administrative centre of the Muslims when they conquered Iraq. It was founded in 15/638 as a garrison town by 'Umar ibn al-Khaṭṭāb.

kūra (plural *kuwar*)**:** from the Greek *chora*, an administrative district.

al-Lāt: female idol worshipped by the pagan Arabs in the Ḥijāz in the *Jāhilīya*.

al-Lizām: the settlement of affairs, in the *ḥadīth*, it refers to the battle of Badr, which was the means of settling affairs between the Muslims and the pagans.

maghārim: taxes not sanctioned by Islamic law.

maghāzī: battles, military expeditions.

Majūs: Magian, derived from Syriac *mgōshā*, derived from Old Persian *magush*.

Makhzūm: a powerful clan of Quraysh.

mamlūk: slave, "someone who is owned"; derived from *malaka*, to possess. Synonym of *'abd*, a slave born of free parents. Also: (1) Turkish or Circassian slave soldier; (2) member of a military oligarchy ruling Egypt and Syria (1250 – 1517) and retaining local power in some areas up to the 19th century.

al-Manāt: female idol worshipped by the pagan Arabs in the Ḥijāz in the *Jāhiliya*.

Marwānids: the Umayyad rulers descended from Marwān ibn al-Ḥakam, who assumed power in 64/685 and were overthrown by the 'Abbasids in 132/750.

marzpān: (*marzbān*) military governor of a later Sasanian frontier district.

Māturīdite: someone who follows the Māturīdite school of *kalām*, which is very similar to the Ash'arite school.

mawālī: the plural of *mawlā*.

mawlā (plural *mawāli*)**:** a person with whom a tie of *walā'* has been established, usually by having been a slave and then set free. It was also used for a type of political patronage.

Miḥna: the Inquisition instituted by the 'Abbasid khalif al-Ma'mūn, which required all important people to publicly state that they believed that the Qur'ān was created, even if they did not.

milla: religion, creed, faith or spiritual community. In Turkey, *millet* was used for the various religious groups within the empire.

miṣr (plural *amṣār*)**:** a garrison city and administrative capital.

al-Miṣrān: the two great cities: Kūfa and Baṣra.

al-mubayyiḍa: "the white ones", the 'Alids, because of the colour of their flag to contrast with the black of the 'Abbasids. Also the followers of al-Munaqqa' who wore white garments.

Muhājirūn: the Companions of the Messenger of Allah who accepted Islam in Makka and made *hijra* to Madina.

al-Munaqqa': a name meaning "the veiled". His actual name is unclear. He came from a village of Marv. He revolted against the 'Abbasid regime in the time of al-Manṣūr. He called on his followers to obey the laws of Mazdak. He was defeated in 162 or 163 (778/779) after a two year campaign.

Muqawqīs: the title of the Byzantine viceroy of Egypt.

Murābiṭūn: those who hold fast together in the Cause of Allah with the aim of establishing the *Dīn* of Allah, derived from the word *'ribāṭ'*. Also the name of a North African/Andalusian dynasty known often as the Almoravides, which lasted between 431/1039 and 539/1145.

al-musawwida: "the black ones," meaning the Abbasids because of their black flags. Eventually al-Ma'mūn adopted the colour green to put an end to the partisanship of the white and black flags.

Musaylima: a false Prophet of the Banū Ḥanīfa in Yamāna who was one of the leaders of the Ridda.

al-Mutalaththimūn: "the Veiled ones," the name of the Murabitun, because the Ṣanhāja tribes covered their faces like the Tuareg and were therefore very distinct in Andalusia.

Muwaḥḥidūn: the name of the North African/Andalusian dynasty, known often as the Almohads, which lasted between 524/1130 and 667/1269.

muwallad: a Muslim from native Spanish stock.

muwashshaḥa: a post classical form of Arabic poetry arranged in stanzas which was very popular in Andalusia.

Nahrawān: a decisive battle fought in 38/658 following the Battle of Ṣiffin (37/657) in which 'Alī, the fourth khalif, and his army annihilated most of the Khārijites.

Najaf: city in Iraq where 'Alī was assassinated (40/661); hence, a Shi'a pilgrimage center.

Najāshī: the Negus, king of Ethiopia.

Najd: the region around Riyāḍ in Saudi Arabia.

naqīb (plural *nuqabā'*)**:** a person responsible to the goverment for the group of which he is a member, an official in charge of a military division at Basra and Kūfa in the time of Ziyād ibn 'Ubaydullāh; a person heading a group of six persons in an expedition (tribal chiefs).

nasab: genealogy.

Negus: (Arabic *najāshī*); a generic term for the King of Abyssinia.

Nihāwand: the decisive battle fought near Hamadan in 22/642 which marked the final defeat of the Persians by the Muslims.

nuṣub: the singular of *anṣāb. An-Nuṣub* were stone alters at fixed places or graves, etc., whereon sacrifices were slaughtered during fixed periods of occasions and seasons in the name of idols, jinn, angels, pious men, saints, etc., in order to honour them, or to expect some benefit from them.

qādī al-jamā'a: "Qadi of the Community". Andalusia was divided into three major judicial areas, each with a *qādī al-jamā'a*. These three were based at Seville, Cordoba and Murcia.

Qādisīya: a decisive four day battle fought against the Persians in Iraq in 15/636.

Qaḥṭān: (Biblical Joktan), the ancestor of the southern Arabs.

Qarn: the *mīqāt* of the people of Najd between Ṭā'if and Makka.

qāṣṣ (pl. *quṣṣāṣ*)**:** Muslim popular preacher and storyteller.

Qaswā': the Prophet's she-camel.

Qayrawān: also spelled Qairouan or Kairouan, a town in north-central Tunisia. It was founded in 50/670 on the site of the Byzantine fortress of Kamouinia, and served as the camp from which the offensive was launched that resulted in the Islamic conquest of the Maghrib. Qayrawān was chosen as the capital of the Maghrib by the first Aghlabid ruler in about 182/800. Subsequently, it served (with Mahdīya) as the political centre through the Fāṭimid and Zīrid dynasties into the eleventh century. It has since declined into an isolated market town.

Qayṣar: "Caesar", a generic term for the ruler of the Romans.

qiṣaṣ al-anbiyā': stories of the Prophets.

qiṣṣa: a popular story, connected narrative or piece of propaganda.

Qubā: a village on the outskirts of Madina (originally about 5 km/3 miles) where the first mosque in Islam was built, also known as the Masjid at-Taqwā (Mosque of Fear of God).

Quraysh: one of the great tribes of Arabia. The Prophet Muḥammad belonged to this tribe, which had great powers spiritually and financially both before and after Islam came. Someone from this tribe is called a Qurayshī.

rabaḍ: suburb of a city.

Rāshidūn: "the Rightly-guided," the first four khalifs of Islam: Abū Bakr, 'Umar, 'Uthmān and 'Alī.

rawādif: later immigrants, late-comers to garrison cities after the conquest.

ribāṭ: the stronghold traditionally used by the Muslims to prepare for their *jihād* against the enemies of Islam, situated on exposed points of the frontier.

Ridda: the defection of various Arab tribes after the death of the Prophet, may Allah bless him and grant him peace, which brought about the Ridda War.

rizq: rations issued to soldiers.

ar-Rūm: the Romans or Byzantines; also *Sūra* 30 of the Qur'ān.

sābiqa: seniority in Islam, hence *as-sābiqūn al-awwalūn*, "the first foremost ones", those Muhājirūn and Anṣār who accepted Islam before the conquest of Makka and strove with their lives and their property in the Cause of Allah.

Safavids: Iranian dynasty that ruled Persia from 907/1501 to 1145/1736.

ṣāḥib ash-shurṭaī chief of police.

ṣā'ifa: summer expedition of the Muslims.

Ṣakb: the Prophet's stallion at the Battle of Uhud.

Saljuqs: see *Seljuqs*.

sanjak: the domain under the control of a beylerbey.

sardar: a Persian title, used also in India and Turkey, meaning a prince with a military command.

Sarīf: a place six miles away from Makka.

Sawād: lit. "the Black", fertile agricultural region of south-central Iraq which is 'black' with date-palms. When it was first conquered by the Muslims, 'Umar ibn al-Khaṭṭāb decided not to divide it among the fighters, but to levy the *kharāj* tax on it instead.

Seljuqs: also Saljuqs, Seljuks. A dynasty of Oghuz Turkmen who first appeared in Transoxiana and Khorasan in the 5th/11th century, establishing an empire in 431/1040 which extended from Central Asia to the Byzantine marches in Asia Minor. It was a cohesive *Sunnī* state under the nominal authority of the 'Abbasid khalifs at Baghdad. After the death of Mālikshāh in 485/1092, internal conflict led to the fragmentation of the Seljuks' central authority into smaller units.

Shām: the territory north of Arabia which is now divided into Syria, Palestine, Lebanon and Jordan.

sharaf al-'aṭā': the highest stipend paid out in the Muslim army.

shūra: "consultation". In early Islamic history, this designates the board of electors that was constituted by 'Umar to elect his successor. Thereafter *shūra* variously designated a council of state, or advisers to the sovereign, a parliament (in modern times), and sometimes a court of law with jurisdiction over claims made by citizens and public officials against the government.

Shu'ūbīya: nationalism, ethno-centricity; from a ninth century literary and political movement in which Persians sought equal power and status with the Arabs.

Ṣiffīn: a place in Syria where, in 38/657, a battle between 'Alī ibn Abī Ṭālib and Mu'āwiya took place.

Sijilmāsa: a great wealthy city on the edge of the desert which was built in 140/757 by Midrār ibn 'Abdullāh. It was on the gold route.

sikka: the die with which coins were minted, and hence the coins themselves.

sipahi: Ottoman horseman supported by land grants in exchange for military service; see *timar*.

ṣiqlabī (plural *ṣaqāliba*)**:** Slav, originally used for slave soldiers from eastern Europe, later for all white slave soldiers and mercenaries.

sīra: "conduct, behaviour, way of acting", hence a biography, particularly the biography the Prophet.

siyāsa: rule or governance, as contrasted with Divine *Sharī'a*.

Sufyānids: those Umayyads who were descended from Abū Sufyān. It designates the Umayyad khalifs Mu'āwiya, Yazīd and Mu'āwiya II.

sūq: market.

Syr Darya: The Jaxartes, a major river, which flows through the territory of Kazakhstan.

Ṭabaqāt: chronicles, biographies arranged according to generations.

Tabūk: a town in northern Arabia close to Jordan. In the ninth year after the *Hijra*, the Messenger of Allah, hearing that the Byzantines were gathering a large army to march against the Muslims, led a large expedition, in his last campaign, to Tabūk, only to find the rumours premature.

Ṭā'if: an important town in the mountains, fifty miles to the east of Makka.

Talas, Battle of: a battle which took place northeast of Tashkent in which the Chinese armies were crushed by the Arabs and retreated behind the Great Wall. It marks the end of Chinese power in Central Asia.

ṭālib: student.

Tan'īm: a place towards the north of Makka outside the sanctuary from where Makkans may assume the state of *iḥrām* to perform *'umra.*

taqīya: "prudent fear", not expressing one's true beliefs publicly out of fear of persecution.

tawqī'a (*tawqī'āt*)**:** the instructions or decisions of a ruler or official written at the bottom of a petition presented to him.

Tawwābūn: a group of Shi'a who in 64-5/684-5, marched from Kufa to fight an Umayyad army in the Battle of 'Ayn al-Warda and were virtualy exterminated. Their name was chosen from the Qur'ān 2:54. They were trying to purge their shame at having failed to help al-Ḥusayn at Karbalā'.

Ṭayyiba: "the good", another name of Madina.

Thabīr: a mountain near Makka.

Thawr: a well-known mountain at Madina. (See *Jabal Thawr*).

thughūr: outer northern frontiers, particularly the Byzantine border, and the borders between the Christians and Muslims in Andalusia.

timar: land grant by Ottoman sultans for military service.

ṭulaqā': "freed", used for those persons who had embraced Islam on the day of the conquest of Makka.

al-'Udwa: "the bank", the land on the other side of the Strait of Gibralter, the term by which the Andalusians designated what is now Morocco.

Uhud: a mountain just outside Madina where five years after the *Hijra*, the Muslims lost a battle against the Makkan idolaters. Many great Companions, and in particular Ḥamza, the uncle of the Prophet, were killed in this battle.

'Ukāz: in the Hijāz in the region of Ṭā'if, southeast of Makka where a fair was held once a year at the beginning of Dhū'l-Qa'da. It lasted for weeks. The Prophet stopped it because of the pagan elements it embodied.

'Umar ibn al-Khaṭṭāb: the second khalif of the Muslims, between 13/634 and 23/644, renowned for his justness and refusal to compromise the *Dīn*. He asked Allah for martyrdom in the Cause of Allah in Madina and his request was granted after he was fatally stabbed by a Persian slave while doing the dawn prayer. He is buried next to Abū Bakr.

Umayyads: the Muslim dynasty of khalifs who ruled in Damascus from 40/661 onwards until they were overthrown by the Abbasids in 132/750.

Uṣūlī: a school among the Shi'a who recognise only the Qur'ān and *ḥadīth* as sources of *fiqh*.

'Uthmān ibn 'Affān: the third khalif of the Muslims, between 23/644 and 36/656, renowned for his modesty. He ensured that the Qur'ān in its written form was accurate and preserved. He was murdered in his house by rebels while he was reciting the Qur'ān.

al-'Uzza: female idol worshipped by the pagan Arabs in the Ḥijāz in the *Jāhilīya*.

Wādī'l-Qurā: located near the Gulf of 'Aqaba north of the Red Sea where a Jewish settlement was located in the time of the Prophet.

Wahhābī: member of a sect dominant in Arabia whose earlier followers supported the family of Sa'ūd and helped bring the Ottoman khalifate to an end.

Wāsiṭ: a military and commercial city in Iraq, especially important under the Umayyads. Wāsiṭ was established as a military encampment in 83/702 on the Tigris River, between Baṣra and Kūfa, by al-Ḥajjāj. Through its location on the Tigris, at the centre of a network of roads radiating to all parts of Iraq, Wāsiṭ became a great shipbuilding and commercial centre. It disappeared after a shift in the course of the Tigris, sometime in the 15th century CE.

wazīr: vizier, chief minister.

wufūd: the plural of *wafd*, delegations.

Yalamlama: the *mīqāt* of the people of Yemen.

Yarmūk: an important battle between the Muslims and the Byzantines in 13/636.

Yathrīb: the ancient name for Madina.

Zanj: the black tribes of East Africa (hence Zanzibar).

Zaydites: a branch of the Shi'a deriving from Zayd ibn 'Alī and hence called Fivers as they have five Imāms.

zunnār: a special belt worn by non-Muslims to distinguish them visually from Muslims.

Some Notable Historians

al-Bakrī: Abu 'Ubayd 'Abdullāh ibn 'Abdu'l-'Azīz, one of the most important sources for the history of western Sudan. He was born to a princely family in Andalusia and moved to Cordoba. He lived most of his life in Cordoba and Almería and was known as a geographer, theologian, philologist and botanist. He died in 487/1094. Few of his works remain, one of which is *Kitāb al-masālik wa'l-mamālik* (Book of Routes and Realms) which is incomplete.

al-Balādhurī: Aḥmad ibn Yaḥyā ibn Jābir, (d. 279/892). The author of *Ansāb al-Ashrāf* and *Futūḥ al-Buldān.* He may have been of Persian origin but spent most of his life in Baghdad. He was one of the first to combine materials from *sīra* and other sources into a historical narrative.

adh-Dhahabī: Muḥammad ibn Aḥmad, great Turkoman Muslim scholar, born in Damascus in 673/1274, who wrote a hundred books, including the twenty-three volume biographical collection, *Siyar a'lam an-Nubalā'* and the thirty-six volume *Ta'rīkh al-Islām al-Kabīr* (Major History of Islam). He died in Damascus in 748/1347.

ad-Dīnawarī: Abū Ḥanīfa Aḥmad ibn Dāwūd, (d. c. 282/895). He wrote *al-Akhbār aṭ-Ṭiwāl* (Extended Histories) a universal history in a single volume. Although he cites reports from both sides, he chooses his preferred version of events, mainly for literary reasons. He also uses non-Muslim, mainly Persian sources.

Ibn 'Abd al-Ḥakam: Muḥammad ibn 'Abdullāh. He was an eminent Mālikī *faqīh* in Egypt. People travelled to him. He was a close friend and follower of ash-Shāfi'ī. He wrote many books including *Aḥkām al-Qur'ān, Kitāb al-Majālis*, *ar-Radd 'alā ash-Shāfi'ī,* and *ar-Radd 'alā ahl al-'Iraq*. He died in 257/871.

Ibn A'tham al-Kūfi: a Shi'ite historian who wrote an extensive *Kitāb al-Futūḥ* which he wrote in 204/819, which makes him earlier than al-Balādhurī. He combines all the traditions together into a single narrative. He died around 214/829.

Ibn al-Athīr: 'Izz ad-Dīn Abū'l-Ḥasan 'Alī ibn Muḥammad ash-Shaybānī, (555/1160 – 630/1233). A historian who was born in Mosul. He has one of the most impartial accounts of history, *al-Kāmil fī't-Ta'rīkh*, which was begun as an abridgement of aṭ-Ṭabarī's *Ta'rīkh*. He also wrote *Usd al-Ghāba*.

Ibn Hishām: 'Abdu'l-Malik (d. 208/834) The author of *Sīrat Muḥammad,* a re-working of the *Kitāb al-Maghāzī* of Ibn Isḥāq, the earliest biography of the Prophet.

Ibn 'Idhārī: Aḥmad ibn Muḥammad al-Marrakūshī, Spanish historian in the late 7th/13th century, author of *al-Bayān al-Mughrib*. It is one of the best sources of information on the dynasties of Andalusia and North Africa.

Ibn Isḥāq: Abū 'Abdullāh Muḥammad. A great scholar who grew up in Madina. He has rare *ḥadīths* which are sometimes disacknowledged because of his vast memory. Mālik ibn Anas is reported as having accused him of being a Shi'ite and inventor of legends. He went to Egypt and Iraq. He wrote *Kitāb al-Maghāzī* which is the earliest biography of the Prophet. He wrote it for the second 'Abbasid khalif, al-Manṣūr. His work has perished and what we have is the re-working of Ibn Hishām. Aṭ-Ṭabari also quotes from him. He died c. 150/767 in Baghdad, having been invited there by al-Manṣūr.

Ibn Kathīr: 'Imād ad-dīn Ismā'īl ibn 'Umar ibn Kathīr, Abū'l-Fidā', born in 701/1302 in a village outside Damascus. He moved to Damascus at the age of five. He was widely travelled and studied with many famous scholars, including Ibn Taymiyya. He was a Shāfi'ī scholar with books with expertise in various areas. He was greatly respected. His history is entitled *al-Bidāya wa'n-Nihāya*. He died in Damascus in 774/1372.

Ibn Khaldūn: 'Abdu'r-Raḥman ibn Muḥammad, generally known as Ibn Khaldūn after a remote ancestor, was born in Tunis in 732/1332 to a family that had earlier emigrated there from Seville in Muslim Spain. Ibn Khaldūn is universally recognized as the founder and father of sociology and sciences of History. He is best known for his famous *Muqaddima*, (Prolegomena), the introduction to the seven volume *al-'Ibar,* the world's first work on social theory. He was a philosopher and historian who travelled over North Africa and Andalusia where he held several government positions. He went to Egypt where the Mamlūk aẓ-Ẓāhir made him the chief Mālikī *qāḍī*, but was dismissed for preferring his native Tunisian dress to customary official robes. He died in Cairo in 808/1406.

Ibn Khallikān: Abū'l-'Abbās Aḥmad ibn Muḥammad (d. 681/1282), a Muslim judge and author of a classic Arabic biographical dictionary which covers all fields, *Wafayāt al-a'yān*. Ibn Khallikān studied in Irbil, Aleppo, and Damascus.

Ibn Khayyāṭ: Khalīfa**,** Shabāb, a Baṣran historian and *muḥaddith*. He died in 240/854, wrote *Kitāb aṭ-Ṭabaqāt*. His *Ta'rīkh* is the oldest of histories, covering 1 AH to 230 AH. He makes use of *isnād* and includes information from Umayyad narrations.

Ibn Taghrībirdī: Abū'l-Maḥāsin Yūsuf: born in Cairo, prob. 812/1409-10. His father was a senior Mamlūk amīr who was commander-in-chief of Egyptian armies and governor of Damascus under aẓ-Ẓāhir Barqūq. He died in 874/1470. He has a biographical collection, *al-Manhal as-Sāfī* and *an-Nujūm az-Zāhira*.

al-Jahshiyārī: Muḥammad ibn 'Abdūs, (d. 331/942), author of *Kitab al-Wuzarā' wa'l-Kuttāb*, an extensive work and administrative account. It begins in pre-Islamic times, going through the secretaries of the Prophet and khalifs until his own times. It is really a history of administration.

al-Madā'inī: Abū'l-Ḥasan 'Alī ibn Muḥammad, famous early historian, (c. 132/749-50 to 228/843). He wrote a history on the khalifs and a book on campaigns, both of which are lost. He is the undisputed authority on the early history of the Arabs in Khurasan. He used Makkan and Madinan accounts.

al-Maqqarī: Abū'l-'Abbās Aḥmad ibn Muḥammad (d. 1041/1631). His family was originally from Maqqara, twelve miles southeast of Msila, Algeria, but he lived for many years at Tlemcen. He wrote a history of Andalusia, *Nafḥ aṭ-Ṭīb*, which was a rather romantic account which has been translated by P. de Gayangos as *History of the Mohammaden Dynasties in Spain*.

al-Maqrīzī: Taqī'd-dīn Aḥmad ibn 'Alī, (766/1364 – 845/1441). A very productive writer and one of the most famous historians of the

Mamlūk period. He was born and died in Cairo. He studied with Ibn Khaldūn when he was there. His main work was *al-Khiṭaṭ*.

al-Mas'ūdī: Abū'l-Ḥasan 'Alī ibn al-Ḥusayn. He was a descendant of 'Abdullāh ibn Mas'ūd, the Companion. An expert geographer, a physicist and historian, al-Mas'ūdī was born in the last decade of the 9th century CE in Baghdad, his exact date of birth being unknown. He was a Mu'tazilite who explored distant lands and died at Cairo, in 345/956. He travelled extensively. In Baṣra he completed his book *Murūj adh-Dhahab*, in which he has described his experience of various countries, peoples and climates. In Cairo he wrote his second extensive book *Murūj al-Zaman* in thirty volumes in which he describes in detail the geography and history of the countries that he had visited. His first book was completed in 332/943. Mas'ūdi is referred to as the Herodotus and Pliny of the Arabs. By presenting a critical account of historical events, he initiated a change in the art of historical writing, introducing the elements of analysis, reflection and criticism. He was the first author to make mention of windmills, which were invented by the Muslims of Sijistān. He also made important contributions to music and other fields of science He had 'Alid tendencies, and only two works are left, *Murūj adh-Dhahab* and *Kitāb at-Tanbīh*.

Muḥammad ibn Sa'd: Abū 'Abdullāh, the famous reliable Imām and *mawlā* of the Banū Hāshim, known as the *kāṭib* (scribe) of al-Wāqidī. He is the author of the *Ṭabaqāt*. He died in 230/844-5 at the age of 62. He was born in 148/764-5.

Naṣr ibn Muzāḥim al-Minqarī: (c. 120/738 – 212/827), an Arab of Tamīm and the author of *Waq'at Ṣiffīn* ("The Battle of Ṣiffīn") the earliest Shi'ite historical source. He was from Kūfa, and settled in Baghdad where he studied under Sufyān ath-Thawrī. He was a perfumer and wrote several other books.

as-Suyūṭi: Jalāl ad-dīn'Abdu'r-Raḥmān ibn Abī Bakr, born in 849/1445. A Shāfi'ī *mujtahid*, Sufi, *ḥadīth* scholar and historian. He wrote books on almost every subject. He died in 911/1505.

aṭ-Ṭabari: Muḥammad ibn Jarīr, the well-known historian and Qur'ān commentator, especially known for his large history. He was from Tabaristan and was born in 224/839 and died in 310/923. His history is a universal history, covering ancient nations, Biblical peoples, ancient Iran and the history of the Islamic world to 302/915.

al-Wāqidī: Abū 'Abdullāh Muḥammad ibn 'Umar, a freed man of Madina. A corn-merchant who, after heavy losses, moved to Baghdad. He became qāḍī in 'Askar al-Mahdi in Baghdad. He died in 207/823 while still qāḍī. He wrote a *Kitāb Ṣiffīn, Kitāb ar-Ridda, al-Maghāzī* and a number of other books. His reliability was criticised.

al-Ya'qūbī: Aḥmad ibn Abī Ya'qūb (d. 284/897), a historian and geographer. He was pro-Alid and anti-Zubayrid, but served the Abbasid khalifs. His history puts stress on economic factors. He covers scientific and philosophical works and is the sole Muslim source for the nomenclature of the Khazar kings. His history is narrative. He wrote a *Ta'rīkh* and *Kitāb al-Buldān.*

Yāqūt: ibn 'Abdullāh al-Ḥamawī ar-Rūmī, by origin a Greek. He was born in 575/1179. He was captured in Byzantine territory and sold to a Syrian merchant in Baghdad who gave him a good education and later sent him to trade on his behalf. He was freed in 596/1199 and continued to travel, exploring libraries. He began *Mu'jam al-Buldān* in 608/1212 and continued to put the finishing touches to it up to his death in Aleppo in 626/1229.

Some Early Historical Sources

A'māl al-A'lām: "Deeds of the Great" by Ibn al-Khaṭīb (d. 774/1374), the wazīr of Granada and a contemporary of Ibn Khaldūn. *A'māl al-A'lām* is a general Muslim history in three parts: the Muslim East, Spain and North Africa and Sicily. The third part was not properly completed. The third part is translated by R. Castrillo as *Historia medieval islamica de Norte de Africa y Sicilia.*

Ansāb al-Ashrāf: "Lineage of the Nobles" by al-Balādhurī (d. 279/892), a fairly objective history, one-third of which is on the Umayyads. It contains a wealth of historical information.

al-Bidāya wa'n-Nihāya fī't-Ta'rīkh: "The Beginning and the End on History" by Ibn Kathīr (d. 774/1374), a large universal history.

Futūḥ al-Buldān: by al-Balādhurī (d. 279/892) on the Muslim conquests. Translated by Philip Hitti as *The Origins of the Islamic State*, it is indispensible for the history of the Muslim conquests. Al-Balādhurī made personal inquiries from local sources and so he has more primary information. He is more interested in the east. He has the most comprehensive account of the advance of the Arab armies in the east.

Futūḥ Miṣr wa'l-Maghrib: "Conquests of Egypt and the Maghrib" by Ibn 'Abd al-Ḥakam (d. 257/871). He was devoted to the study of *ḥadīth* and his account of the conquests of Egypt and the Maghrib is one of a traditionist, giving the *isnād* of each piece of information. It is translated into French by Gateau as *Conquête de l'Afrique du Nord et de l'Espagne*. It is also translated into Spanish by E. Vidal Beltran.

al-Imāma wa's-Siyāsa: "The Imamate and Politics", attributed to Ibn Qutayba (d. 276/889), (although there is some debate about this.) It is also known as *Ta'rīkh al-Khulafā'*. It deals with the history of Islam under the Rāshidūn Khalifs and Umayyads, with some observations on the 'Abbasids.

al-Kāmil fī't-Ta'rīkh: "The Complete Book on History" by Ibn al-Athīr (d. 630/1233) Begun as an abridgement of aṭ-Ṭabarī's *Tarīkh*, it is one of the best known and most impartial and readable accounts. He continued on from aṭ-Ṭabarī until 628/1230-1. He does not mention his sources for the last 300 years. The passages which deal with North Africa and Spain were translated into French by E. Fagnan as *Annales du Maghreb et de l'Espagne.*

Kitāb al-Bayān al-Mughrib: "The Astonishing Explanation of the Kings of Spain and North Africa" by Ibn 'Idhārī al-Marrākushī (late 7th/13th cent). It is one of the best sources of information, being a compilation of earlier books.

Kitāb al-Masālik wa'l-Mamālik: "Book of Routes and Realms" by al-Bakrī (d. 487/1094). One of the most important sources for the history of the western Sudan. There is a French translation by Monteil.

Kitāb as-Sulūk: "Book of Entrance to the Knowledge of the Dynasties of the Kings" by al-Maqrīzī (d. 845/1441), a history of Egypt from Salāḥ ad-dīn in 564/1169, with some introductory remarks on earlier times. It ends in 844/1440-1 and was continued by Ibn Taghrībindī. So it is the complete history of the Ayyūbids and Bahrī Mamlūks and part of the Burjī Mamlūks. A lot of it is translated as *Histoire des sultans mamluks de l'Égypte* by Quatremère.

al-Maghāzī: "Expeditions" by al-Wāqidī (d. 207/823). An account of the military expeditions of the Prophet. He may well be earlier than Ibn Isḥāq and his sources come from a different line than Ibn Isḥāq.

al-Muqaddima: by Ibn Khaldūn (d. 808/1406), the "Introduction" to his universal history, *Kitāb al-'Ibar. Kitāb al-'Ibar* is particularly useful for North African history. The *Muqaddima* is translated by Rosenthal.

Murūj adh-Dhahab: by al-Mas'ūdī (d. 345-956). In it he describes his experience of various countries, peoples and climates. He chooses what was a more modern approach than aṭ-Ṭabarī and selects one version of an event. There is a partial translation as *The Meadows of Gold* and a full French translation called *Les Prairies d'Or.*

Nafḥ aṭ-Ṭīb: by al-Maqqarī (d. 1041/1631), it has been translated by P. de Gayangos as *History of the Mohammaden Dynasties in Spain.*

Sīra: by Ibn Hishām (d. 218/833). He re-worked the *Kitāb al-Maghāzī* of Ibn Isḥāq, the earliest biography of the Prophet. It is one of the best existing authorities on the life of the Prophet. It has been translated into English by Guillaume.

Ṭabaqāt Ibn Sa'd: "Generations" by Muḥammad ibn Sa'd (d. 230/844-5), a compilation of earlier information with biographies on the Prophet, the Companions and later generations. It is tradition-based. Volumes 7 and 8 have been published as *The Men of Madina, Vol. 1* and *The Women of Madina* respectively.

Tajārib al-Umam: "Experiences of the Nations" by (Ibn) Miskawayh (d. 421/1030). The first part is dependent on aṭ-Ṭabarī, but the later part extends to the death in 372/983 of the Būyid 'Aḍud ad-Dawla, whose confidant he was. From 340/951 he depends on eye-witnesses. The concluding part is available in translation as *The Eclipse of the Abbasid Caliphate.*

Ta'rīkh al-Islām: "The History of Islam" by adh-Dhahabī (d. 748/1348), a very extensive work of history from which he extracted shorter works. One of them, *Kitāb Duwal al-Islām,* is translated as *Les dynasties d'Islam.* His *History* does contain some things which are not mentioned in aṭ-Ṭabarī. He relies a lot on the *Ṭabaqāt* of as-Sulamī.

Ta'rīkh al-Khulafā': "The History of the Khalifs" by as-Suyūṭī (d. 911/1505), a history of those called khalifs. The part covering the first khalifs has been published as *The History of the Khalifahs who took the right way.*

Ta'rīkh Madīnat Dimashq: "History of the City of Damascus" by Ibn 'Asākir (502/1106 – 572/1176), a local history of Damascus which is very biographical.

Ta'rīkh aṭ-Ṭabarī: his "World History" which covers Biblical Prophets, early rulers, Sasanian history and Islamic history, ending at 310/922. It is very detailed, but it should be noted that aṭ-Ṭabari had pro-Alid sympathies. He also follows the manner of the traditionists, and gives all versions of an event which he has. It has been translated by various authors as a series.

Ta'rīkh al-Umam: "History of Kings of the Earth and Prophets" by Ḥamza al-Iṣfahānī (d. 356/967). It is rather like a textbook which covers the history of past peoples. He is very careful about his sources.

Wafayāt al-A'yān: "Deaths of Notables and News of the Sons of the Times," written by Ibn Khallikān between 654/1256 and 672/1274. A biographical dictionary written in the Mamlūk period. It is valuable because he used sources which are now lost. There is an old English translation by de Slane called *Ibn Khallikān's Biographical Dictionary.*

Waq'at Ṣiffīn: "The Battle of Ṣiffīn" by Naṣr ibn Muzāḥim (d. 212/827). The earliest Shi'ite historical source, which is an account of the battle between Mu'āwiya and 'Alī in 37/657.

az-Zāhira fī Mulūk Miṣr wa'l-Qāhira: "The Brilliant Stars in the Kings of Egypt and Cairo" by Ibn Taghrībirdī, covers Egyptian history from the Arab conquest to 872/1468. A translation of the period dealing with the Circassian Mamluks (784/1382 – 872/1468) has been translated by William Popper as *History of Egypt.*

Eschatology

akhbār al-ghayb: Prophetical reports of previously unrecorded events.

Ākhira: the Next World, what is on the other side of death, the Hereafter, the dimension of existence after this world.

'Arsh: the Throne. It is the ceiling of all creatures and the greatest of them. The Throne contains immense expanses, height and resplendent beauty, but it is beyond the power of any human being to describe it or imagine its form. Knowledge of it is with Allah alone. The light of the Throne is from the Light of the Noble Face of Allah. The Throne has bearers who carry it and Allah Almighty is settled on it, in a way that is beyond definition or concept.

Aṣḥāb al-Mash'ama: "the Companions of the Left", the people of the Fire (See Qur'ān 56:9).

Aṣḥāb al-Maymana: "the Companions of the Right", the people of the Garden (See Qur'ān 56:8).

'Azrā'īl: the Angel of Death, one of the four archangels.

Bāb ar-Rayyān: "The Gate of the Well-Watered", a special gate of the Garden by which the people of fasting enter.

barzakh: the interspatial life in the grave between death in this world and resurrection on the Day of Rising.

ba'th: the arousing or bringing the dead back to life at the end of the world.

al-Bayt al-Ma'mūr: "the Visited House", Allah's House above the seventh heaven.

dabba: the beast which will arise from the earth, (see Qur'ān 27:82). It is one of the signs of the approach of the Last Hour.

Dajjāl: the false Messiah whose appearance marks the imminent end of the world. The Arabic root means "to deceive, cheat, take in".

Dukhān: "smoke"; the name of *Sūra* 44 of the Qur'ān, one of the signs before the End of the world.

Firdaws: Paradise.

al-fitan wa ashrāṭ as-sā'a: the trials and the signs of the Hour. Also known as *āyāt as-sā'a*, "the signs of the Hour".

al-Ghāshīya: "The Overwhelmer", one of the names for the Day of Judgement and the name of *Sūra* 88 of the Qur'ān.

al-ghurr al-muḥajjalūn: "those with shining white on their foreheads, wrists and ankles", a name that will be given on the Day of Resurrection to the Muslims because the parts of their bodies which they used to wash in ablution will shine then.

Ḥamalat al-'Arsh: "the bearers of the Throne", the eight angels who are the bearers of the Divine Throne.

Hārūt and Mārūt: the two angels mentioned in the Qur'ān (2:102) in Babel from whom people learned magic. Some commentators state that they are two kings rather than two angels (*malik* rather than *malak*).

Ḥawḍ: the watering-place or Basin of the Prophet in the Next World, whose drink will refresh those who have crossed the *Sirāṭ* before entering the Garden.

al-Hāwīya: the abyss, bottomless pit, Hell.

al-Ḥuṭama: "that which breaks to pieces", the seventh and deepest level of the Fire (See Qur'ān 104:4-9).

houri: see *ḥūr*.

ḥūr: houris, pure maidens in Paradise, literally "the white ones", often said to refer to the contrast between the intense white and the intense blackness of the eyes, or it means having eyes like gazelles. The singular is *ḥawrā'*.

Iblīs: the personal name of the Devil. He is also called Shayṭān or the "enemy of Allah".

'Illīyūn: "the High Places", a name for the upper part of the Heavens, where the register of people's good actions are kept, or a name for the register itself. (See Qur'ān 83:18-19).

Isrāfīl: the archangel who will blow the Trumpet to announce the end of the world.

Jahannam: Hell, Gehenna.

al-Jaḥīm: Hellfire.

Janna: the Garden, Heaven, Paradise.

Jibrīl: or Jibrā'īl, the angel Gabriel who brought the revelation of the Qur'ān to the Prophet Muḥammad, may Allah bless him and grant him peace.

jinn: a class of being created from smokeless fire who are generally invisible to human beings. There are many types of them, like the *'ifrīt* and the *ghūl*, which lures travellers to their death in the wilderness.

al-Karrūbiyūn: the Cherubim, the angels who are the closest to the Throne-bearers and praise Allah constantly night and day. Their name is either derived from *karb* or "sorrow", because of the intensity of their fear of Allah, or from *kurb*, meaning "nearness" and "strength" because of their constancy in worship.

al-Kathīb: the Slipping Sand-Heap, the heap where all souls will assemble in the Next World, each taking its place according to its spiritual rank.

kātibūn: the recording angels. (See Qur'ān 82:10-12).

Kawthar: "Abundance", a river in the Garden.

kirām kātibīn: "the noble scribes", the two angels who sit on the human being's shoulders to record his actions. (See Qur'ān 82:11).

kismet: this word for "fate" comes from the Arabic *qisma*, meaning "part" or "portion", and was changed via Persian and Turkish.

al-Kursī: the Footstool (as distinct from the Throne (*'Arsh*)) although the *Āyat al-Kursī* (2:255) is referred to as the Throne verse. The Footstool is 'under' the Throne and is far smaller than it, "like a ring lying buried in the middle of the desert" (*ḥadīth*). The place of the Divine Command and Prohibition, the realm of the universe and the seven heavens, in both the Seen and the Unseen.

al-Lawḥ al-Maḥfūẓ: the Preserved Tablet in the Unseen which is also referred to as the *Umm al-Kitāb*, the place of recording what will be, the repository of Destiny.

al-Ma'ād: "the returning" to life after death; the life-to-come; the Hereafter.

al-Mahdī: "the Divinely Guided", the descendant of the Prophet who will return at the end of time to establish justice.

maḥshar: the place of gathering on the Day of Judgement.

al-Mala' al-A'lā: the heavenly host, the angels.

malā'ika: angels, the plural of *malak* (*muqarrabūn*: the angels brought near to Allah; *al-karrūbiyūn* (Cherubim) who praise Allah constantly night and day); *ḥāfiẓūn* (guardian angels). The ten individual angels mentioned are Jibrīl, Mikā'īl, Isrāfīl, 'Azrā'īl, Munkar, Nakīr, Riḍwān, Mālik, and the two guardian angels who record each person's actions.

Malakūt: the angelic world.

Mālik: the angel in charge of Hell.

Malik al-Mawt: the Angel of Death, 'Azra'īl.

al-Maqām al-Maḥmūd: the highest place in Paradise, which will be granted to the Prophet Muḥammad and none else.

mārid: a strong and rebellious type of jinn.

al-Masīḥ: the Messiah, 'Īsā son of Maryam.

al-Masīḥ ad-Dajjāl: the anti-Messiah, the Antichrist.

mawāzīn: the plural of *mīzān*, the scales or balances set up to weigh people's actions on the Day of Judgement.

Mawqif: "the Standing" for judgement on the Day of Rising.

Mikā'īl: the archangel Michael. He is entrusted with the rain, wind and clouds by which land, plants and animals are brought to life.

Munkar and Nakīr: the two angels who come to question a person in the grave about his or her beliefs and actions while in this world.

muqarrabūn: "those who are drawn near", those who are nearest to Allah. The angels who are *muqarrabūn* are also called *al-'alawīyūn*, "the highest".

nafkha: a blast of the Trumpet. There will be two blasts. At the first all in the heaven and earth will die, and at the second all will rise.

an-Nār: the Fire, Hell.

al-Qāri'a: "The Crashing Blow", one of the names of the Last Day and the name of *Sūra* 101 of the Qur'ān.

al-Qiyāma: the arising and standing of people at the Resurrection, and the name of *Sūra* 75 of the Qur'ān.

ar-Rayyān: the name of one of the gates of Paradise through which only the people who often observe fasting will enter. Once all the fasters have entered it, it will be locked.

Riḍwān: the angel in charge of admitting people to the Garden.

as-Sā'a: the Final Hour (the Day of Judgement).

sābiqūn: "those who outstrip the rest", in drawing near to Allah.

ṣāḥib ash-shimāl: "companion of the left", one of the recording angels; also an inhabitant of the Fire.

ṣāḥib aṣ-Ṣūr: "the possessor of the Trumpet", meaning the angel Isrāfīl.

ṣāḥib al-yamīn: "companion of the right", one of the recording angels; also an inhabitant of the Garden.

aṣ-Ṣa'īr: raging fire, a name for Hell.

Salsabīl: the name of a fountain in Paradise mentioned in the Qur'ān in 76:18.

Saqar: scorching Fire, a name for Hell.

shafā'a: intercession, particularly the intercession of the Prophet Muḥammad on the Last Day.

Sidrat al-Muntahā: "The Lote-Tree of the Boundary" or "Lote Tree of the Uttermost Limit", a lote tree above the seventh heaven near the Paradise, denoting the limit of Being and the cessation of form itself; the place at which the knowledge of every creature, even the angels close to Allah, stops. (See Qur'ān 53:14).

Sijjīn: the register where the actions of the evil are recorded, or the place where the register is kept. Some say it is a stone underneath the lowest earth. (See Qur'ān 83:7-8)

Ṣirāṭ: the narrow bridge which spans the Fire and must be crossed to enter the Garden. It is described as sharper than a sword and thinner than a hair. It will have hooks over it to catch people as they cross it.

Tasnīm: the name of a fountain in Paradise.

Ṭūbā: a state of blessedness in the Garden.

Yājūj wa Mājūj: (or Ya'jūj wa Ma'jūj) the people of Gog and Magog who are to burst forth near the end of time to wreak destruction.

Yawm al-Ba'th: the Day of Rising, another name for the Day of Judgement.

Yawm ad-Dīn: the Day of Judgement.

Yawm al-Faṣl: "the Day of Dividing", another name for the Day of Judgement.

Yawm al-Ḥisāb: "The Day of Reckoning".

Yawm al-Qiyāma: "the Day of Rising", the Day of Standing.

Zabānīya: "the violent thrusters", the angels who thrust people into Hellfire, who are nineteen in number.

az-Zaqqūm: a tree with bitter fruit which grows at the bottom of the Fire. Its fruit resembles the heads of devils.

Terms relating to Morals and Ethics

adab: correct behaviour, both inward and outward, good deportment.

adīb: someone who is characterised by *adab*, someone well-disciplined.

'adl: justice, fairness, equitableness, the mean between excess and falling short.

akhlāq: the plural of *khuluq*, meaning trait of character. In the plural it means ethics, morality. The Prophet said, "I was sent to perfect good character (*akhlāq*)."

amal: false hope, remote expectation, as in having a false expectation of the importance of worldly things; or else true hope in Allah.

al-Amāna: the trust, or moral responsibility or honesty, and all the duties which Allah has ordained. (See Qur'ān 33:72). *Amāna* also means trustworthiness, faithfulness, honesty.

amīn (plural *umanā'*)**:** a trustworthy person. The Prophet was known as "al-Amīn".

barr: pious, dutiful to one's parents; one who behaves with kindness and gentleness and is truthful.

baṣīra: insight, discernment.

birr: kindness, solicitous regard for parents and others, piety towards Allah, gentle behaviour and regard for others, obedience to Allah.

bukhl: niggardliness, stinginess, avarice; denying the poor any one's excess wealth; withholding that which it is not lawful to withhold.

dahā': political finesse which consists of intelligence combined with cunning and accurate forward planning.

dunyā: this world, not as a cosmic phenomenon, but as imagined and experienced. (See *khayāl*).

faḍā'il: virtues, excellent qualities. It is the plural of *faḍīla*.

faḥshā': something abominable or obscene, meaning anything forbidden by Allah. It can also designate fornication or foul language.

faqīh an-nafs: "an expert on the self", a term used by al-Ghazālī for someone with expertise and understanding of the art of purifying the self.

fāsiq (plural *fussāq*)**:** sinner, deviant, fornicater, profligate.

firāsa: the science of recognising a person's inward qualities by studying the outward appearance; intuitive knowledge of human nature.

fisq: deviant behaviour, leaving the correct way or abandoning the truth, disobeying Allah, immoral behaviour.

fiṭra: the first nature; the natural, primal condition of mankind in harmony with nature.

furqān: discrimination, distinguishing the true from the false. It is also a name given to a Divine revealed book.

futuwwa: chivalry; placing others above one's self as manifested in generosity, altruism, self-denial, indulgence for people's shortcomings. Also a term for the guilds in Asia Minor.

ghaḍḍ al-baṣar: lowering the eyes, a virtue required in the presence of members of the opposite sex.

al-ghazw al-fikrī: cultural aggression.

ghība: backbiting, slander, mentioning anything about a person that he would dislike to hear, even if it is true.

ghibṭa: the desire for a blessing which someone else has without desiring that it should pass away from the person who has it.

ghīra: This word covers a wide range of meanings: it can mean jealousy as regards women and it is also a feeling of great fury and anger when one's honour and prestige is injured or challenged. It can be positive or negative depending on the circumstances.

ghurūr: self-delusion, beguilement, as when someone is deceived by the appearance of worldly things or by Shayṭān.

ḥadīth an-nafs: the chatter of the self which goes on inside one's head.

ḥasad: envy of what someone else has and wishing that they did not possess it and would lose it. (Compare with *ghibṭa*).

ḥasana (plural *ḥasanāt*)**:** a good deed.

hawā: passion, desire (usually not praiseworthy) for self-gratification, inclination to something enjoyed by animal appetites; also used in the plural (*ahwā'*), meaning opinions which have moved away from the truth.

ḥayā’: this denotes a cluster of several concepts: modesty, diffidence, shyness, self-respect, scruples.

ḥikma: wisdom, that which acts as a curb and prevents a person from ignorant behaviour; knowledge of the true nature of things and acting accordingly.

ḥilm: forbearance, self-restraint.

iḥsān: virtue, doing the best.

iḥtimāl: endurance, forbearance.

ikhlāṣ: sincerity, pure unadulterated genuineness.

iqtiṣād: moderation, adopting a middle course, being frugal. In modern terms, it is used to mean ‘economics’.

istiqāma: rectitude, rightness, integrity, the state of being correct and sound in one’s being and behaviour.

istiqrār: persistence, stability, constancy.

istislām: submission, acceptance.

īthār: altruism, putting others before oneself.

ithm: wilful transgression, sin.

jahl: ignorance, lack of knowledge, also rashness, arrogance.

karam: nobility.

madhmūm: blameworthy.

maḥmūd: praiseworthy, commendable.

manāqib: virtues, glorious deeds.

muḥasaba: self-examination, examining one’s deeds and taking account of them.

muḥsin (plural *muḥsinūn*)**:** someone who does what is good.

munkar: any action or behaviour which is unacceptable or disapproved of by sound intellects; anything which is declared to be hateful, unseemly, foul, immoral, objectionable or reprehensible.

murū’a: manly virtue or moral probity, behaving in a manner which comprises all the virtues: manliness, courage, generosity, honour, refraining from doing secretly what one would be ashamed to do publicly, etc.

mutafahhish: a person who conveys evil talk.

nafth: literally “spitting”, often meaning to cast something into the mind.

namīma: tale-bearing, to quote someone's words to another in a way that worsens relations between them.

nasīḥa (plural *naṣā'iḥ*)**:** good advice, sincere conduct.

nifāq: hypocrisy.

qinā'a: contentedness, frugality and temperance; being satisfied with what one has.

raḥma: mercy.

rayb: a doubt which creates disquiet, mental agitation, and suspicion.

riḍā: being well-pleased and content with what Allah decrees.

riyā': showing off, doing actions for the sake of being seen to do them.

riyāḍa: self-discipline, training and discipline.

sa'āda: happiness.

ṣabr: patience, fortitude, steadfastness.

sahr: sleeplessness.

sakīna: an enveloping stillness which Allah sends down on the hearts.

ṣalāḥ: goodness, righteousness, virtue.

ṣāliḥāt: righteous actions, good deeds.

shahwa: appetite, passion, desire, sexual and aggressive instincts.

shakk: doubt.

shukr: thankfulness, gratitude.

ṣiddīq: a man of truth, sincerity is his condition, a name of respect given to Abū Bakr.

ṣidq: truthfulness.

siyar: types of conduct.

ṭabī'a: nature, natural constitution, the aggregate of the natural constituent parts of something.

tadbīr: management, planning; to study, consider and comprehend something and then act accordingly.

ta'dīb: reprimand.

tahdhīb: refining and improving character.

taqwā: fearful awareness of Allah and acting accordingly.

tarbīya: education.

tawāḍu': humility.

tawakkul: confidently putting one's trust and reliance in Allah. It is the realisation that Allah provides for you.

tazkīya: "purification" in a moral and ethical sense, the continual psychological and moral process of purifying the soul of base qualities and desires. It is commanded in the Qur'ān in 91:7-10.

thabāt: steadfastness; possessing steadiness in battle or speech and self-restraint.

uns: fellowship, sociableness, inclination to company.

wafā': faithfulness, fidelity, discharging obligations and living up to promises.

warā': scrupulousness, being cautious about one's actions.

wāṣil: one who keeps good relations with his kith and kin.

Specific Topics

Qur'ānic Terms
Ḥadīth Terms
Fiqh
Kalām and Philosophy
Ṣūfism

Terms related to Qur'ānic recitation or *tafsīr*

adab of Qur'ān recitation: the *adab* of Qur'ān recitation includes the following: the intention should be sincerely for Allah and not to please others; the reciter must be pure in body, clothes and place; one begins by seeking refuge with Allah; it should be done with fear and humility and distinct pronunciation, and with awareness of the meanings of what is being recited; the recitation should be neither too soft nor too loud.

aḥkām al-Qur'ān: legal judgements which are derived from the Qur'ān.

aḥruf: the seven different modes in which the Qur'ān was revealed.

'āmm: generally applicable, in reference to a Qur'ānic ruling.

aqlāb: modification. This occurs when *nūn* or *tanwīn* is followed by *ba'*. The *nūn* becomes a *mīm*. Thus *min ba'd* becomes *mim ba'd.*

asbāb an-nuzūl: the historical circumstances leading up to a revelation or in which particular *āyāt* were revealed; situational exegesis.

a'ūdhu billāhi min ash-shayṭān ar-rajīm: the Arabic expression "I seek protection in Allah from the accursed Shayṭān." One says this before beginning to recite the Qur'ān.

āya(t) (plural *āyāt*)**:** verse of the Qur'ān; a sign of Allah.

Āyāt al-Aḥkām: verses which give rulings with a legal connotation.

Āyat al-Kursī: the Throne Verse: Qur'ān 2:255. Also called *Āyat al-Ḥifẓ*, the *Āyat* of Preservation. (See *Kursī*)

Āyat as-Sayf: the Verse of the Sword: Qur'ān 9:5.

balāgha: the clear and perspicuous style of the Qur'ān.

basmala: the expression, "In the name of Allah, the All-Merciful, the All-Compassionate".

bāṭin: inwardly hidden.

bāṭinī: inward, esoteric.

bayān: clarification, elucidation: either of the substance of a meaning in the Qur'ān or of the meaning of that substance.

bayyina (plural *bayyināt*)**:** a piece of evidence which is clear and demonstrates the truth; testimony. Such clear demonstrative evidence reinforces belief. *Bayyināt* can be either verses of the Qur'ān or natural phenomena.

bismi'llāh ar-Raḥmān ar-Raḥīm: the *basmala*: "In the name of Allah, the All-Merciful, the All-Compassionate".

al-Burūj: the the Constellations of the Zodiac; the name of *Sūra* 85 of the Qur'ān.

dhikru'llāh: "remembrance of Allah".

dirāya: deduction (as *istinbāṭ*): analysis of Scripture.

dukhān: "smoke", the name of *Sura* 44 of the Qur'ān, one of the signs before the End of the world.

fāṣila (plural *fawāṣil*)**:** the final words of the verses of the Qur'ān which resemble rhyme.

Fātiḥa: the first *sūra* of the Qur'ān.

al-Furqān: that which separates truth from falsehood; hence the Qur'ān.

gharā'ib al-Qur'ān: the study of obscure or unusual words in the Qur'ān. *Gharā'ib* is the plural of *gharīb*.

al-Ghāshiya: "The Overwhelmer", one of the names for the Day of Judgement and the name of *Sūra* 88 of the Qur'ān.

ghunna: nasalisation, to pronounce the letter from the nose, usually the letter *nūn* or *tanwīn*.

ḥadhf: ellipsis.

ḥadr: rapid recitation of Qur'ān.

ḥāfiẓ: someone who has memorised the Qur'ān.

ḥarf (plural *aḥruf*)**:** one of the seven modes or manners of readings in which the Qur'ān was revealed.

ḥarf wa jarḥ: "letters and sounds", the Qur'ān when it is is articulated.

Ḥawāmīm: the seven *sūras* which begin with *Ḥā Mīm* (40 – 46).

ḥizb (plural *aḥzāb*)**:** a sixtieth part of the Qur'ān.

hudā: guidance; al-Hudā is a name for the Qur'ān.

ḥurūf al-muqaṭṭa'āt (or *ḥurūf al-fawātiḥ*)**:** the opening letters at the beginning of twenty-nine *sūras*. Fourteen letters are used in various combinations. These fourteen are: *alif*, *ḥā'*, *rā'*, *sīn*, *shīn*, *ṣād*, *ṭā'*, *'ayn*, *qāf*, *kāf*, *lām*, *mīm*, *nūn*, *hā'*, and *yā'*.

'ibāra an-naṣṣ: explicit meaning of a given text which is borne out by its words.

idghām: In Qur'ān recitation, to assimilate one letter into another. Thus *an-ya'bud* becomes *ay-ya'bud*, *qad tabayyan* becomes *qat-tabayyan*, etc.

i'jāz: inimitability of the Qur'ān. There have been three ways of stating it. The argument of *ṣarfa*: Allah turns people away from imitating the Qur'ān, associated with the Mu'tazilite an-Naẓẓām (d. c. 241/835); the contents of the Qur'ān make it inimitable, stated by al-Jāhiẓ (d. 271/864); and the third is based on the inimitability of the language itself, which no one can imitate even if they try to do so.

ikhfā': not full articulation in recitation.

iltifāt: shift in talking in one person to another (i.e. from the singular to the plural).

imāla: "leaning forward", after soft consonants, e.g. in *Allāh* and in *lillāh*, the double *l* becomes softened and the following long *a* is subject to *imāla*.

imām: the codex of the Qur'ān which 'Uthmān had compiled and checked.

iqtiḍā' an-naṣṣ: the required meaning of a given text.

i'rāb: grammatical inflection; the rules for the vowel endings.

ishāra an-naṣṣ: alluded meaning of a text.

Isrā'īliyāt: Israelite traditions; pre-Islamic Biblical or other such materials.

istināf (or *ibtidā'* in az-Zamakhsharī)**:** disjunctive syntax, meaning that the "*wāw*" begins an entirely new sentence.

iẓhār: clear articulation of the letter without nasalisation. This occurs when *nūn* or *tanwīn* is followed by one of six guttural letters (*hamza, hā', 'ayn, ḥā', ghayn* and *khā'*).

jahr: recitation of the Qur'ān out loud during *ṣalāt*.

jam': collection of the Qur'ān into a single volume.

jumal al-farā'iḍ: highly general statements in the Qur'ān.

juz' (plural *ajzā'*)**:** a thirtieth part of the Qur'ān.

kalām Allah: "the speech of Allah", e.g. the Qur'ān.

khafī: hidden, obscure, also refers to a category of unclear words.

khāṣṣ: a text which is specifically applicable, particular.

khatm: or *khatma*, lit, 'seal'; the recitation of the entire Qur'ān from beginning to end.

al-Kitāb: "the Book"; e.g. the Qur'ān.

lafẓ (plural *alfāẓ*)**:** actual articulated expression.

laḥn al-khiṭāb: parallel meaning, if the understood meaning of a text is equivalent to the pronounced meaning.

madda: prolongation. There are three letters which are subject to prolongation in recitation of the Qur'ān: *alif, wāw* and *yā'*.

mafhūm al-mukhālafa: divergent meaning, an interpretation which diverges from the obvious meaning of a given text.

mafhūm al-muwāfaqa: harmonious meaning, an implied meaning which is equivalent to the pronounced text.

maḥdhūf: elided and implied, a rhetorical device.

makhārij: plural of *makhraj*, articulation, phonetics.

mansūkh: what is abrogated or superseded, particularly with regard to earlier Qur'ānic *āyāt* and *ḥadīth* which were subsequently replaced by later ones, thereby altering the legal judgements or parameters which had initially been expressed in the earlier ones.

maqlūb: inversion, a type of metaphor. This can be by describing something by its opposite (antiphrasis) and by a reversal of the natural order (hysteron proteron).

mathal: parable, example.

Mathānī: lit. "the often recited", said to be the first long *sūras*, or the *Fātiḥa* and also various other things. (See Qur'ān 15:87).

al-Mi'ūn: *sūras* of a hundred *āyāt* or more.

mu'ānaqa: "embracing" a word or phrase in the Qur'ān which can be considered as referring to the preceding or the following word, e.g. In 2:2, *fīhi* (therein) can refer to the word before, *"lā rayba fīhi"* (No doubt in it) or to the word after, *"fīhi hudā"* (guidance in it). In some Qur'āns there are three dots before and after the phrase and *mīm-'ayn* written in the margin.

Mu'awwidhatān: the last two *sūras* of the Qur'ān, the two *sūras* of seeking refuge with Allah from the evil which He has created.

mubālagha: hyperbole.

mubham: ambiguous, vague.

Mufaṣṣal: the *sūras* of the Qur'ān starting from *Sūrat Qaf* (50) to the end of the Qur'ān.

mufassirūn (singular *mufassir*)**:** those who make *tafsīr.*

muḥkam: perspicuous, a text conveying a firm and unequivocal meaning.

mu'jiza: miracle, something which it is usually impossible to accomplish. This term is used for the miracles performed by the Prophets. The Qur'ān is the greatest miracle of the Prophet.

muqaddar: an implied text. It is not actually there, but implied by the context.

mursalūn: "those sent", meaning the Messengers.

muṣḥaf (plural *maṣaḥif*)**:** a copy of the Qur'ān.

mutashābih: intricate, unintelligible, referring to a word or text whose meaning is not totally clear.

naskh: abrogation.

naskh al-ḥukm wa't-tilāwa: supersession of both the ruling and the recitation.

naskh al-ḥukm dūna't-tilāwa: supersession of the ruling but not the recitation.

naṣṣ: unequivocal, clear injunction, an explicit textual meaning.

niṣf: half of a *juz'*.

nujūm: instalments in the Revelation (as opposed to its being revealed all at once).

nuzūl: the revelation of the Qur'ān.

pārah: Persian and Urdu for *juz'*.

qāri' (plural *qurrā'*)**:** one who recites the Qur'ān.

al-Qāri'a: "The Crashing Blow", one of the names of the Last Day and the name of *Sūra* 101 of the Qur'ān.

qirā'a (plural *qirā'āt*)**:** the method of recitation, punctuation and localisation of the Qur'ān. There are seven main readings: Abū 'Amr ibn al-'Alā', Ḥamza, 'Āsim, Ibn 'Āmir, Ibn Kathīr, Nāfi' and al-Kisā'ī. The two most used today are the *qirā'a* of 'Asim in the *riwaya* of Ḥafs (d. 190/805) and that of Nāfi' in the *riwāya* of Warsh (d. 197/812).

al-qirā'āt as-sab': the seven accepted variant readings of the Qur'ān. Also the title of a famous book on the subject by Ibn Mujāhid.

qiṣaṣ al-anbiyā': stories of the Prophets.

qurrā': the plural of *qāri'*, Qur'ān reciter. There is sometimes confusion about whom is being referred to when this term is used because *qurrā'* is also used to designate those who had not taken part in the *Ridda*, namely the *Ahl al-Qurā*, or "people of the towns".

rasm: the orthography of the Qur'ān; the usage of the letters in copies of the Qur'ān where they are written differently than the normal written usage.

rāwī (plural *ruwā*)**:** transmitter.

riwāya: transmission of a particular reading of the Qur'ān. Ḥafs and Warsh are the most in use today.

rub': a quarter of a *juz'*.

Rūḥ al-Qudus: "the Spirit of Purity", the angel Jibrīl.

Sab' al-Mathānī: 'the seven often repeated ones,' usually meaning the seven *āyāt* of the *Fātiḥa*.

Sab' aṭ-Ṭiwāl: the first seven long *sūras* of the Qur'ān.

saj': rhymed prose in which consecutive clauses end in a similar sound but not in a similar poetic measure.

sakīna: calmness, tranquillity, the Shechina (See Qur'ān 2:248).

shādhdh: one of the rarer readings of the Qur'ān.

shāhid: singular of *shawāhid*.

shawāhid: illustrations from Arabic poetry or other quotations to illustrate an uncertain linguistic usage.

ṣila: elision.

sirrī: silent recitation of the Qur'ān during *ṣalāt*.

siyāq: context.

ṣuḥuf: pages, books, epistles, the plural of *ṣaḥifa*; the *ṣuḥuf* of Ibrāhīm and Mūsā means the Revelations which they received. (See Qur'ān 87:18-19).

sūra (plural *suwar*)**:** chapter of the Qur'ān. The Qur'ān is composed of 114 *sūras*.

suwar: plural of *sūra*.

tadwīr: medium speed recitation of Qur'ān.

tafsīr: commentary of explanation of the meanings of the Qur'ān. Firstly there is *tafsīr bi'l-ma'thūr* (*tafsīr* by what has been transmitted, as is seen in the *tafsir* of Ibn Kathīr), which conveys past opinions and secondly *tafsīr bi'l-ma'qūl wa bi'd-darāya* (*tafsīr* by logic and comprehension), which involves interpretation. The second form of *tafsīr* is further divided into *at-Tafsīr al-Lughawī* (linguistic *tafsīr* as in *al-Kashshāf*); *at-ta'wīl, falsafa wa't-taṣawwuf* (allegorical, philosophical and Sufic like *Mafātiḥ al-Ghayb* of ar-Rāzī); *al-Isrā'īliyāt* (based on Jewish sources, like *Tafsīr Ibn Ḥayyān*); *Tafsīr āyāt al-aḥkām* (verses which contains judgements (like *Aḥkām al-Qur'ān* by Ibn al-'Arabī); *tafsīr ar-riwāya wa'd-darāya* (commentary through narration and proof like *Tafsīr Ibn Kathīr*), and *tafsīr bi'r-ra'y*, based on individual interpretation.

taḥaddī: the challenge issued to people to compose something like the Qur'ān. No one has been able to do so.

taḥrīf: distortion, perversion of the meaning of something or misconstruing it, also altering the pronunciation of a word to alter its meaning.

tajwīd: the art of reciting the Qur'ān, giving each consonant its full value.

takrār: repetition.

tanjīm: graduality of revelation as it is revealed in stages.

tanwīn: nunnation.

tanzīl: "sending down", revelation.

taqdīm wa ta'khīr: "advancing and delaying"; a common rhetorical device in the Qur'ān in which the normal order is reversed with what should come last coming first, transposition. Grammatically this figure of speech is called a hysteron proteron. (See *maqlūb*).

taqdīr: restoring the full meaning of the text by holding certain 'missing' words to be 'understood'.

ta'rīḍ: allusion by way of euphemism or circumspection.

ṭarīq (plural *ṭuruq*)**:** one of the transmissions of a particular *riwāya*.

tartīb an-nuzūl: the order of revelation.

tartīb at-tilāwa: the order of recitation.

tartīl: slow recitation of the Qur'ān.

taṭbīq: parallelism.

ta'wīl: interpretation, allegorical interpretation.

tawkīd: emphasis.

tawrīya: synonym of *ta'rīḍ*.

thumn: an eighth of a *juz'*.

tilāwa: recitation of the Qur'ān.

aṭ-Ṭiwāl: the long *sūras*.

'ulūm al-Qur'ān: "the sciences of the Qur'ān".

Umm al-Qur'ān: "the Mother of the Qur'ān", the opening *sūra* of the Qur'ān which is called *al-Fātiḥa*. Also said to be its source in the Unseen.

waḥy: revelation.

wajh (plural *wujūh*)**:** aspect.

waqf: a stop in recitation. There are various signs which indicate different weights of stopping when reciting the Qur'ān. A necessary stop is indicated in Ḥafs by a *mīm*, and by a *ṣād* in Warsh.

Yā Sīn: *Sūra* 36, the heart of the Qur'ān.

ẓāhir: apparent, probablistic, a *ẓāhir* text can mean one of two or more things.

ẓāwāhir: plural of *ẓāhir*.

ziyāda: pleonastic embellishment, the addition of a superfluous word or preposition which has no effect on the actual meaning.

Prophets, Places and and People Mentioned in the Qur'ān

'Ād: an ancient people in southern Arabia to whom the Prophet Hūd was sent. It takes its name from 'Ād, who was in the fourth generation after Nūḥ (the son of 'Aws son of Aram son of Sām son of Nūḥ). They were prosperous, tall in stature and great builders. It is possible that the tracts of sands (*al-Aḥqāf*, Qur'ān 46:21) where they lived were irrigated. They had become haughty and disobedient to Allah, and suffered first a three year drought and then Allah destroyed them with a violent destructive westerly wind. Their city was possibly Iram of the Pillars. (See Qur'ān 89:6-8).

'Adn: Eden, part of Paradise.

Alaysa': a disciple of Ilyās, the Prophet Elisha.

al-Aḥqāf: "the Sand Dunes", the tracts of sand dunes where the people of 'Ād lived, next to Ḥadramawt and Yemen. Also the title of Sūra 46 of the Qur'ān.

Asbāṭ: Tribes (of Israel).

Aṣḥāb al-Ayka: "the People of the Thicket". Ayka may be a place or a description. Their prophet was Shu'ayb and the description of them corresponds to the people of Madyan.

Aṣḥāb al-Kahf: the Seven Sleepers, the seven believers who slept for 309 years (in a cave near Ephesus) and who attained high status because of their emigrating to another place in order not to lose their faith when disbelievers invaded their land. Mentioned in *Sūrat* 18:9-27 of the Qur'ān.

Aṣḥāb al-Ukhdūd: the people of the Ditch, the Christians of Najrān who were burned alive by Dhū Nuwas in Yemen in about 525 CE after he had failed to force them to convert to Judaism. (See Qur'ān 85:4-9).

Āsiya: the wife of Pharaoh mentioned in the Qur'ān in 66:11. She is considered to be one of the four perfect women, (the others being Maryam, Khadīja and Fāṭima).

Ayyūb: the Prophet Job.

Āzar: the father of the Prophet Ibrāhīm. His name was Terah (or Tarah). Various explanations were given for this: either it was a nickname or a title.

al-'Azīz: "the notable", the title of the high court official of Egypt who purchased the Prophet Yūsuf – and whom the Prophet Yūsuf eventually became.

Bakka: the ancient name of Makka.

Bilqīs: the Queen of Sabā' or Sheba.

Binyāmīn: Benjamin, the younger brother of the Prophet Yūsuf.

Dā'ūd: the Prophet David. 'The fast of Dā'ūd' is to fast every other day.

Dhū'l-Kifl: a Prophet mentioned in the Qur'ān in 21:85, possibly Ezekiel.

Dhū'n-Nūn: "He of the Whale", Jonah or Yūnus.

Dhū'l-Qarnayn: "the two-horned", a name given to a great ruler in the past who ruled all over the world, and was a true believer. It is often thought to refer to Alexander the Great. His story is mentioned in the Qur'ān (18:83-99).

Fir'awn: Pharaoh.

Ḥābīl and Qābīl: Cain and Abel.

Hājar: Hagar, the mother of Ismā'īl, from whom the Prophet Muḥammad is descended.

Hāmān: the minister of Pharaoh mentioned in the Qur'ān.

Ḥanna: Anna, the name given by commentators for the wife of 'Imrān and the mother of Maryam.

Hārūn: the Prophet Aaron, the brother of Mūsā.

Hārūt and Mārūt: the two angels mentioned in the Qur'ān (2:102) in Babel from whom people learned magic. Some commentators state that they are two kings rather than two angels.

ḥawāriyyūn: the disciples of the Prophet 'Īsā.

Ḥawwā': Eve. This name appears in *Ḥadīth.*

al-Ḥijr: "the rocky tract", a town in Arabia about 150 miles north of Madina, where the people of Thamūd lived. Also the title of *Sūra* 15 of the Qur'ān.

Hūd: the Prophet sent to the people of 'Ād. His tomb is traditionally located in Hadramawt.

hudhud: the hoopoe, mentioned in the Qur'ān (27:20-22).

ḥūr: the plural of *ḥawrā'*, the maidens in Paradise, the black iris of whose eyes is in strong contrast to the clear white around it.

Iblīs: the personal name of the Devil. It means "seized by despair". He is also called Shayṭān or the "enemy of Allah".

Ibrāhīm: the Prophet Abraham.

Idrīs: the Prophet, possibly Enoch.

Ilyās: also Ilyāsīn, the Prophet Elijah or Elias.

'Imrān: the Biblical Amran, the father of Mūsā and Hārūn. Also the name of Maryam's father.

Injīl: the Gospel, the revelation given to the Prophet 'Īsā.

Irām: possibly Aram, probably in reference to the Aramaeans; or else the dam of Irām which engulfed the ancient city of Ma'rib in Yemen in about 120 CE, the city from which it is said Bilqīs originally came.

Irmiyā': Jeremiah.

'Īsā: the Prophet Jesus.

Isḥāq: the Prophet Isaac.

Ishbā': Elizabeth, the name given by various commentators for the mother of the Prophet Yaḥyā.

Ismā'īl: the Prophet Ishmael.

Isrāfīl: the archangel who will blow the Trumpet to announce the end of the world.

Isrā'īl: Israel, the Prophet Ya'qūb or Jacob.

Jaḥannam: Hell, Gehenna.

Jālūt: the Biblical Goliath.

Janna: the Garden, Paradise.

Jibrīl: or Jibrā'īl, the angel Gabriel who brought the revelation of the Qur'ān to the Prophet Muḥammad, may Allah bless him and grant him peace.

Jūdī: Mount Ararat, where the Ark landed.

Kalimatu'llah: "the word of Allah", meaning the Prophet 'Īsā.

Kalīmu'llāh: "the one to whom Allah spoke directly", a title of the Prophet Mūsā.

Kawthar: "Abundance", a river in the Garden; also the name of *Sūra* 108 of the Qur'ān.

Khalīl: "Friend", a title of the Prophet Ibrāhīm.

Laylat al-Qadr: the Night of Power, mentioned in *Sūra* 97 of the Qur'ān.

Luqmān: a figure in the Qur'ān, a sage, the source, some say, of Aesop's fables.

Lūt: the Prophet Lot.

Madyan: Midian, the people to whom the Prophet Shu'ayb was sent.

Majūs: Magians, Zoroastrians.

Mārūt: see *Hārūt and Mārūt.*

Maryam: Mary, the mother of 'Īsā.

al-Masīḥ: the Messiah, 'Īsā, son of Maryam.

Mikā'īl: (or Mīkāl), the archangel Michael.

Mūsā: the Prophet Moses.

al-Mu'tafika: "the Overwhelmed Ones", the cities of Sodom and Gomorrah.

Nār: the Fire, Hell.

Nūḥ: the Prophet Noah.

Qārūn: the Biblical Korah, mentioned in *Sūra* 28:76-84. He was famed for his incredible wealth and became arrogant on account of it. Allah caused the earth to swallow him up.

Qītmīr: the traditional name given to the dog of the Seven Sleepers. (See *Aṣḥāb al-Kahf*).

Qiyāma: the arising of people at the Resurrection on the Last Day.

ar-Raqīm: the tablet which contained the story of the Seven Sleepers, or possibly the name of their dog. (See *Qītmīr*).

ar-Rass: "the men of ar-Rass", a people mentioned in the Qur'ān who were destroyed. Ar-Rass is possibly the name of a well.

ar-Rūḥ al-Amīn: "the Trusty Spirit," meaning Jibrīl; also known as *ar-Rūḥ al-Qudus*, "the Spirit of Purity".

Sabā: Sheba.

Sābi'ūn: Sabeans, a group of believers. It is not entirely clear who they were. Possibly they were Gnostics or Mandaeans.

Ṣāḥib al-Ḥūt: "the man of the fish", the Prophet Yūnus.

Ṣāliḥ: the Prophet sent to the people of Thamūd.

Salsabīl: the name of a fountain in Paradise mentioned in the Qur'ān in 76:18.

as-Sāmirī: the Samaritan who made the Golden Calf.

Saqar: a place in Hell.

Sara: Sarah, the mother of Isḥāq, from whom the Prophet 'Īsā is descended.

Seven Sleepers: the People of the Cave mentioned in *Sūra* 18 who are known as the "Seven Sleepers of Ephesus." (See *Aṣḥāb al-Kahf*).

Shu'ayb: the Prophet Jethro.

Sidrat al-Muntahā: "The Lote-Tree of the Boundary" or "Lote Tree of the Uttermost Limit", a lote tree above the seventh heaven near the Paradise, denoting the limit of Being and the cessation of form itself; the place at which the knowledge of every creature, even the angels close to Allah, stops. (See Qur'ān 53:14).

Sulaymān: the Prophet Solomon.

Tābūt: the Ark of the Covenant.

Ṭālūt: the Israelite king Saul.

Tawra: the Torah, the Divine Revelation given to the Prophet Mūsā.

Thamūd: a people to whom the Prophet Ṣāliḥ was sent, possibly a group of Nabateans. Madā'in Ṣāliḥ is located at al-Ḥijr in Najd about 180 miles north of Madina. The inscriptions on the tombs there date from 3 BC to 79 CE which are probably after the culture which once flourished there was destroyed.

Ṭūbā: a state of blessedness in the Garden.

Tubba': a South Arabian people, probably the Ḥimyarites, of whom this was the title of their kings.

aṭ-Ṭūr: the Mount, the name of *Sūra* 52 of the Qur'ān, refers to Mount Sinai.

Ṭuwā: the valley in which Allah spoke to Mūsā.

ulū'l-'azm: "the Prophets with resolve", who are Ādam, Nūḥ, Ibrāhīm, Mūsā, 'Īsā and Muḥammad.

Umm al-Qurā: Mother of cities, i.e. Makka.

'Uzayr: Ezra.

Yāfith: Japheth.

Yaḥyā: the Prophet John the Baptist, the son of Zakariyyā.

Ya'qūb: the Prophet Jacob, also called Isrā'īl.

al-Yasā': the Prophet Elisha.

Yūnus: the Prophet Jonah.

Yūsha': Joshua.

Yūsuf: the Prophet Joseph.

Zabānīya: "Violent thrusters", the angels who thrust people into Hellfire, who are nineteen in number.

Zabūr: the Psalms of Dā'ūd.

Zakariyyā: the Prophet Zacharia, the father of Yaḥyā, John the Baptist, and guardian of Maryam.

Zulaykhā: the name given for the wife of the 'Azīz in the story of the Prophet Yūsuf.

Qur'anic commentators (*Mufassirūn*)

'Abdullāh ibn 'Abbās: ibn 'Abd al-Muṭṭalib al-Ḥāshimi, Abū'l-'Abbās, the son of the uncle of the Prophet. He was born when the Banu Hāshim were in the ravine three years before the *Hijra*. He is called the "sage of the Arabs," "the Sea" and the "Doctor (*ḥibr*) of the Community". He went on expeditions in North Africa with 'Abdullāh ibn 'Amr ibn al-'Aṣ in 27/647. He was tall with reddish fair skin and of heavy build. The Prophet made supplication for him, rubbed his head and spat into his mouth and said, "O Allah, give him understanding in the *dīn* and the knowledge of interpretation." He led the *ḥajj* in the year 'Uthmān was murdered. He died in 68/687-8 at the age of 71 in at-Ṭā'if.

'Alī ibn 'Īsā ar-Rummānī: a Mu'tazilite born in Iraq in 295/908 and died in 386/996. He wrote *an-Nukat fi i'jāz al-Qur'ān*, the earliest complete text in support of the *i'jāz al-Qur'ān.*

Al-Baghawī: al-Ḥusayn ibn Mas'ūd, born in Bagha, an Imam in various fields. He was known to his contemporaries as "the Reviver of the *Dīn*". He has a sixteen volume *Sharḥ as-Sunna*, dealing with Shāfi'ī *fiqh* and the basis for it. He has a *tafsīr* entitled *Lubab aṭ-Ṭa'wil.* He died in Marw in 510/1117.

al-Baqillānī: Muḥammad ibn aṭ-Ṭayyib, the Qāḍī and Imām of the people of the *Sunna*, d. 403/1013. He was born in Baṣra in 338/950 and became one of the foremost scholars in *kalām*. He was a Mālikī *faqīh* and an Ash'arite *mutakallim*. He wrote *I'jāz al-Qur'ān*. He was sent by 'Aḍud ad-Dawla as an envoy to the Byzantines in Constantinople where he debated with Christian scholars in the presence of the emperor.

al-Bayḍawi: 'Abdullāh ibn 'Umar, born in Bayḍa, near Shiraz. When "al-Qāḍī" (the Judge) is mentioned in *tafsīr*, he is the one who is meant. He was qāḍī in Shiraz for a time. His chief work was *Anwār at-Tanzīl*. He died in Tabriz in 685/1286.

Ibn ‘Aṭiyya: Abū Muḥammad ‘Abdu'l-Ḥaqq ibn Ghālib al-Andalusī (481/1088-9 – c. 542/1147). A North African who abridged all the commentaries and selected the most likely interpretations in *al-Muḥarrir al-Wajīz*. This book is in general circulation in the western Islamic world. Al-Qurṭubī adopted his method.

Ibn Juzayy: Muḥammad ibn Aḥmad, Abū'l-Qāsim ibn Juzayy al-Kalbī of Granada, born in 693/1294, a Mālikī scholar and Imām in *tafsīr* and *fiqh*. He wrote the well-known *tafsīr*, *at-Tashīl fi ‘Ulūm at-Tanzīl*. He died in 741/1340.

Ibn Kathīr: ‘Imād ad-dīn Ismā‘īl ibn ‘Umar ibn Kathīr, Abū'l-Fidā', born in 701/1302 in a village outside Damascus. He moved to Damascus at the age of five. He was widely travelled and studied with many famous scholars, including Ibn Taymiyya. He was a Shāfi‘ī scholar with books with expertise in various areas. He was greatly respected. He has a well-known *tafsīr*. He has little respect for the intellectual tradition. He dislikes polyvalent readings and argues for a single ‘correct’ reading and hence he is somewhat dogmatic: it might even be said that he impoverishes the text by removing the layered meaning. His desire is also to include all of the relevant *ḥadīths* relevant to the text. He died in Damascus in 774/1372.

Ibn Mujāhid: Aḥmad ibn Mūsā at-Tamīmī: the chief of the reciters, and the first to compile the seven recitations in *al-Qirā'āt as-Sab‘a*. He was born in 245/859 and died in 324/935.

al-Maḥallī: Jalāl ad-dīn, the shaykh of as-Suyūṭī, who began a *tafsīr* which as-Suyūṭī finished which is known as the *Tafsīr al-Jalālayn*, d. 863/1459.

Muqātil ibn Sulaymān: born in Marw, where he taught, and then moved to Basra during the Abbasid Civil war. He later moved to Baghdad and then back to Baṣra where he died in 150/767. Although he is renowned for his knowledge of *tafsīr*, and his *tafsīr* appears to be the earliest in existence, he is often viewed unfavourably, but the reason is not entirely clear. His *tafsīr* is full of narrative embellishments (part of the criticism of him may be due to his use of Jewish and Christian material in this respect). He was also criticised for borrowing interpretations from earlier sources indirectly (without ‘listening’ to them) and without *isnād*. He was also a

Zaydī and Murji'ite. He wrote on abrogation, recitations, and other Qur'ānic subjects.

al-Qurṭubī: Muḥammad ibn Aḥmad ibn Abī Bakr, Abū 'Abdullāh al-Anṣārī al-Qurṭubī, of Cordoba, an ascetic Mālikī scholar and *hadīth* scholar, one of the greatest Imams of *tafsīr* who divided his days between writing and worship. His twenty volume *tafsīr* is called *al-Jāmi' li-Aḥkām al-Qur'ān*. He delights in the grammatical and rhetorical virtuosity in the various readings which enhances the possibilities of the meanings of the text. He enjoys the diversity of the different readings and the opportunity to construct and refute well-expressed arguments, and explores its layered meanings. He disdained self-importance and wore a simple caftan and cap. He travelled to the east and settled in Munya Abi'l-Khusayb in Upper Egypt where he died in 671/1273.

ar-Rāzī: Al-Fakhr, Muḥammad ibn 'Umar, Imām of *tafsīr* who was unique in his time in judgement and transmission and basic sciences. A Shāfi'ī *mujtahid* who worked to preserve the religion of the *Ahl as-Sunna* from the deviations of the Mu'tazilites, Shi'ites, etc. He wrote a thirty-two volume *tafsīr*, *Mafātiḥ al-Ghayb.* He was a Qurashī from Tabaristan, born in Rayy. He died in Herat in 606/1210.

as-Sulamī: Abū 'Abdu'r-Raḥmān Muḥammad ibn al-Ḥusayn, a shaykh of the Sufis and author of a book on their history, ranks and *tafsīr*. He wrote the *Ṭabaqāt aṣ-Ṣūfiya* and *Ḥaqā'iq at-Tafsīr*. He was born in Nishapur in 325/936 and died in 412/1021.

as-Suyūṭi: Jalāl ad-dīn'Abdu'r-Raḥmān ibn Abī Bakr, born in 849/1445. A Shāfi'ī *mujtahid*, Sufi, *ḥadīth* scholar and historian. He wrote books on almost every subject. Raised as an orphan in Cairo, he memorised the Qur'ān by the age of eight and proceeded to devote himself to study. At the age of forty he abandoned the company of men for the solitude of the Garden of al-Miqyas by the Nile, avoiding his prior friends, and proceeded to write nearly six hundred books. Wealthy Muslims and princes visited him, but he put them off and refused to visit the Sultan. His books include a *ḥadīth* collection, *Jāmi' al-Jawāmi'*, the *Tafsīr al-Jalālayn* (completing a manuscript by his shaykh, Jalāl ad-dīn al-Maḥallī), and *Tadrīb ar-Rāwī*. He died in 911/1505.

aṭ-Ṭabari: Abū Ja'far Muḥammad ibn Jarīr, one of the scholars and author of famous books. He was from Tabaristan. He was born in 224/839 and died in 310/923. He has a massive and widely-used *tafsīr* of the Qur'ān called *Jāmi' al-Bayān* which is known as *Tafsīr aṭ-Ṭabarī*. It contains a large number of *ḥadīths*, but it is also a structured work which deals with methodological issues. He discusses linguistic concerns, the various readings, and the issue of interpretation by personal opinion (*ra'y*). He divides the Qur'ān into verses which can only be interpreted by the Prophet; verses of which only Allah knows the interpretation; and those which can be interpreted by people with proper knowledge of the language.

Ṭāwūs ibn Kaysān: 'Abdu'r-Raḥmān ibn Kaysān al-Yamānī. He was called Ṭāwūs (Peacock) because he was "the Peacock of the Qur'ān reciters." He was a Persian and the leader of the Followers in being a proof of knowledge. He was righteous and ascetic. The authors of the *Sunan* and others transmit from him. He died in Makka and was buried in 106/724-5. He went on *ḥajj* forty times and prayed *Ṣubḥ* with the *wuḍū'* he had done for *'Ishā'* of the previous night for a period of forty years.

ath-Tha'ālibī: Abū Zayd 'Abdu'r-Raḥmān b. Muḥammad (d. 875/1470-1) wrote *al-Jawāhir al-Ḥisān fī Tafsīr al-Qur'ān*. He was interested in stories, narrative variants and their various authorities. He attempts to convey the richness of the narrative tradition.

Ubayy ibn Ka'b: al-Anṣāri al-Bukhārī. One of the Anṣār of Khazraj, "the Master of the reciters". He was one of those at the second Pledge of 'Aqaba. He was present at Badr and all the battles. 'Umar, the second khalif, called him "the master of the Muslims". Ubayy was one of the select few who committed the Qur'ānic revelations to writing and had a *muṣḥaf* of his own. He acted as a scribe for the Prophet, writing letters for him. At the demise of the Prophet, he was one of the twenty-five or so people who knew the Qur'ān completely by heart. His recitation was so beautiful and his understanding so profound that the Prophet encouraged his companions to learn the Qur'ān from him and from three others. He was the first to write for the Prophet. He died in 29 or 32 AH while 'Uthmān was khalif.

al-Wāḥidī: 'Alī ibn Aḥmad Abū'l-Ḥasan an-Nīsabūrī. A grammarian and commentator, he wrote a classical *tafsīr* on which as-Suyūṭī drew extensively. He died in 468/1076. He wrote *al-Basīt*, *al-Wasīt*, *al-Wajīz*. He dealt with *asbāb an-nuzūl*.

az-Zamakhsharī: Abū'l-Qāsim Maḥmūd b. 'Umar, a Persian-born Arabic scholar. Born in 467/1075 in Khwarizim. He was a Mu'tazilite. He died in 538/1144. His famous commentary on the Qur'an is called *al-Kashshāf.*

Zayd ibn Thābit: Abū Khārija, born in Madina eleven years before the *hijra* and raised in Makka, he was one of the scribes who recorded the Qur'ān. His father was killed when he was six and he emigrated at the age of eleven to Madina. When 'Umar travelled from Madina, he left Zayd in his place until he returned. Ibn 'Abbās used to visit him to learn from him. He wrote out the Qur'ān in the time of Abū Bakr and copied out the copies of the Qur'ān for 'Uthmān. When he died in 45/665, Abū Hurayra said, "The scholar of this nation has died today."

Some Classical *Tafsīrs* of the Qur'ān

Aḥkām al-Qur'ān: "Rulings of the Qur'ān" by Qāḍī Ibn al-'Arabī (d. 543/1148). There are several books with this title by different authors. Essentially it presents the *āyats* which contain legal judgements and explains them. It is very systematically formulated.

Anwār at-Tanzīl: "The Light of Revelation and Secrets of Interpretation" by al-Bayḍawī. He condensed the *tafsīr* of az-Zamakhsharī in places and expanded it in other places, removing its Mu'tazilite aspects and overtones.

Ḥaqā'iq at-Tafsīr: "The Truths of *Tafsīr*" by Abū 'Abdu'r-Raḥmān as-Sulamī (325/936 - 412/1021) He quotes extensively from the *tafsīr* of Ibn 'Aṭā', an earlier Sufi (d. 309/922) and companion of al-Junayd, and seeks to bring out the mystical allusions in the Qur'ān.

Jāmi' li-Aḥkām al-Qur'ān: "Collection of the Rulings of the Qur'ān" by al-Qurṭubī, an extensive and very popular *tafsīr* in twenty volumes.

al-Kashshāf: "The Unveiler" by az-Zamakhsharī (d. 538/1144), a Mu'tazilite commentary on the Qur'ān. It has a dogmatic position and is characterised by his own view-point. However, he has a brilliant grasp of grammar and lexicology.

Mafātiḥ al-Ghayb: "Keys to the Hidden," by ar-Rāzī (d. 606/1210), unfinished but expanded by his pupils. It is also called at-*Tafsīr al-Kabīr,* or "The Great *Tafsīr"* because of its size. He brings in philosophical thought and other elements. He offers independent suggestions in careful arguments. He was criticised for exceeding the realm of actual *tafsīr* and going into philosophy.

aṣ-Ṣāwī: the gloss of Aḥmad aṣ-Ṣāwī al-Mālikī on the *Tafsīr al-Jalālayn*. This actually makes the *Jalālayn* more usable because it explains words and grammatical usages and expands on it. It is in four volumes (which includes the text of the *Jalālayn*).

Tafsīr al-Jalālayn: "Commentary of the two Jalāls," Jalāl ad-Dīn as-Suyūṭī's (d. 911/1505) completion of the *tafsīr* of his teacher, Jalāl ad-dīn al-Maḥallī (d. 863/1459). A paraphrase of the text of the Qur'ān with linguistic explanations and material from *ḥadīth* and variants. It is also known as *al-Itqān fi 'Ulūm at-Tafsīr* ("The Perfection of the Sciences of *Tafsīr*").

Tafsīr al-Qur'ān: by Ibn Kathīr, a synopsis of earlier material in an accessible form, which made it popular. He relies totally on *ḥadīth* material without any opinion of his own.

Tafsīr aṭ-Ṭabarī: Its actual title is *Jāmi' al-Bayān*. Aṭ-Ṭabarī's commentary on the Qur'ān is a compendium of earlier interpretations with his own opinions interspersed. It is valued but very large (thirty volumes).

at-Tashīl fi 'Ulūm at-Tanzīl: "Facilitation of the Sciences of Revelation" by Ibn Juzayy. It is very succinct and comprehensive, quite densely packed into two volumes. It is one of the best of the smaller *tafsīrs*.

Qirā'āt of the Qur'ān

The *qirā'āt* or the readings, or methods of recitation, are named after the leader of a school of Qur'ān reciters. Each *qirā'a* derives its authority from a prominent leader of recitation in the second or third century *hijrī* who in turn trace their *riwāya* or transmission back through the Companions of the Prophet. For instance, in the back of a Warsh Qur'ān, one is likely to find "the *riwāya* of Imām Warsh from Nāfi' al-Madanī from Abū Ja'far Yazīd ibn al-Qa'qa' from 'Abdullāh ibn 'Abbās from Ubayy ibn Ka'b from the Messenger of Allah, may Allah bless him and grant him peace, from Jibrīl, peace be upon him, from the Creator." Or in a Ḥafs Qur'ān you will see "the *riwāya* of Ḥafs ibn Sulaymān ibn al-Mughīra al-Asadī al-Kūfī of the *qirā'a* of 'Āṣim ibn Abī'n-Nujūd al-Kūfī from Abū 'Abdu'r-Raḥmān 'Abdullāh ibn Ḥabīb as-Sulamī from 'Uthmān ibn 'Affān and 'Alī ibn Abī Ṭālib and Zayd ibn Thābit and Ubayy ibn Ka'b from the Prophet, may Allah bless him and grant him peace."

There are seven *mutawātir* transmissions of the Qur'ān:

I. Nāfi' (d. 169/785) (Madina based)
- A. The *riwāya* of Qālūn
- B. The *riwāya* of Warsh (used in North Africa)

II. Ibn Kathīr (d. 120/737) (Makka based)
- A. The *riwāya* of al-Bazzī
- B. The *riwāya* of Qunbal

III. Abū 'Amr ibn al-'Alā' (d. 154/771) (Baṣra)
- A. The *riwāya* of ad-Dūrī (used in Nigeria)
- B. The *riwāya* of as-Sūsī

IV. Ibn 'Āmir (d. 118/736) (Syria)
- A. The *riwāya* of Hishām
- B. The *riwāya* of Ibn Dhakwān

V. 'Āsim (d. 127/744) (Kūfa)
- A. The *riwāya* of Shu'ba
- B. The *riwāya* of Ḥafs (the most widespread *qirā'a*)

VI. Ḥamza (d. 156/772) (Kūfa)
- A. The *riwāya* of Khalaf
- B. The *riwāya* of Khallād

VII. al-Kisā'ī (d. 189/904) (Baṣra)
- A. The *riwāya* of Abu'l-Ḥārith
- B. The *riwāya* of ad-Dūrī

There are also three additional *mashhūr* tranmissions of the Qur'ān:

Abū Ja'far (d. 130/747)
Ya'qūb (d. 205/820)
Khalaf (d. 229/843)

Ḥadīth

Ḥadīth literature consists principally of records of eyewitness accounts of what the Prophet Muḥammad, may the peace and blessings of Allah be on him, said and did during his lifetime. The *Ḥadīth* have always been carefully distinguished from the Qur'ān which is the revelation which was revealed to the Prophet Muḥammad by Allah through the angel Jibrīl. Thus the *Ḥadīth* literature complements the Qur'ān and even contains commentaries on passages from the Qur'ān – but the two are never confused with each other. The Qur'ān is the Word of God. The *Ḥadīth* contain the words of human beings.

During the early years the *Ḥadīth* were subjected to the most scrupulous checking and verification in the history of recorded scholarship, for a *ḥadīth* which records the words or actions of the Prophet is not accepted as being completely reliable unless it can be traced back through a chain of human transmission made up of reliable people, from person to person, back to someone who was a Companion of the Prophet and who actually witnessed the event or heard the words which the *ḥadīth* describes or relates. The most reliable transmitters of the *Ḥadīth* were those people who loved and feared Allah and His Messenger the most.

After a relatively short time, most of the *Ḥadīth* which had been transmitted orally were recorded in written form, including the details of who all the people in the human chain of transmission were, and the greater the number of different chains of transmission there are for the same *ḥadīth*, the more reliable any particular *ḥadīth* is considered to be. At a later stage, usually during the 1st or 2nd centuries after the death of the Prophet, large collections of the *Ḥadīth* were gathered together in order to ensure that they were not lost.

Among the most important collections of *Ḥadīth* are those made by al-Bukhari and Muslim, which were compiled about two hundred years after the death of the Prophet Muḥammad, and which describe and record every aspect of his life and knowledge. Thus the *Ḥadīth* form an essential part of the record of the teaching and the history and the biography of the Prophet Muḥammad, being as they are reliable contemporary eyewitness accounts.

Ḥadīth Terminology

aḥad (khabar): an isolated *ḥadīth*; a report which is transmitted through a single *isnād* or from a single source.

aḥādith: plural of *ḥadīth*.

Ahl al-Ḥadīth: "the people of *Ḥadīth*", term used for conservative traditionalists, especially during the time of the Mu'tazilite/Ash'arite conflict.

al-akābir 'an al-asāghir: "the greater from the lesser," meaning a senior from a junior narrator, or a prolific from a lesser narrator.

akhbār: plural of *khabar*.

'alī: "high", a short chain of transmission.

alqāb: nicknames (by which transmitters are known).

'arḍ: simply reading out the text to the teacher, or its being read out by an appointed reader.

asānid: plural of *isnād*.

asbāb al-wurūd: the historical circumstances of a *ḥadīth*.

asmā' ar-rijāl: "the names of the men", the study of the lives of the narrators who are the links in the chain of transmission.

athar (plural *āthār*)**:** lit. impact, trace, vestige; synonym of *khabar*, but usually reserved for deeds and precedents of the Companions.

'azīz: "rare, strong", a *ḥadīth* which has only two reporters in the *isnād* at any stage.

balāgha (plural *balāghāt*)**:** a *ḥadīth* in which the *isnād* is not mentioned, but the reporter quotes the Prophet directly. Also called *mu'allaq*.

ḍābiṭ: precise and accurate in reproducing reports.

ḍabṭ: the faculty of retention, the ability of a person to listen to something, comprehend its original meaning and to retain it accurately.

ḍā'if: "weak", the status below *ḥasan*. Usually the weakness is one of discontinuity in the *isnād*.

fard: "single", similar to *gharīb*. It is of three kinds: a single person is found reporting it (like *gharīb*), the people of only one locality relate the *ḥadīth*; or the narrators of one locality report the *ḥadīth* from narrators of another locality (like the people of Makka from the people of Madina).

fiqh al-ḥadīth: the science of *ḥadīths* which deal with legal judgements.

Follower: see *Tābi'ūn*.

gharīb: "strange, scarce". This term is used in the following contexts:

gharīb al-alfāẓ: uncommon words.

gharīb al-matn: uncommon content of the text.

gharīb as-sanad: a *ḥadīth* which has a single reporter at some stage of the *isnād*.

gharīb al-ḥadīth: the study of the linguistic origins of the difficult or uncommon words used in *aḥādith*.

ḥadīth: reported speech of the Prophet.

ḥadīth qudsī: those words of Allah on the tongue of His Prophet which are not part of the Revelation of the Qur'ān.

ḥāfiẓ: a *ḥadīth* master who has memorised at least 100,000 *ḥadīths* – their texts, chains of transmissions and meanings. The plural is *ḥuffāẓ*.

ḥasan: good, excellent, often used to describe a *ḥadīth* which is reliable, but which is not as well authenticated as one which is *ṣaḥīḥ*.

ḥuffāẓ: plural of *ḥāfiẓ*.

i'ḍāl: when two or more links are omitted in the *isnād*.

idrāj: interpolation into a *ḥadīth*.

iḍṭirāb: shakiness in the *isnād*.

ijāza: a certification, by a teacher that a particular student is qualified to teach a particular subject or to transmit a specific book or collection of traditions.

'illa: weakness in an *isnād*.

'ilm al-ḥadīth: knowledge and understanding of the contents of the *ḥadīth*.

'ilm ar-rijāl: knowledge of the identity and reliability of the people who transmitted *ḥadīth*.

'ilm muṣṭalaḥ al-ḥadīth: knowledge of the terminology used to categorise the quality of the *ḥadīth.*

'ilm tadwīn al-ḥadīth: knowledge of when and by whom the *ḥadīth* came to be recorded in written form, and in which books these records are to be found.

imlā': dictation.

inqiṭā': when there is a break in the *isnād.* See *munqaṭi'.*

irsāl: the transmitting by a Follower of a tradition while failing to name the Companion from whom it was transmitted.

isnād (plural *asānid*)**:** the chain of transmission of a tradition, transmitted from individual to individual, from its source to the present.

i'tibār: "consideration," seeking ways of strengthening support for a *ḥadīth* from a single source.

jāmi': comprehensive, a collection which contains *ḥadīths* on all the various subject matters. *Ṣaḥīḥ al-Bukhārī* is a *Jāmi'* but Muslim is not because it does not have a full chapter on *tafsīr.*

jarḥ wa ta'dīl: "wounding and authentication", criticism of the transmitters in an *isnād.*

juz': (plural *ajzā'*) collection of *ḥadīths* handed down on the authority of one individual. Sometimes *juz'* is used for a collection of *ḥadīths* on a particular topic.

khabar (plural *akhbār*): news, report.

al-kutub as-sitta: "the six books", considered to be the most authentic collections of *ḥadīth*: al-Bukhārī, Muslim, Abū Dāwūd, at-Tirmidhī, an-Nasā'ī and Ibn Majah.

majhūl: unknown narrator.

ma'lūl: "defective" although it appears to be sound, it is affected by some infirmity. Also called *mu'allal.*

mansūkh: what is abrogated or superseded, particularly with regard to earlier Qur'ānic *āyats* and *ḥadīth* which were subsequently replaced by later ones, thereby altering the legal judgements or parameters which had initially been expressed in the earlier ones.

maqbūl: "accepted".

maqlūb: "changed, reversed", when the *isnād* of a *ḥadīth* is grafted onto a different text or vice versa, or if the order of a sentence is reversed.

maqṭū‘: "severed", a narration from a *Tābi‘ī* without mentioning the Prophet. Sometimes *munqaṭi‘* is used as a synonym, but *munqaṭi‘* more properly denotes any break at any point in the *isnād.*

marāsil: the plural of *mursal.*

mardūd: "rejected".

marfū‘: "elevated", a narration from the Prophet mentioned by a Companion, e.g. "The Messenger of Allah said…"

ma‘rūf: something whose meaning is well-known.

mashhūr: a *ḥadīth* reported by more than two transmitters. Some say that it is every narrative which comes to be widely-known, whatever its original *isnād.*

matn: the text of a *ḥadīth.*

matrūh: contradicts direct evidence.

matrūk: "abandoned" because the *isnād* contains a known liar.

mawḍū‘: "fabricated, forged", a *ḥadīth* whose text goes against the established norms of the sayings of the Prophet.

mawqūf: "stopped," narration from a Companion without mentioning the Prophet. It can be elevated to *marfū‘* if it is of the nature of "We were commanded to…" and the like.

mu‘allal: "defective" although it appears to be sound, it is affected by some infirmity. Also called *ma‘lūl.*

mu‘allaq: "hanging", missing the whole *isnād* and quoting the Prophet directly. Also known as *balāgha.*

mu‘an‘an: all links in the *isnād* are connected simply by the preposition *‘an* (from) and thus the manner of transmission is not mentioned.

mu‘ḍal: "perplexing", omitting two or more links in the *isnad.*

mudallas: a "concealed" *ḥadīth* is one which is weak due to the uncertainty caused by *tadlīs* which is where the shaykh of transmission is not mentioned and so the chain of transmission is unclear.

mudhākarāt al-ḥadīth: memorisation of *ḥadīth.*

mudraj: "interpolated", an addition or comment by a reporter to the text of the saying being narrated.

muḍṭarib: "shaky", when reporters disagree about a particular shaykh of transmission or some points in the *isnād* or text so that none of the opinions can be preferred over the others.

mufrad: with one narrator, or from one place.

muḥaddith: one who transmits and studies *ḥadīths*.

muj'am: a book arranged in alphabetical order, like the geographical and biographical dictionaries of Yāqūt. Such collections of *ḥadīth* are called *Mu'jam aṣ-Ṣaḥāba*.

mukātaba: to receive written traditions from a scholar, either directly or by correspondence, with or without permission, to narrate them to others.

mukhaththirūn: "reporters of numerous traditions", Companions of the Prophet who reported more than a thousand *ḥadīths*: Abū Hurayra, 'Abdullāh ibn 'Umar, Anas ibn Mālik, 'Ā'isha, 'Abdullāh ibn al-'Abbās, Jābir ibn 'Abdullāh, and Abū Sa'īd al-Khudrī.

mukhtalif: names with the same form that can be read in different ways, e.g. Ḥamīd and Ḥumayd. As *mu'talif*.

munāwala: passing on the text by hand with the approval of the shaykh of transmission.

munkar: "denounced", a narration reported by a weak reporter which goes against another authentic *ḥadīth*.

munqaṭi': "broken", a *ḥadīth* where a link is omitted anywhere before the *Tābi'ī*, i.e. closer to the traditionist reporting the *ḥadīth*.

muqābala wa-taṣḥīḥ: formal system of checking and correcting.

mursal: a *ḥadīth* in which a man in the generation after the Companions quotes directly from the Prophet without mentioning the Companion from whom he received it. (See *irsāl*).

muṣaḥḥaf: traditions which have a mistake in the words or letters of the *isnād* or the *matn*, e.g. Ḥasan is written as Ḥashan.

musalsal: "uniformly-linked" *isnād*, one in which all the reporters use the same manner of transmission.

muṣannaf: a *ḥadīth* collection arranged in topical chapters. The *Muwaṭṭā'* of Imām Mālik is an example of this.

mushkil: containing difficult words or meanings.

mushtarak: with ambiguous words.

musnad: a collection of *ḥadīth* arranged according to the first authority in its *isnād*; also a *ḥadīth* which can be traced back through an unbroken *isnād* to the Prophet.

musnid: also *musnidī*, someone who collected *ḥadīths* into a *Musnad.*

mustadrak: a collection of *ḥadīth* in which the compiler, accepting the preconditions of a prior compiler, collects other traditions which fulfil those conditions but were missed out.

mustakhraj: a collection of *ḥadīth* in which a later compiler collects fresh *isnāds* for traditions.

muṣṭalaḥ al-ḥadīth: classification of the *ḥadīth* as weak, strong, etc.

mutāba'a: "following": following up to see if a *ḥadīth* is reported from someone else.

mu'talif: names with the same form that can be read in different ways, e.g. Ḥamād and Ḥumayd, as *mukhtalif.*

mutawātir: a *ḥadīth* which is reported by a large number of reporters at all stages of the *isnād.*

muttaṣil: "continuous", a *ḥadīth* which has an uninterrupted *isnad.*

mutūn: the plural of *matn.*

naqd: criticism.

naql: transmission.

nāsikh: abrogating. (See *mansūkh*).

naṣṣ: unequivocal, clear injunction; an explicit textual meaning.

nāzil: a long chain of transmission.

nuṣūṣ: plural of *naṣṣ.*

rāwī: a transmitter of reports, oral or written.

riḥla: to travel in search of knowledge, in this case, to collect *aḥādith.* Someone who does this is called *raḥḥāla* or *jawwāl*, "one who travels extensively in search of knowledge". Sometimes they would travel for months in order to listen to a single *ḥadīth.*

rijāl: the men who are the links in the chain of transmission or *isnād* of a *ḥadīth.*

riqāq: *aḥādith* which deal with piety and asceticism, so named because they produce tenderness in the heart.

risāla: a collection of *aḥādith* which deals with one major topic. It can also bc called simply a "book" (*kitāb*).

riwāya: transmission of texts.

riwāya bi'l-ma'na: transmission of meaning.

riwāya bi'l-lafẓ: literal transmission.

ṣadūq: someone who is truthful.

ṣadūq yahim: someone who is truthful but commits errors.

Ṣaḥāba: the Companions of the Prophet.

Ṣaḥābī: a Companion of the Prophet.

ṣaḥīfa: a collection of *ḥadīths* written down by one of the Companions during his lifetime or by their Followers in the next generation. They are also described as *rasā'il* and *kutub.*

ṣaḥīḥ: healthy and sound with no defects, used to describe an authentic *ḥadīth.*

Ṣaḥīḥān: the two *Ṣaḥīḥ* Collections of al-Bukhārī and Muslim.

samā': listening to the teacher, hence it is direct transmission.

shādhdh: an "irregular" *ḥadīth* which is reported by a trustworthy person but which goes against the narration of someone who is more reliable than him.

shāhid: a witness, another narration which supports the meaning of a *ḥadīth* which is being investigated with an entirely different *isnād.*

shawāhid: plural of *shāhid.*

shurūṭ: criteria, the means by which someone classifies *ḥadīths*. It is the plural of *sharṭ.*

Tābi'ūn: the Followers, the second generation of the early Muslims who did not meet the Prophet Muḥammad, may Allah bless him and grant him peace, but who learned the *Dīn* of Islam from his Companions.

Tābi'u't-Tābi'īn: the generation after the *Tābi'ūn,* who did not meet any of the Companions.

tadlīs: describes an *isnād* in which a reporter has concealed the identity of his shaykh. There is *tadlīs al-isnād* where he reports from a shaykh whom he did not hear directly in a manner which suggests that he heard the *ḥadīth* in person. There is *tadlīs ash-shuyūkh* in which the shaykh is not mentioned by name, but by a nickname or alias in order to conceal the shaykh's identity. There is *tadlīs at-tasqīya* in which a trustworthy person relates from a weak person from a trustworthy person and the transmitter deletes the weak link.

taṣḥīf: inadvertently altering the sense of the text by having misread the text.

tawātur: the quality of being *mutawatir.*

thābit: "firm", someone who is a competent transmitter.

thiqa: someone who is trustworthy in transmission.

thiqa thābit: someone who is very reliable, next in rank to a Companion.

ṭuruq (plural of *ṭarīq*)**:** means or paths of transmission.

wijāda: passing on a text without an *ijāza*.

ziyādatu thiqa: an addition by someone who is trustworthy.

Some Important People in the Field of *Ḥadīth*

'Abdu'r-Razzāq ibn Humām: born in 126/743 in Ṣan'ā, Yemen, he began the study of *ḥadīth* at the age of twenty. He produced the earliest *muṣannaf* collection. He died in 211/826.

Abu Dāwūd: Abū Sulaymān ibn al-Ash'ath ibn Isḥaq al-Azdī as-Sijistānī, the author of the *Sunan* and one of the greatest of the scholars of *ḥadīth*. He was born in 203/817 and died on a Friday in the middle of Shawwāl, 275/888 in Baṣra. He was so accomplished in the science of *ḥadīth* that it was said that *ḥadīths* were made pliable for Abū Dāwūd in the same way that iron was made pliable for the Prophet Dā'ūd. He said, "I wrote down 500,000 *ḥadīths* of the Prophet and selected from them those which are in the *Sunan*." He was a pupil of Ibn Ḥanbal.

Abū Nu'aym al-Iṣfahānī: Aḥmad ibn 'Abdullāh ibn Aḥmad al-Iṣfahānī, a notable *ḥadīth* scholar who studied under many excellent men. He wrote various works, including *al-Mustadrak 'alā kull min aṣ-Ṣaḥīḥayn* and *Ḥilya al-Awliyā'*. It is said that it was taken to Nishapur and sold there for 400 dinars. He was born in Rajab, 334/942 and died in Ṣafar, or on 20 Muḥarram, 430/1038 in Isfahan.

Abu Ya'lā: Aḥmad ibn 'Alī at-Tamīmī al-Mawṣulī, author of *Musnad al-Kabīr*. He was a *ḥāfiẓ* of *ḥadīth* who was known as "the *ḥadīth* scholar of Mosul". He died in Mosul in 307/919.

Aḥmad ibn Ḥanbal: Imam of the *Ahl as-Sunna* and founder of the Ḥanbalī school, born in Baghdad in 164/780. He was so devoted to the *Sunna* and *ḥadīth* that he became their Imām in his time. He learned *fiqh* from ash-Shāfi'ī. He died in 241/855.

Al-Baghawī: Abu Muḥammad al-Ḥusayn ibn Mas'ūd, born in Bagha near Herat, a Shāfi'ī Imām in various fields. His father was a furrier. He was known to his contemporaries as "the Reviver of the *Dīn*". He has a sixteen volume *Sharḥ as-Sunna*, dealing with Shāfi'ī *fiqh* and its basis. He has a *tafsīr* entitled *Lubāb at-Ta'wīl*. He died in Marw in 510/1117. He produced the *Masābiḥ as-Sunna* which is a collection of *ḥadīth*.

al-Bayhaqī: Aḥmad ibn al-Ḥusayn, Abū Bakr, born in Khasrajand, a village around Bayhaq near Nishapur. He produced nearly a thousand volumes, and was a Shāfi'ī. Al-Bayhaqī was one of the great Imams in *ḥadīth* and Shāfi'ī jurisprudence. He wrote some important books, such *as-Sunan al-Kubrā, as-Sunan aṣ-Ṣughrā, al-Mabsūṭ,* and *al-Asmā' wa'ṣ-Ṣifāt*. He died in Nishapur in 458/1066.

al-Bazzār: Abū Bakr Aḥmad 'Amr, a *ḥadīth* scholar from the people of Baṣra. He compiled two *Musnads*, a large one called *al-Baḥr al-Kabīr* and a small one (*al-'Ilal*). He died in Ramla in 292/904.

al-Bukhāri: Abū 'Abdullāh Muḥammad ibn Ismā'īl, travelled in search of knowledge to all the men of *ḥadīth* of the cities. He was born in 194/810 in Bukhara. He started to frequent the company of the shaykhs of transmission when he was eleven. He said that he produced the *Ṣaḥīḥ* from the cream of 6,000 *ḥadīths*, and did not write down any *ḥadīth* in it until he had first prayed two *rak'ats*. He died in 256/870.

ad-Dāraquṭnī: 'Alī ibn 'Umar, from Dār al-Quṭn, a part of Baghdad. He was an unrivalled scholar in his era. He had knowledge of traditions and weaknesses and the names of the men and their states in integrity, truthfulness and knowledge of the schools of the *fuqahā'*. He was born in 306/918 and died in 385/995. He has many books, including a *ḥadīth* collection, *as-Sunan*, and *al-Istidrāk* which is about the weakness of some *ḥadīths* in al-Bukhārī. He also has one of the first books on the *qirā'āt*.

ad-Dārimī: Abū Muḥammad 'Abdullāh ibn 'Abdu'r-Raḥmān at-Tamīmī, born in Samarqand in 181/797-8 and died there in 255/869. He travelled widely in search of knowledge and was known for his integrity and scrupulousness. His students included Muslim, Abū Dāwūd, at-Tirmidhī and an-Nasā'ī. He was appointed qāḍī of Samarqand, judged one case and then resigned. He has a *Sunan*.

adh-Dhahabī: Muḥammad ibn Aḥmad, great Turkoman Muslim scholar, born in Damascus in 673/1274, who wrote a hundred books, including *Siyar a'lam an-Nubalā'*. He records the biographies of the narrators of *ḥadīth*. He died in Damascus in 748/1347.

al-Ḥākim: Abū 'Abdullāh Muḥammad ibn 'Abdullāh an-Nīsabūrī, born in 321/933, a Shāfi'ī *faqīh* and *ḥadīth* scholar. He travelled extensively in search of *ḥadīth* and listened to nearly 2,000 shaykhs. He became *qāḍī* of Nishapur in 359 (hence his name "the Judge") and then in Jurjan. He has about 1,500 volumes on *ḥadīth*, of which the most famous is *al-Mustadrak*. He died in Nishapur in 405/1014.

Ibn 'Abdi'l-Barr: an-Numayrī, Abū 'Umar, *ḥāfiẓ* of the Maghrib and Shaykh al-Islām, author of *al-Isti'āb.* He was born in Cordoba in 368/978 and died at the age of 95 in Shatiba in 463/1071. An important *ḥadīth* scholar, Mālikī scholar and author and a *mujtahid*, he was nicknamed the *ḥadīth* Scholar of the West. 'Abdu'l-Barr was the master of the people of his time in memory and precision. He was an expert on genealogy and history. Ibn Ḥazm said, "There is no one with more knowledge of the *fiqh* of *ḥadīth* than him." He wrote a number of works, the most famous of which is *al-Isti'āb.* He travelled throughout Andalusia. He was appointed qāḍī several times. He also wrote the earliest major commentary on the *Muwaṭṭa'* called *al-Istidhkār*.

Ibn Abī Shayba: Abū Bakr ibn Abī Shayba: the author of the *Musnad*, *al-Muṣannaf* and other books. Based in Kūfa, Iraq, Ibn Abī Shayba was a major authority in *ḥadīth*. Abū Zur'a, al-Bukhārī, Muslim, and Abū Dāwūd all related from him. He died in Muḥarram, 235/849.

Ibn 'Adī: 'Abdullāh ibn 'Adī al-Jurjānī, (277/891 – 365/976). He wrote *al-Kāmil,* a general survey of the development of critical assessment of the narrators of *ḥadīth*.

Ibn 'Asākir: 'Alī, (d. 571/1176), author of *Tabyīn* and *Ta'rīkh Dimishq* which contain biographies of transmitters.

Ibn Bābūya: (Ibn Bābawayh) Muḥammad ibn 'Alī al-Qummī, (306/918 – 381/992). He is known also as Shaykh Ṣadūq. Author of the main Shi'ite collections of *ḥadīth*, *Man lā Yahdhuruh al-Faqīh,* which covers only legal matters.

Ibn Ḥajar al-'Asqalānī: Abū'l-Faḍl Aḥmad ibn 'Ali, born in Cairo in 773/1372. Shāfi'ī *faqīh* and *ḥadīth* scholar, he studied under az-Zayla'ī and others, was a qāḍī several times and was known as "Shaykh al-Islam". He wrote *Fatḥ al-Bārī* and died in Cairo in 852/1449.

Ibn Ḥibbān: Muḥammad ibn Ḥibbān at-Tamīmī al-Busti, a Shāfi'ī *ḥadīth* scholar who died in Bust in 354/965. He wrote *Kitāb ath-Thiqāt* and compiled the *Ṣaḥīḥ ibn Ḥibbān*. The *ḥadīths* in this book are arranged neither as in a *muṣannaf* nor as in a *musnad*.

Ibn Kathīr: Ismā'īl ibn 'Umar ibn Kathīr, Abū'l-Fidā', born in 701/1302 in a village outside Damascus where he moved at the age of five. He was widely travelled. He was a Shāfi'ī scholar with books with expertise in various areas, particularly the science of *rijāl*. He has a well-known *tafsīr*. He died in Damascus in 774/1372.

Ibn Khuzayma: Muḥammad ibn Isḥāq, Abū Bakr as-Sulamī, born in Nishapur in 223/838. He was a Shāfi'ī scholar and *mujtahid* and wrote more than 140 books, including his *Mukhtasar al-Mukhtasar* and a *Ṣaḥīḥ* collection. He died in Nishapur in 311/924.

Ibn Mā'in: Yaḥyā ibn Mā'in, Abū Zakariyyā al-Baghdādī, born in Niqya, a village near al-'Anbar in 157/775. He was one of the great Imams of *ḥadīth* and knowledge of its narrators, known as "the Master of *ḥadīth* Masters." His father left him a fortune which he spent on gathering *ḥadīths*. He said, "I have written a million *ḥadīths* with my hand." He lived in Baghdad and wrote several books on *ḥadīth* and died while on *ḥajj* in 233/848.

Ibn Majah: Muḥammad ibn Yazid ar-Rabī', Abu 'Abdullāh al-Qazwīnī, of Qazwin, born in 209/824. He was a *ḥadīth* master and *mufassir* who travelled in search of knowledge and composed his *Sunan*. He died in 273/886.

Ibn Sa'd: see Muḥammad ibn Sa'd.

Ibn aṣ-Ṣalāḥ: Abū 'Amr 'Uthmān ibn 'Abdu'r-Raḥmān ash-Shahrazūrī, known as Ibn aṣ-Ṣalāḥ. He died in 643/1245. He wrote a book on the science of *ḥadīth, Kitāb 'Ulūm al-Ḥadīth*. He was a great authority in Damascus.

Isḥāq ibn Rahawayh: at-Tamīmī, called Abū Ya'qūb, the scholar of Khurāsān in his time and the "Amīr al-Mu'minīn" in *ḥadīth*. He was originally from Marw, born in 161/778. He revived the *Sunna* in the east. He travelled throughout the lands to gather *ḥadīth*. Whenever he heard anything he remembered it and did not forget it. Ibn Ḥanbal, al-Bukhāri, Muslim, at-Tirmidhī, an-Nasā'ī and others took from him. Aḥmad ibn Ḥanbal said, "I do not know of Ibn Rahawayh's equal in Iraq." Abū Zur'a said, "I never met anyone with a better memory than Isḥāq." Abū Ḥātim said, "His precision and freedom from error are a marvel, besides the memory he has been endowed with." He has a four volume *Musnad*. He lived in Nishapur and died there in 238/853.

Mālik ibn Anas: Abū 'Abdullāh al-Aṣbaḥi al-Ḥimyarī, born in Madina, the famous Imām of Madina in *fiqh* and *ḥadīth*. One of the four great Imāms. Ash-Shāfi'ī was one of his pupils. He had great knowledge and embodied the *Dīn*. He compiled the *al-Muwaṭṭā'*. He died in Madina in 179/795.

al-Mizzī: Jamāl ad-Dīn, the famous traditionist. His two major works are: the *rijāl* work, *Tahdhīb al-Kamāl fī Asmā' ar-Rijāl*, and *Tuḥfat al-Ashrāf bi-Ma'rifa'l-Aṭraf*. The second work is of great utility for analysis of the *isnāds* of *ḥadīths*. (d. 742/1341).

Muḥammad ibn Sa'd: Abū 'Abdullāh, the famous reliable scholar, the *mawlā* of the Banu Hashim, known as the *kaṭīb* or scribe of al-Wāqidī, author of the *Ṭabaqāt*. He died in 230/845 at the age of 62.

Muslim: Abū'l-Ḥusayn Muslim ibn al-Ḥajjāj al-Qushayrī an-Nīsābūrī, born in Nishapur in 204/820. He was a Shāfi'ī scholar and *ḥadīth* master. He came to Baghdad more than once and transmitted *ḥadīth* there. He composed his *Ṣaḥīḥ* from 3,000 *ḥadīth*s, and it is said to be the soundest book of *ḥadīth*. He died in 261/875.

an-Nasā'ī: Abū 'Abdu'r-Raḥmān Aḥmad ibn 'Alī ibn Shu'ayb, born in 215/830 in Nasā. He studied with the great scholars and went to those who were mentioned as having knowledge in his time. He was a Shāfi'ī and wrote on the rites of *ḥajj* according to the Shāfi'ites. He used to fast every other day and loved women, having four wives and many slave-girls. He wrote many books on the virtues of the Companions, especially on 'Alī. He was skilled in the science of *ḥadīth* and unique in memorisation and precision. He compiled one of the Six *Ṣaḥīḥ* Collections of *ḥadīth*: the *Sunan*. His *Sunan* is the one with the fewest weak *ḥadīths* after the two main *Ṣaḥīḥ* collections. He was murdered in 303/915 in Damascus because of his love for 'Alī by the remnants of the Khārijites.

an-Nawawī: Yaḥyā ibn Sharaf, Abū Zakariyyā, born in the village of Nawa on the Horan Plain of southern Syria in 631/1233. He was the Imām of the later Shafi'ites and wrote many books: *Minhāj aṭ-Ṭālibīn, Kitāb al-Adhkār, Riyāḍ aṣ-Ṣāliḥīn* and other books. He lived very simply. After twenty-seven years in Damascus, he returned home and died at the age of 44 in 676/1277.

ar-Ramhurmuzī: Abū Muḥammad (d. c. 370/981), the first writer to compile a comprehensive work on the science of *ḥadīth* entitled *Kitāb al-Muḥaddith al-Fāṣil.*

ash-Shawkānī: Muḥammad ibn 'Alī, born in Shawkan, near Khawlan, Yemen in 1173/1760. An important scholar, he was educated in Ṣan'ā' where he became a qāḍī. He wrote 114 books, especially an eight volume commentary on *ḥadīth* called *Nayl al-Awṭār*. He died in 1250/1834.

as-Suyūṭī: Jalālu'd-dīn, 'Abdu'r-Raḥmān ibn Abī Bakr, born in 849/1445. A Shāfi'ī *mujtahid*, Sufi, *ḥadīth* scholar and historian who wrote books on almost every subject. Raised as an orphan in Cairo, he memorised the Qur'ān by the age of eight and proceeded to study intensively. At the age of forty he abandoned the company of men for the solitude of the Garden of al-Miqyas by the Nile, avoiding his former friends. He wrote nearly six hundred books. Wealthy Muslims and princes tried to visit him, but he put them off and refused to visit the ruler. His books include his *ḥadīth* work, *Jāmi' al-Jawāmi'*, the *Tafsīr al-Jalālayn* (completing a manuscript by his teacher, Jalālu'd-dīn al-Maḥallī), and *Tadrīb ar-Rāwī*. He died in 911/1505.

aṭ-Ṭabarānī: Sulaymān ibn Aḥmad, Abu'l-Qāsim, born in Acre in 260/873. A great *ḥadīth* master and *mufassir*, he travelled to listen to *ḥadīth* for sixteen years, meeting about a thousand shaykhs of transmission. He travelled from Syria in quest of *ḥadīth*s, and his journey lasted thirty-three years. He settled in Isfahan where he related *ḥadīths* for sixty years and produced three *ḥadīth* collections, the largest of which is the twenty-five volume *al-Muj'am al-Kabīr.* He died in Isfahan in 360/971.

at-Tayālisī: Abū Dāwūd Sulaymān ibn Dāwūd ibn al-Jārūd al-Fārisī. He was an outstanding scholar. Al-Qallās and Ibn al-Madīnī both said that they had never met anyone with a better memory than him. Ibn Mahdī said, "He is the most truthful of people." He wrote from a thousand shaykhs. He was born in 133/750 and died in 201/818 at the age of sixty-eight. He has a *Musnad*, the earliest *musnad* still extant.

at-Tirmidhī: Abū ʻĪsā ibn Muḥammad ibn ʻĪsā, he was born in 209/824 and is one of the great scholars. He was proficient in *fiqh* and had many books on the science of *ḥadīth*. His book *aṣ-Ṣaḥīḥ* is one of the best and most useful books. It is properly entitled *al-Jāmiʻ*. He also has *ash-Shamāʻil an-Nabawīyya*. It is said, "Whoever has this book in his house, it is as if he had the Prophet speaking." He died in Tirmidh in 279/892.

Major Collections of *Ḥadīth*

Arbā'īn: "The Forty *Ḥadīth*" by an-Nawawī (d. 676/1277), perhaps the most popular small collection of *ḥadīths*.

Fatḥ al-Bārī: by Ibn Ḥajar al-'Asqalānī (d. 852/1449), a fourteen volume commentary on *Ṣaḥīḥ al-Bukhārī*. It is sometimes described as the work by which Muslim scholars repaid the debt they owed to al-Bukhāri.

al-Jāmi' as-Saghīr: by as-Suyūṭī (d. 911/1505), a large compilation of *ḥadīth* which as-Suyūṭī completed in 907/1502. It is arranged alphabetically without *isnād*. He also has the *Jām' al-Jām'* and *al-Jāmi' al-Kabīr*.

Jāmi' of at-Tirmidhī: (d. 279/892) contains about 4,000 *ḥadīths*. After each *ḥadīth* he comments on its legal usage and the quality of its *isnād*. He has personal notes on almost every page which mention the degrees of authenticity of the *ḥadīth*, the different versions of a single report, as well as the various currents of thought and practice in the Islamic world of his time. This makes his *Jāmi'* unique.

Maṣābīḥ as-Sunna: by al-Baghawī (d. 510/1117), a collection of 4,719 *ḥadīths*. It is arranged by topic, but he omitted the *isnāds* as they were taken from well-known collections. It was designed to give people guidance in their daily lives. The *Mishkāt al-Masābiḥ* is an expanded version of it.

Mishkāt al-Maṣābīḥ: by Walī'd-dīn al-Khaṭīb at-Tabrīzī. At-Tabrīzī revised and expanded *Masābiḥ as-Sunna* by al-Baghawī, mentioning the sources and weight of the *ḥadīths* cited and adding more traditions on the topics.

Musnad Aḥmad: collected by Aḥmad ibn Ḥanbal (d. 241/855). It is the most important and exhaustive of the *Musnad* works. His aim was to collect all traditions which were likely to prove genuine if tested and could serve as a basis for argument. He never claimed that all it included was genuine or reliable, but anything not in it had no force. His *Musnad* was respectively transmitted by his son 'Abdullāh (d.

290/903) and the latter's student, Abū Bakr al-Qati'ī (d. 368/979), both of whom added some *ḥadīths*. It contains a total of 30,000 *ḥadīths* (with 10,000 repetitions) narrated by 700 Companions.

Musnad of Abū Dāwūd aṭ-Ṭayālisī: (d. 201/818). It contains 2,767 *ḥadīths* with full *isnāds* on the authority of 281 Companions, and is said to be the first *musnad*. The *ḥadīths* are arranged by names, beginning with the first four khalifs, then those who were at the Battle of Badr, the Muhājirūn, the Anṣār, women, and the youngest Companions. This arrangement was done by his student Ibn Ḥabīb who compiled the *ḥadīths* he had received from him. If there is any doubt in the text, it is pointed out. Sometimes the character of the transmitters is mentioned and sometimes comments about the transmissions are made. It is the oldest *musnad* still extant.

Muṣannaf: by 'Abdu'r-Razzāq ibn Humām (d. 211/826). This is the earliest *muṣannaf* work in existence. It is divided into topical chapters, ending with the virtues of the Prophet Muḥammad (*shamā'il*). A more exhaustive example is the thirteen volume *Muṣannaf* by Ibn Abī Shayba (d. 235/849).

al-Mustadrak 'alā aṣ-Ṣaḥīḥayn: by al-Ḥākim an-Nīsābūri (d. 405/1014). He used *ḥadīths* which he considered met the criteria of al-Bukhari and Muslim.

al-Muwaṭṭā': of Mālik ibn Anas (d. 179/795), the oldest and most authentic collection of *ḥadīth* and *fiqh*.

Riyāḍ aṣ-Ṣāliḥīn: an-Nawawī (d. 676/1277), a famous collection of *ḥadīths* arranged by subject. It is a selection from the *Ṣaḥīḥ* and a couple of other works on *ḥadīth* accompanied by relevant Qur'ānic *āyats*.

Ṣaḥīḥ al-Bukhārī: (d. 256/870). Generally accepted to be the most reliable and most prestigious of the collections of *ḥadīth*. It is a *Jāmi'* collection and a *muṣannaf*. Al-Bukhārī was said to have revised it three times. Al-Bukhārī sought to list only *ḥadīths* which possessed uninterrupted chains of credible authorities. He wished to impress the contents on the reader and to that end divided the book into more than a hundred chapters with 3,450 sub-sections, each with a heading to indicate the contents.

Ṣaḥīḥ ibn Ḥibbān: (d. 354/965). The *ḥadīths* in this book are arranged neither as in a *muṣannaf* nor as in a *musnad*. His collection contains

2,647 *ḥadīths* that do not appear in the collections of either al-Bukhārī or Muslim.

Ṣaḥīḥ Muslim: (d. 261/875). It is considered to be one of the two most reliable collections of *ḥadīth*. It includes 12,000 *ḥadīths* (with 4,000 repetitions). Since it does not contain a complete chapter on *tafsīr*, it is not considered a *Jāmi'*. Muslim is stricter than al-Bukhārī in pointing out the differences between narrations and has a better arrangement of the *ḥadīths*.

Sunan of Abū Dāwūd: (d. 275/888). One of the Six Collections, it contains 4,800 *ḥadīths* mostly on legal matters. It was the first book of its type in *ḥadīth* literature and is considered the best *Sunan*. The author often points out the weaknesses and peculiarities in *ḥadīths* and their *isnāds* or expresses his preference among the variants of a *ḥadīth*. It is one of the most comprehensive collections.

Sunan of ad-Dāraquṭnī: (d. 385/995). He used *ḥadīths* which he considered met the criteria of al-Bukhari and Muslim and adds *isnāds* and alternate versions and notes about the narrators. Its reliability is second only to the Sound Six Collections. It was the basis for the collections of al-Baghawī and at-Tabrīzī.

Sunan of ad-Dārimī: (d. 255/869). This book is a *muṣannaf* which is also called *al-Musnad al-Jāmi'*, a misnomer. It contains 3,550 *ḥadīths* plus comments on the narrators and on legal points. It has an introductory chapter on pre-Islamic times and traditions connected to the life and character of the Prophet. It is thought of as reliable and is one of the earliest extant *Sunan* collections. It is an important collection and some considered it to be one of the Six.

Sunan of Ibn Majah: (d. 273/886). It contains 4,341 *ḥadīths*. Of these, 3,002 appear also in the collections of al-Bukhārī, Muslim, at-Tirmidhī, Abū Dāwūd, and Nasā'ī. It is one of the Six, although it is considered less authentic than the *Muwaṭṭā'*. It contains many *ḥadīths* which are forged and he did not mention his criteria for selection.

Sunan of an-Nasā'ī: (d. 303/915). His *Sunan* is the one with the fewest weak *ḥadīths* after the two *Ṣaḥīḥ* collections. The *Sunan* which is one of the Six is *al-Mujtabā* or *as-Sunan aṣ-Ṣughrā*, which is a synopsis of a large collection of *ḥadīths* which he considered to be fairly reliable. In the smaller collection he only included those *ḥadīths* which he considered to be reliable.

as-Sunan al-Kubrā: by al-Bayhaqī (d. 458/1066). The *ḥadīths* in this compilation are arranged according to their legal import. They include traditions that were not available from earlier compilations.

Tadrīb ar-Rāwī: by as-Suyūṭī (d. 911/1505), the classic commentary on the sciences of *ḥadīth*. It is an extensive commentary on the *Taghrīb* of an-Nawawī.

Tahdhīb al-Aḥkām: by Muḥammad b. al-Ḥasan aṭ-Ṭūsī (385/995 – 460/1068) It contains 13,590 *ḥadīths* and is one of the main Shi'ite collections.

at-Targhīb wa't-Tarhīb: by Ibn Ḥajar al-'Asqalānī (d. 852/1449), a small collection arranged according to topics.

Traditional Ranking of Ḥadīth Collections

1. The Most Reliable Collections:
Al-Muwaṭṭā', *Ṣaḥīḥ al-Bukhārī* and *Ṣaḥīḥ Muslim.*[1]

2. The Four *Sunan* Collections:
Abū Dāwūd, an-Nasā'ī, at-Tirmidhī and Ibn Majah.

"The Four" are: *Ṣaḥīḥ al-Bukhārī*, *Ṣaḥīḥ Muslim*, the *Sunan* of Abū Dāwūd and the *Sunan* of an-Nasā'ī.

"The Sound Six": are *Ṣaḥīḥ al-Bukhārī, Ṣaḥīḥ Muslim*, the *Sunan* of Abū Dāwūd, the *Sunan* of an-Nasā'ī, the *Jāmi'* of at-Tirmidhī and the *Sunan* of Ibn Majah.

1. Although the *Muwaṭṭā'* is the oldest and most reliable collection, it is not mentioned as one of the "Four" or the "Six" since its *ḥadīths* are found in the two *Ṣaḥīḥ* collections.

General Terms used in *Fiqh*

ābiq: a runaway slave.

adab al-qāḍī: the duties of the judge.

'adāla: uprightness of character, justice, balance and observance of the requirements of the *dīn*. It is a legal term which denotes certain qualities which are preconditions for being allowed to be a witness. Someone who possesses these qualities is called *'adl*.

'adl: justice; an upright and just person.

al-aḥkām al-khamsa: "the five values", the categories of *farḍ* or *wājib*, *mandūb*, *mubāḥ*, *makrūh*, and *ḥarām*.

al-aḥkām as-sulṭānīya: governmental principles, governmental and administrative law.

ahlīya: legal capacity, also called *kafā'a*.

ahlīya al-adā': an active legal capacity which can incur rights as well as obligations.

ahlīya al-wujūb: a receptive legal capacity which is good for receiving entitlements but cannot incur obligations.

'anat: fornication. (cf. *zinā*).

'āqila: the paternal kinsmen of an offender who are liable for the payment of blood money.

'aqīqa: a sacrifice in celebration of the birth of a child on the eighth day.

arsh: compensation given in the case of someone's injury caused by another person.

awqāf: (plural of *waqf*) pious foundations.

bāligh: someone who is an adult.

al-barā'a al-aṣilīya: presumption of innocence or freedom from liability.

bāṭil: null and void.

bayyīna: oral testimony.

bint labūn: a two-year-old she-camel. The proper age for a camel paid in *zakāt* for 36 to 45 camels.

bint makhad: a one-year-old she-camel. The proper age for a camel paid in *zakāt* for 25 to 35 camels.

bulūgh: the age of sexual maturity.

ḍamān: guarantee.

ḍarar: damage.

ḍarūra: necessity.

ḍarūra malji'a: pressing necessity, also called *muliḥḥa.*

dhimma: obligation or contract, in particular a treaty of protection for non-Muslims living in Muslim territory.

dhimmī: a non-Muslim living under the protection of Muslim rule.

dhihār: see *ẓihār.*

dhū maḥram: a male, whom a woman can never marry because of close relationship (e.g. a brother, a father, an uncle etc.); or her own husband.

ḍimār: a bad debt; property which has slipped out of one's possession with little chance of recovery (like fugitive slaves). According to the Mālikīs, if it is gold or silver, *zakāt* is paid for one year only on it when it is removed. If it is cattle, then it is for all the past years.

diya: financial compensation (blood money) for homicide or injury.

faqīh (plural *fuqahā'*)**:** a man learned in the knowledge of *fiqh* (see below) who by virtue of his knowledge can give a legal judgement.

far': a branch or sub-division, and (in the context of *qiyās*) a new legal case.

farā'iḍ: plural of *farīḍa,* shares of inheritance; religious obligations.

farḍ al-'ayn: an individual obligation.

farḍ al-kifāya: also *farḍ kafā'ī*, a collective obligation, something which is obligatory for the community as a whole and is satisfied if one adult performs it.

fāsid: irregular, invalid, corrupt, void, deficient.

fāsiq (plural *fussāq*)**:** a person not meeting the legal requirements of righteousness. The evidence of such a person is inadmissible in court.

fatāwā: plural of *fatwā.*

fatwā: an authoritative statement on a point of law.

fay': spoils taken without fighting. It goes to the Muslim treasury, the *Bayt al-Māl.*

fidya: a ransom, compensation paid for rites or acts of worship missed or wrongly performed because of ignorance or ill health.

fiqh: the science of the application of the *Sharī'a.* A practitioner or expert in *fiqh* is called a *faqīh.*

fiqh al-aqallīyāt: "jurisprudence of [Muslim] minorities", a new name for an old area of jurisprudence that used to be called *fiqh an-nawāzil*, or "jurisprudence of momentous events".

fiqh an-nawāzil: "jurisprudence of momentous events", an area of *fiqh* covered mostly by the Mālikīs, which is concerned with the *fiqh* for Muslims living in a minority situation.

fisq: the testimony of someone who is *fāsiq*, who behaves in a manner which can be described as *fisq*, is not accepted as evidence in court. This involves committing a major sin or persisting in minor ones.

fuqahā': plural of *faqīh.*

ghanīma: booty, weapons, horses and all moveable possessions taken in battle from unbelievers.

gharaḍ: motive, individual interest.

ghaṣb: usurpation, unlawful appropriation of property, without the permission of its owner and without stealthiness.

ghulūl: stealing from the war booty before its distribution.

ghusl: major ablution of the whole body with water required to regain purity after menstruation, lochia and sexual intercourse.

ḥabūs: habous, another term for *waqf.*

hadath: minor ritual impurity requiring *wuḍū'*: passing wind, urination, defecation, vomiting.

ḥadd (plural *ḥudūd*)**:** Allah's boundary limits for the lawful and unlawful. The *ḥadd* punishments are specific fixed penalties laid down by Allah for specified crimes.

ḥakam: an arbiter.

ḥalāl: lawful in the *Sharī'a.*

ḥaraj: an impediment.

ḥarām: unlawful in the *Sharī'a.*

ḥarbī: a belligerent.

ḥaṣan: an adjective describing a married person, from *ḥiṣn*, a fortress. A person who has become *muḥṣin* by marriage is subject to the full *ḥadd* punishment of death for *zinā*.

ḥayḍ: menstruation.

hiba: a gift.

ḥiḍāna: custody of minors.

ḥīla: legal evasion. The plural is *hiyal*.

ḥill: the boundaries of a Ḥaram.

ḥima: fence, protective zone, pasture-land devoted solely to grazing livestock from the *zakāt* or to be used in *jihād*.

ḥiqqa: a three-year-old she-camel. The proper age for a camel paid in *zakāt* for 46 to 60 camels.

ḥirāba: highway robbery, brigandage. There is a lot of diversity between the schools as to what this applies to. It involves armed robbery. Mālik says that it can take place inside a town, but Abū Hanīfa says that it must be outside of it. The penalties vary according to the severity of the offence. Ad-Dāsūqī, a Mālikī *faqīh*, says that rape under force of arms is *ḥirāba*.

ḥirz: a place where property is customarily kept, like a house, shop, tent.

ḥisba: lit. computation or checking, but commonly used in reference to what is known as *amr bi'l-ma'rūf wa'n-nahy 'an al-munkar*: promotion of good and prevention of evil.

ḥiyal: legal devices, evasions, observing the letter, but not the spirit of the law.

ḥujja (plural *ḥijaj*)**:** courtroom evidence.

ibāḥa: permissibility.

'Īd: a festival, either the festival at the end of Ramaḍān or at the time of the *Ḥajj*.

'Īd al-Aḍḥa: the *Ḥajj* festival which takes place on the 10th of the month of Dhū'l-Ḥijja.

'Īd al-Fiṭr: the festival at the end of the fast of Ramaḍān on the 1st of the month of Shawwāl.

'idda: a period after divorce or the death of her husband during which a woman must wait before re-marrying.

iḍtirār: compulsion.

ifṭār: breaking the fast.

iftirāsh: a form of sitting in the prayer in which you sit on the left foot which is on its side, while the right foot is resting upright on the bottom of its toes with the heel up. (Cf. *tawarruk*).

iḥdād: the period of mourning observed by a widow.

iḥrām: a state in which one is prohibited to practise certain deeds that are lawful at other times, necessary when performing the rites of *'umra* and *ḥajj*.

iḥṣān: the state of being *muḥṣin*, an unblemished reputation sexually of someone who is or has been married.

iḥtibā': a sitting posture, putting one's arms around one's legs while sitting on the hips.

iḥyā' al-mawāt: "revival of dead lands", bringing wasteland into cultivation.

ijbār: the power of compulsion exerted on someone unable to manage their own affairs.

ikrāh: duress, undue influence.

īlā': a vow by a husband to abstain from sexual relations with his wife. If four months pass, it is considered a divorce. (See *ẓihār*).

īmā': implication, implicit indication.

imām: Muslim religious or political leader; leader of Muslim congregational worship. The plural is *a'imma*.

imsāk: in fasting, it is abstinence from things which break the fast.

imtithāl: compliance.

iqāma: the call which announces that the obligatory prayer is about to begin.

iqrār: confession; approval, acknowledgement.

irtidād: apostasy.

'Ishā': the night prayer.

ishtimāl aṣ-ṣammā': wearing clothes in the following two ways:

1. Covering one shoulder with a garment and leaving the other bare.
2. Wrapping oneself in a garment while sitting in such a way that nothing of that garment covers one's private parts.

istiftāḥ: the opening supplication recited at the beginning of the prayer (which is not done by Mālikīs).

istiḥāḍa: bleeding from the womb of a woman outside her ordinary periods.

istijmār: wiping the anus with stones.

istimrār: continuity.

istinjā': washing the private parts with water.

istinshāq: drawing water up the nose which is part of *wuḍū'*.

Istisqā': the Rain prayer of two *rak'ats*, performed outside the town, with two *khuṭbas* after which those present turn their cloaks the other way around.

i'tikāf: seclusion, while fasting, in a mosque, particularly in the last ten days of Ramadan.

'itq: manumission of a slave.

jadha'a: a four-year-old she-camel. The proper age for a camel paid in *zakāt* for 61 to 75 camels.

jā'iz: permitted, another term for *mubāḥ*.

jam': joining two *farḍ* prayers together, which is permitted when travelling or in extremely bad weather. The prayers which may be joined are *Ẓuhr* and *'Aṣr*, and *Maghrib* and *'Ishā'*.

jam' taqdīm: 'early' combination of two *farḍ* prayers.

jam' ta'khīr: 'delayed' combination of two *farḍ* prayers.

jamā'a: the main body of the Muslim community; also designates the group prayer.

janāba: major ritual impurity requiring a *ghusl*: intercourse, sexual discharge, menstruation, childbirth.

janābāt: penalties, torts.

janāza: funeral.

jawrab: socks (not to be confused with *khuff*, leather socks).

jizya: a protection tax payable by non-Muslims as a tribute to the Muslim ruler.

julūs: sitting, particularly the sitting position in the prayer. (cf. *qu'ūd*).

junub: being in a state of *janāba*.

kafā'a: legal capacity, also called *ahlīya*.

kafan: the shroud for the dead.

kaffāra: atonement, prescribed way of making amends for wrong actions, especially missed obligatory actions.

kanz: hoarded up gold, silver and money, the *zakāt* of which has not been paid.

karāha (plural *karāhiyya*)**:** abhorrence, abomination.

khitān: circumcision.

khiṭba: marriage proposal.

khiyāna: breach of trust.

khuff: leather socks.

khul': a form of divorce initiated by the wife from her husband by giving him a certain compensation, or by returning back the *mahr* which he gave her.

khums: the fifth taken from the booty which is given to the ruler for distribution.

khuṣūma: litigation, quarrel.

khuṭba an-nikāḥ: a speech delivered at the time of concluding the marriage contract.

kitāba: a contract by which a slave acquires his freedom against a future payment, or instalment payments, to his master.

kusūf: solar eclipse.

li'ān: mutual cursing, a form of divorce which involves oaths taken by the wife and husband when he accuses her of committing adultery and she denies it. They can never remarry after this.

luqaṭa: an article found (lit. 'picked up'). The finder must advertise the article for a year unless it is insignificant or perishable.

mabrūr: accepted, as in an accepted *ḥajj.*

maḍārr: harmful.

mafqūd: a missing person whose whereabouts is unknown.

mafrūḍ: obligatory.

maḥkama: court, tribunal.

mahr: dower given by a husband to his wife on marriage.

maḥram: a person with whom marriage is forbidden.

Majalla: a uniform codification of the laws of contract and obligation based on Ḥanafi law, published between 1286/1869 and 1293/1876.

makrūh: abominable, reprehensible in the *Sharī'a*, disliked but not forbidden.

mamnū'a: prohibited in the *Sharī'a*.

maqdūr: within one's capability.

ma'qula (plural *ma'āqil*)**:** blood money.

mas'ala (plural *masā'il*)**:** issue, problem, case, a matter proposed for determination.

masḥ: wiping over leather socks when doing *wuḍū'* rather than washing the feet.

masnūn: *sunna*.

mawālī: the plural of *mawlā*.

mawāt: barren uncultivated land.

mawlā (plural *mawālā*)**:** a person with whom a tie of *walā'* has been established, usually by having been a slave and then set free. It is also used for a type of political patronage.

mayyit: a corpse, a dead body of a human being.

maẓālim: "injustices", complaints, esp. the appellate court for the redress of grievances.

mu'allafa al-qulūb: giving a share of the *zakāt* to reconcile people's hearts. This share was discontinued by 'Umar ibn al-Khaṭṭāb on the basis of *siyāsa shar'īyya*.

mubāḥ: permissible, permitted; something for which there is neither reward nor punishment. Also called *jā'iz*.

mudabbar: a slave who has been given a *tadbīr*, a contract to be freed after his master's death.

mufsida: what invalidates acts of worship in the *Sharī'a*.

muftī: someone qualified to give a legal opinion or *fatwā*.

muḥallil: a man who marries a woman who has been trebly divorced on the condition that he then divorce her in order that her first husband can remarry her. Marriage solely for this purpose is not permitted.

muḥdith: someone in a state of minor ritual impurity. (See *ḥadath*).

muḥṣan: (or *muḥṣin*) a person who has been married. (See *ḥaṣan*).

muḥṣana: the feminine of *muḥṣan*. As well as meaning a person guarded by marriage, it also refers to a chaste unmarried free woman, who is sexually protected, as opposed to an unmarried slave woman over whom her master has sexual rights.

mukallaf: a competent person in full possession of his faculties; subject of legal obligation, personally obligated.

mukātab: a slave who has been given a *kitāba*, a contract to buy his freedom.

muqāsama: taking part of a governor's wealth when he retires to be used for the good of the community.

muqtadī: "one appointed", the person who stands behind the Imām in the prayer and calls out the *iqāma* and *takbīr*.

murtadd: an apostate, recanter.

muṣallā: a place for praying. *'Īd* prayers are normally held outside the mosque at a *muṣallā*; the term is sometimes used for a prayer mat.

mustaḥabb: what is recommended, but not obligatory in acts of worship in the *Shari'a*.

musta'man: a non-Muslim who has entered *Dār al-Islām* under an *amān* or safe-conduct.

mut'a: temporary marriage, which is forbidden in Sunnī *fiqh*; severance gift after divorce.

mu'takif: one who is in a state of *i'tikāf*.

nadhr: a vow.

nādiḥa: a camel used for agricultural purposes.

nafaqa: maintenance, adequate support (especially of immediate family.)

nafī: banishment; negation.

nafila (plural *nawāfil*)**:** supererogatory act of worship.

nahd: sharing the expenses of a journey or gathering the journey food of the travellers together to be distributed among them in equal shares.

naḥr: the slaughtering of camels only, done by cutting the carotid artery at the root of the neck; the Day of Naḥr is the 10th of Dhū'l-Ḥijja on which the pilgrims slaughter their sacrifices.

nahy: prohibition.

najāsa: impurity.

najis: impure, the opposite of *ṭāhir*. There are variations in opinion as to what are *najasāt*. However, wine and other intoxicants are regarded as *najis* by all *fuqahā'*.

naw': species.

nawāfil: plural of *nafila*.

naẓar: examination, reasoning.

nifās: lochia, bleeding after childbirth.

niṣāb: minimum. The minimum for the *ḥadd* of theft is three *dirhams* or a quarter of a *dinar*; and there are various minimums for *zakāt* becoming payable: in money it is 200 dirhams or 20 dinars, in produce 5 *wasqs*, and in livestock 5 camels, 30 cattle, and 40 sheep or goats.

niyāba: proxy, representation.

nushūz: violation of marital duties on the part of of the husband or wife.

nusk: religious act of worship.

nusuk: a sacrifice.

qabḍ: when standing in prayer, to place the right hand on the back of the left hand or on the wrist. This is done by Shāfi'īs, Ḥanbalīs, Ḥanafīs, and some Mālikīs. It is considered *sunna* and not *wājib*.

qaḍā': belated performance of an obligation; the office of qāḍī; the decision of the qāḍī.

qadhf: slanderous accusation; accusing a chaste person of fornication. Unless the accusation is supported by the testimony of four male witnesses, the penalty is eighty lashes.

qāḍī (plural *quḍā*)**:** a judge, qualified to judge all matters in accordance with the *Sharī'a* and to dispense and enforce legal punishments.

qar' (plural *qurū'*)**:** a term used in reference to *'idda* which either means becoming pure after a menstrual period, or the menstrual period itself. (See Qur'an 2:228).

qarā'in al-aḥwāl: circumstantial evidence.

qasāma: an oath taken by fifty members of a tribe or locality to refute accusations of complicity in unclear cases of homicide.

qāsim: distributer, as of *zakāt*.

qibla: the direction faced in the prayer by Muslims which is towards the Ka'ba in Makka. Their first *qibla* had been towards Jerusalem and so the early Muslims had prayed towards two *qiblas*, a quality which is sometimes used to describe the fact that they became Muslim early on.

qinn: a slave who was born a slave.

qiṣāṣ: retaliation.

qiyām: standing, particularly the standing position in the prayer.

qudra: power, ability, capacity.

qunūt: a supplication said in the prayer, particularly in the standing position after *rukū'* in the *Ṣubḥ* prayer.

qurū': the plural of *qar'*.

qussām: plural of *qāsim.*

qu'ūd: sitting position during the prayer.

raḍā': or *riḍā'* or *raḍā'a*, suckling, which produces an impediment to marriage of foster-kinship.

rajm: stoning to death.

rak'a(t): a unit of the prayer consisting of a series of standings, bowing, prostrations and sittings.

rātib (plural *rawātib*)**:** a regular form of litany; or the regular Imām in a mosque who receives a regular salary from the treasury.

riḍā': see *raḍā'*.

ridda: apostasy.

rifq: leniency.

rikāz: treasure buried in pre-Islamic times which is recovered without great cost or effort.

rukhṣa: concession or concessionary law, law which is modified due to the presence of mitigating factors; legal allowance.

rukn (plural *arkān*)**:** essential ingredient; used to describe the five essential 'pillars' of Islam.

rukū': bowing, particularly the bowing position in the prayer.

ruqba: kind of gift in the form of a house given to somebody to live in as long as he is alive.

ṣadaq: another word for *mahr*.

sadl: when in the standing position, to pray with the arms at one's sides. This is done by most Mālikīs and the Shi'a.

saḥw: forgetting; here it means forgetting how many *rak'ats* a person has prayed in which case he should perform two additional prostrations of *saḥw* to compensate.

sā'iba: a she-camel which used to be let loose in free pastures in the name of idols, gods, and false deities.

sajda: the act of prostration.

salab: belongings (arms, horse, etc.) of a deceased warrior killed in a battle.

Ṣalāt al-Ḥāja: the prayer of need, asking for that need to be fulfilled, which consists of four to twelve *rak'ats*.

Ṣalāt al-Khawf: the shortened fear prayer which is done in times of danger.

sariqa: theft.

ṣawāfī: state lands.

shaf': a supererogatory prayer of two *rak'ats* performed with the *witr*.

shahāda: bearing witness, particularly bearing witness that there is no god but Allah and that Muḥammad is the Messenger of Allah. It is one of the pillars of Islam. It is also used to describe legal testimony in a court of law.

shahāda az-zūr: perjury, false testimony.

shāhid (plural *shuhūd*)**:** a witness.

sharṭ (plural *shurūṭ*)**:** qualification, precondition.

shighār: a forbidden form of marriage agreement whereby a man gave his daughter in marriage to another man who in return gave his daughter in marriage to him, without either of them paying any *mahr* to their respective brides.

shuf'a: the right of pre-emption in property.

shūrā: consultation.

shurṭa: urban police.

sirq: theft.

sujūd: prostration.

ṣulḥ: reconciliation, or comprehensive peace settlement.

sulṭān: an abstract noun meaning power, especially that of government. It has come to designate a king or ruler who governs by virtue of his power.

sunan: plural of *sunna*; also collections of *ḥadīth*.

Sunna: the customary practice of a person or group of people. It has come to refer almost exclusively to the practice of the Messenger of Allah and of the first generation of Muslims.

sutra: an object placed in front of someone praying so that people will pass beyond it and not come between him and the *qibla*.

ta'addī: violation of trust; delict.

ta'āruḍ: conflict of evidence.

tabdīl: substitution, replacement of an old custom with a new one.

tadbīr: a contract given by a master to a slave whereby the slave will be freed after the master dies. *Tadbīr* also means management, direction.

ta'dīya: transferrability.

tafwīḍ: delegation of authority, proxy.

taghyīr: change and difference in customs.

tahajjud: voluntary prayers performed at night between *'Ishā'* and *Fajr*.

ṭahāra: purification, purity.

ṭāhir: pure.

taḥīyat al-masjid: "the greeting of the mosque", two *rak'ats* which are prayed on entering a mosque.

taḥlīl: an intervening marriage contracted for the sole purpose of legalising remarriage between a divorced couple; saying, *"lā ilaha illā'llāh"*, "There is no god but Allah". (See *muḥallil*).

taḥṣīl: actualising, obtaining.

takattuf: another term for *qabḍ*. Most Shi'a call it *takfīr* (covering) and claim that it is *ḥarām*.

takbīr: saying "*Allāhu Akbar*", "Allah is greater".

takbīr al-iḥrām: the *takbīr* which begins the prayer.

taklīf: liability, obligation.

taklīf mā lā yuṭāq: impossible obligation.

ṭalāq: divorce.

ṭalāq al-bā'in: final irrevocable divorce.

ṭalāq ar-rāj'ī: a divorce which can be revoked (e.g. the first or second pronouncement).

tanfīdh: implementation, execution.

tarabbus: waiting, observing.

tarāwīḥ: prayers at night in Ramaḍān.

tarjī‘: repeating the *shahāda* in the *adhān* in a loud voice after first saying it in a low voice.

tark al-ḥuẓūẓ: forgoing lawful rights.

tartīb: proper sequence of actions in the prayer, *wuḍū'*, *ḥajj* or any other act of worship.

tashahhud: lit. to make *shahāda*. In the context of the prayer, it is a formula which includes the *shahāda* and is said in the final sitting position of each two *rak‘at* cycle.

tashīl: convenience, facilitation.

taslīm: the greeting, "*As-salāmu ‘alaykum*.". It terminates the prayer.

taṭawwu‘: voluntary.

tawaqquf: conditionality.

tawarruk: a form of sitting in the prayer with the left buttock on the ground and the left foot under the right thigh, emerging from under the right ankle, while the right foot is resting upright on the bottom of its toes with the heel up. The other form is *iftirāsh*. Mālik says that *tawarruk* is *sunna* in both *tashahhuds* while Abū Ḥanīfa says that *iftirāsh* is *sunna* in both.

tayammum: purification for prayer with clean dust, earth, or stone, when water for *ghusl* or *wuḍū'* is either unavailable or would be detrimental to health.

ta‘zīr: deterrence, discretionary penalty determined by the qāḍī.

tazkīya: compurgation, testing the reliability of a witness, cross-examination.

umm walad: a slavegirl who had born her master's child. She cannot be sold and becomes free upon her master's death. The child is free from birth.

‘uqūbāt: plural of *‘uqūba* (lit. punishment), penal or criminal law.

wājib: a necessary part of the *Sharī‘a* but not obligatory, although it is sometimes used as a synonym for *farḍ*.

wakīl: person who is an authorized representative, agent or proxy.

walā': the tie of clientage established between a freed slave and the person who frees him, whereby the freed slave becomes integrated into the family of that person.

walī: a guardian who is responsible for another person.

waqf: also *habous*, an unalienable endowment for a charitable purpose which cannot be given away or sold to anyone.

witr: lit. "odd", a single *rak'at* prayed immediately after the *shaf'* which makes the number of *sunna* prayers uneven. The Ḥanafīs consider that it consists of the three *rak'ats* prayed together with a single *salām*. It is considered *wājib*.

wuḍū': ritual washing with water to be pure for the prayer of hands, mouth, nostrils, face, forearms, head, ears and feet.

yamīn (plural *aymān*)**:** oath. Oaths form a complementary role to evidence in Islamic law. If a person is accused of an offence without the evidence of sufficient witnesses of good standing, he or she may swear an oath as to his or her innocence to avert punishment.

zakāt: one of the five pillars of Islam. It is a wealth tax paid on certain forms of wealth: gold and silver, staple crops, livestock, and trading goods. As regards its distribution, see Qur'ān 9:60.

zakāt al-fiṭr: a small obligatory head-tax imposed on every Muslim who has the means for himself and his dependants. It is paid once yearly at the end of Ramaḍān.

ẓihār: an oath by the husband that his wife is like his mother's back, meaning she is unlawful for him. It was a form of divorce in the *Jāhiliyya*, not permitted in Islam.

zinā: unlawful sex, adultery, fornication.

Uṣūl al-Fiqh Terms

'adāt: customary usage, a legal principle in the Mālikī school. "Those obligations which aim at the protection of human life, the intellect faculty and other things in this world." (ash-Shāṭibi).

adilla: plural of *dalīl*, proofs, items of evidence.

aḥkām: the plural of *ḥukm*: laws, values and ordinances.

al-aḥkām at-taklīfiyya: legal values resulting directly from commands which impose obligations.

Ahl ar-ra'y: people of opinion. It is used to refer to people who make use of the principle of *ra'y* to arrive at rulings.

a'immat al-madhāhib: plural of *imām al-madhhab*; Imams of the legal Schools.

'amal: action, normative practice, precedent, juridical practice.

'amal ahl al-Madīna: the normative practice of the people of Madina (meaning the first three generations), one of the fundamental principles of Mālikī *fiqh*.

amāra (plural *amārāt*)**:** evidence or an indication which leads to a speculative reasoning, as opposed to *dalīl*, which leads to a definitive ruling.

'āmm: generally applicable, in reference to a Qur'ānic ruling.

amr (plural *awāmir, umūr*)**:** command, matter, affair.

amr bi'l-ma'rūf wa'n-nahy 'an al-munkar: promotion of good and prevention of evil. This is a duty for all Muslims which is prescribed in the Qur'ān.

al-amr al-mujtami' 'alayhi: "The generally agreed-on way of doing things with us", an expression used by Imām Mālik to denote the consensus of the people of Madina.

asbāb: legal causes, plural of *sabab*.

al-asbāb wa'l-wasā'iṭ: literally "causes and means", intermediary causes.

Aṣḥāb ar-Ra'y: speculative jurists. (See *Ahl ar-ra'y*).

ashbāh wa naẓā'ir: "resemblances and similarities", the study of the semantic structure of the law.

aṣl (plural *uṣūl*)**:** root on whose basis analogy is sought, primary principle, textual basis.

athar (plural *āthār*)**:** lit. impact, trace, vestige; also deeds and precedents of the Companions.

'azīma: strict or unmodified law which remains in its original rigour due to the absence of mitigating factors. Regularity, not opting for allowance or discretion permitted by the Lawgiver in performing an obligation.

bayān: clarification, elucidation: either of the substance of a meaning in the Qur'ān or of the meaning of that substance.

daf' al-ḥaraj: removal of hardship.

dalāla: explanation, clarification. Indication, signification, textual implication. Sub-categories of this vary according to school. For instance, the Ḥanafīs have four categories while the Shāfi'īs have five.

dalāla aṣlīya: essential signification.

dalāla al-iqtiḍā': the required meaning indicated by the text.

dalāla al-ishāra: alluded meaning.

dalāla al-mafhūm: implied meaning.

dalāla al-manṭūq: pronounced meaning of a text. This is sub-divided into *dalāla al-iqtiḍā'* and *dalāla al-ishāra.*

dalāla an-naṣṣ: inferred or implied meaning of a text.

dalāla tābi'a: subordinate denotation.

dalālāt: textual implications.

dalīl (plural *adilla*)**:** proof, indication, evidence; also a guide.

ḍarūra: overriding necessity.

ḍarūrī: necessary, a priori, a grade of *maṣlaḥa*, "Indispensible in sustaining the good (*maṣāliḥ*)." (ash-Shāṭibi).

aḍ-ḍarūrīyāt al-khamsa: "the five essential values": religion, life, intellect, lineage, and property. The objectives (*maqāṣid*) of the *Sharī'a* involve the promotion and protection of these values. The principle of *maṣāliḥ mursala* is based on achieving the realisation of these values.

dawr: arguing in a circle.

faḥwā al-khiṭāb: superior meaning, when the implied meaning of a text is superior to the pronounced meaning.

fatḥ adh-dharā'i': "facilitating the means"; it entails making the means to what is obligatory also obligatory.

furū': (the plural of *far'*) branches or subsidiaries, such as *furū' al-fiqh*, that is, the branches of *fiqh*.

ghalbat aẓ-ẓann: predominant probability, most likely to happen.

ghayr mu'akkada: a *sunna* which is *ghayr mu'akkada* is one which was done sometimes but not regularly. (cf. *mu'akkada*).

ḥāja: general need.

ḥājī: "Those *maṣāliḥ* which are needed in order to extend the purpose of the objectives and to remove the strictness of the literal sense, the application of which leads mostly to impediments and hardships and eventually to the disruption of the objectives." (ash-Shāṭibi). Such things are supplementary to the five essential values and their neglect would lead to hardships.

ḥaqīqī: literal, real, original.

ḥaqq al-'abd: right of man, or private right; the right of the injured person to demand redress.

ḥaqq Allāh: right of Allah or public right; the punishment which the judge must inflict for certain crimes.

ḥujja (plural *ḥijaj*)**:** courtroom evidence; also an authority.

ḥujjīya: producing the necessary proof or authority to validate a rule or concept.

ḥukm (plural *aḥkām*): law, value or ruling of the *Sharī'a*. *Ḥukm* is the legal ruling on the status of something. The five values are: 1) obligatory (*farḍ* or *wājib*); 2) *sunna* or recommended (*mandūb*); 3) permissible (*mubāḥ*); 4) offensive (*makrūh*); and 5) unlawful (*ḥarām*).

al-ḥukm at-taklīfī: defining law, law which defines rights and obligations.

al-ḥukm al-waḍ'ī: declaratory law, that is, law which regulates the proper implementation of *al-ḥukm at-taklīfī*, such as by expounding the conditions, exceptions and qualifications thereof.

'ibāra an-naṣṣ: explicit meaning of a given text which is borne out by its words.

iḍṭirārī: (obligation) imposed on man without his choice.

iḥtiyāṭ: caution, precautionary measure.

ijmā': consensus, particularly the consensus of the people of knowledge among the Muslims on matters of *fiqh*. There are several sub-categories of *ijmā'*: *ijmā' muḥaṣṣal* (acquired consensus) which is concluded directly by the *mujtahid*; *ijmā manqūl* (transmitted consensus) which is established by means of reports; *ijmā' ahl al-Madīna* (consensus of the Madinans), a principle of Mālikī *fiqh*; *ijmā' ṣarīḥ* (explicit consensus), expressed by all; and *ijmā' sukūtī* (tacit or presumptive consensus) on which some give an opinion while the rest are silent.

ijtihād: to struggle, to exercise personal judgement in legal matters. The most basic form of *ijtihād* is to form an analogy based on a legal cause (*'illa*).

ijtihād bayānī: "explanatory *ijtihād*", the *ijtihād* which involves interpreting source materials and existing evidence.

ijtihād maṣlaḥī: legal reasoning on the basis of *maṣlaḥa*.

ikhtilāf: controversial questions, juristic disagreement.

ikhtiṣāṣ: restrictive interpretation.

'ilal: plural of *'illa*.

'illa: underlying reason, effective cause, *ratio legis*. *Ma'na* and *sabab* are synonyms.

iqrār: approval, affirmation.

iqtidā': following, authority.

iqtiḍā' an-naṣṣ: the required meaning of a given text.

ishāra: textual indication.

ishāra an-naṣṣ: alluded meaning of a text.

istidlāl: deductive reasoning.

istiḥsān: to deem something good, juristic preference; to decide in favour of something which is considered good by the jurist, over and against the conclusion that may have been reached by analogy.

istikhrāj: extraction of rulings from the sources.

istinbāṭ: inference, deducing a somewhat hidden meaning from a given text.

istiṣḥāb: presumption of continuity, or presuming continuation of the *status quo ante.* There are various types of *istiṣḥāb*: *istiṣḥāb al-'adam al-aṣilī* (presumption of original absence) in which the fact that a law did not exist in the past leads to the presumption that it is still non-existent unless the contrary is proved; *istiṣḥāb al-wujūd al-aṣilī* (presumption of original presence) which is like the saying "possession is nine-tenths of the law"; *istiṣḥāb al-ḥukm* (presumed continuity of laws and principles), in which the provisions of the *Sharī'a* are presumed to apply unless there is contrary evidence (both in judgements and in areas which are not subject to judgement); and *istiṣḥāb al-waṣf* (continuity of attributes), e.g. water is pure unless there is evidence to the contrary.

istiṣlāḥ: consideration of public interest; to decide in favour of something because it is considered good (*maṣlaḥa*), and more beneficial than anything decided otherwise. A method of interpreting already existing rules by disengaging the spirit of these rules from the letter of the law so that exceptions and extensions are reached which command practical utility and correspond to the fundamental goals of the law.

jawāz 'aqlī: logical possibility.

jumal al-farā'iḍ: highly general statements in the Qur'ān.

jumhur: dominant majority.

jumla: general, unspecific.

khabar: news, report.

khabar wāḥid: isolated *ḥadīth*; a report coming down by a single *isnād* or from a single source. (Also called *khabar al-khāṣṣa.*)

khafī: hidden, obscure, also refers to a category of unclear words.

khāṣṣ: specifically applicable, particular.

lā ḍarar wa lā ḍirār: "Do not inflict injury nor repay one injury with another," a *ḥadīth* which is the basis for the legal principle of *al-maṣāliḥ al-mursala.*

laḥn al-khiṭāb: parallel meaning, if the understood meaning of a text is equivalent to the pronounced meaning.

lā madhhabī: someone who does not believe in adhering to a *madhhab.*

maḍarra: harm.

madhhab: a school of law founded on the opinion of a *faqīh*. The four main schools now are Ḥanafī, Mālikī, Shāfi'ī and Ḥanbalī. There are also *madhhabs* which have ceased to exist: the Awzā'ī, Ẓāhirī, Jarīrī and the *madhhab* of Sufyān ath-Thawrī. The Shi'a also designate their *fiqh* as the 'Ja'farī *madhhab'* after Ja'far aṣ-Ṣādiq.

mafhūm al-mukhālafa: divergent meaning, an interpretation which diverges from the obvious meaning of a given text. It has several categories.

mafhūm al-muwāfaqa: harmonious meaning, an implied meaning which is equivalent to the pronounced text.

mafsada: evil, namely anything which violates *aḍ-ḍarūrīyāt al-khamsa*, the five essential values of religion, life, intellect, lineage and property; the opposite of *maṣlaḥa*.

maḥkūm fīh: the subject matter of *ḥukm*; the acts, rights and obligations which constitute the subject-matter of a command, prohibition, or permissibility.

majāzī: metaphorical.

ma'na (plural *ma'ānī*)**:** In *fiqh*, a causal factor. Otherwise, 'meaning'.

ma'na ifrādī: individual meaning.

ma'na tarkībī: contextual meaning.

manāfi': (personal) advantages.

manāṭ: anchor, basis of a rule.

mandūb: commendable, recommended.

manfa'a: benefit, utility.

mansūkh: what is abrogated or superseded, particularly with regard to earlier Qur'ānic *āyats* and *ḥadīths* which were subsequently replaced by later ones, thereby altering the legal judgements or parameters which had initially been expressed in the earlier ones.

maqṣid (plural *maqāṣid*)**:** intention, goal, end, objective.

maṣāliḥ mursala: considerations of public interest, human welfare, utility, welfare not explicitly supported by the text. This is a major principle in Mālikī and Ḥanbalī *fiqh*.

mashhūr: famous or widely ascribed to.

maskūt 'anhu: matters on which the Lawgiver is silent.

maṣlaḥa: considerations of public interest, human welfare, utility, welfare, human good. "What concerns the subsistence of human life, the wholeness of his way of life, and the acquiring of what man's emotional and intellectual faculties require of him in their absolute sense." (ash-Shāṭibi).

maṣlaḥa mulghā: a nullified or discredited benefit. The Lawgiver has nullified it explicitly or by an indication.

mu'akkada: a *sunna* which is *mu'akkada* is an emphatic one, also known as *sunna al-hudā*, one regularly done. (cf. *ghayr mu'akkada*).

mu'amālāt: secular transactions, "acts concerning those *maṣāliḥ* of men that concern his fellow beings." (ash-Shāṭibī).

mu'āriḍāt: plural of *mu'āriḍa*, countervailing considerations.

mubīn: clear, evident.

muḥkam: perspicuous, a word or text conveying a firm and unequivocal meaning.

mujmal: ambivalent, requires details and explanation, ambiguous, referring to a category of unclear words.

mujtahid: someone qualified to carry out *ijtihād*.

mujtahid muṭlaq: the absolute *mujtahid* who is able to undertake *ijtihād* in all aspects of the *dīn*, like the founders of the various schools. Such a person is also called *mujtahid fī'sh-Shar'*.

mujtahid madhhab: the *mujtahid* of the school who makes *ijtihād* only within his own *madhhab*. (like Qāḍī Ibn 'Arabī, al-Muzanī, Ibn Taymiyya, and Zufar).

mujtahid mas'ala: the *mujtahid* in a specific issue, e.g. a person able to take *ijtihād* in one special area e.g. economics, contracts, marriage etc. (like Abū Bakr al-Abharī, al-Marwazī and Abu'l-Ḥasan al-Karkhī).

mujtahid mukharrij: one of those who practise *takhrīj*, who do not extrapolate rulings (*aḥkām*) but who are conversant enough with their subject to indicate which view is preferable and suitable.

mujtahid murajjiḥ: someone who is competent to make comparisons and distinguish the correct, preferred (*rājih*) and agreed upon views from weak ones (like al-Qurṭubī, Ibn Qudāma, an-Nawawī, and al-Marghīnānī).

mujtahid muṣaḥḥiḥ: someone who can distinguish between the apparent and the obscure views. Textbook writers fall into this category.

mulā'im: suited, consistent.

munāsaba: appropriateness.

munāsib: appropriate, in harmony with the basic purpose of the law; suitable.

munḍabiṭa: stipulative.

muqābala wa-taṣḥīḥ: formal system of checking and correcting.

muqaddima: prerequisite.

muqallid: a person who practises *taqlīd*, not performing *ijtihād* himself but instead following the legal opinion already arrived at by a *mujtahid*.

muqārin: associative.

muqayyad: restricted, qualified, conditional.

murā'āt al-khilāf: allowance for disagreeing opinion.

mursal: a *ḥadīth* in which a man in the generation after the Companions quotes directly from the Prophet without mentioning the Companion from whom he received it. (See *irsāl*).

mushāwara: consultation.

mushāwir: consultant, the *muftī* appointed to assist the qadi.

mushkil: difficult, also a category of unclear words.

mushtarak: homonym, a word or phrase imparting more than one meaning.

mutafaqqih: a beginner in a *madrasa*.

mutawātir: a *ḥadīth* which is reported by a large number of reporters at all stages of the *isnād*.

muṭlaq: unrestricted, unqualified, absolute, simple.

naql: transmission.

nāsikh: that which abrogates.

naskh: abrogation.

naṣṣ: unequivocal, clear injunction, an explicit textual meaning.

naẓar: examination, reasoning, intellectual examination, thinking upon a thing and trying to understand it.

naẓar fī'l-maẓālim: investigation of complaints.

naẓāra: debate.

nāzila: unprecedented legal question.

nāẓir: philosopher, debater, investigator.

naẓẓār: someone who examines and decides questions of theology and jurisprudence.

nuṣūṣ: plural of *naṣṣ*.

nuẓẓār: plural of *nāẓir.*

qaḍā' bi't-ta'addī: judicial decision by extension of the original ruling.

qānūn: (from Greek 'canon'); civil law.

qaṭ'ī: definitive, decisive, free of speculative content.

qawā'id: foundations, general legal precepts which clarify the method of using *ijtihād* in a school; also the links which connect minor questions.

qiyās: logical deduction by analogy, one of the four main fundamental principles which can be utilised in reaching a judgement.

qiyās al-adnā: analogy of the inferior, the *'illa* is less evident in the new than in the original case.

qiyās al-awlā: analogy of the superior, the *'illa* is more evident in the new than in the original case.

qiyās jālī: *a fortiori* analogy.

qiyās al-musāwī: analogy of equals, the *'illa* is equally evident in the new and in the original case.

qiyās naẓarī: theoretical analogy.

quwwa: effectiveness.

raf' al-ḥaraj: removal of hardship.

rājiḥ: preponderant, preferable.

ra'y: opinion, personal discretion, a legal decision based on the use of common sense and personal opinion, used where there is no explicit guidance in the Qur'ān and *Sunna* and where it is not possible to use analogy.

rijāl: men, plural of *rajul*, used of the men who are the links in the chain of transmission or *isnād* of a *ḥadīth*.

riwāya: transmission of texts.

rukhṣa: concessionary law based on extenuating circumstances.

sabab (plural *asbāb*)**:** cause, means of obtaining something. It is usually used to describe the cause of acts of devotion whereas *'illa* is not.

sadd adh-dharā'i': to block the means which might possibly lead to undesired consequences.

sāḥib: lit. companion, also a graduate student in a *madrasa*.

ṣaḥīḥ: healthy and sound with no defects, used to describe an authentic *ḥadīth*.

samā': hearing something from someone.

sanad: basis, proof, authority.

as-ṣidr wa'l-taqsīm: another term for *takhrīj al-manāt*.

ṣifa ḥukmīya: legal qualification.

siyar: types of conduct.

siyāsa: a decision based on public interest.

siyāsa shar'īya: administration of justice according to Islamic law.

ta'abbud: special act of worship; obedience, bondage to Allah, "Recourse only to what the Lawgiver has determined." (ash-Shāṭibī). "Non-intelligibility of meaning." (ash-Shāṭibī).

ta'āruḍ: conflict, when two pieces of evidence of equal strength conflict and appear to cancel each other out.

ta'diya: transferability of the *'illa*. It must have an objective quality which can be applied to other cases (e.g. the principle of 'intoxication' can be transferred from wine to other intoxicating substances.)

taḥqīq al-manāṭ: refinement of the basis of the ruling.

taḥsīnīya (plural *taḥsīnāt*)**:** a grade of *maṣlaḥa*, "To adopt what conforms to the best of practice, to avoid such manners as are disliked by the wise people." (ash-Shāṭibī).

tajzi'a: the division of *ijtihād* into different categories (see under *ijtihād*).

takālif 'aynīya: specific individual obligations.

takālif kifā'īya: general societal obligations.

takhfīf: alleviation, laxity, commutation.

takhrīj: extrapolation.

takhrīj al-manāṭ: deduction of the basis of a ruling.

takhṣīṣ: enhanced degree of specification.

takhyīr: choosing between two or more alternatives.

takmīlī: complementary.

ṭālib: a seeker of knowledge, a student.

talfīq: legal eclecticism, picking different judgements from different schools.

ta'līl: determination by the cause of command by logical and linguistic analysis.

tanqīh al-manāṭ: refinement of the basis of the ruling.

taqdīr: restoring the full meaning of the text by holding certain words to be 'understood'.

taqdīrī: hypothetical.

taqlīd: imitation; following the opinion of a *mujtahid* without considering the evidence (*dalīl*).

ṭard: examination of a problem from all sides.

tarjīh: preponderance, a process only exercised by the most qualified jurists.

tarjīh al-adilla: weighing probative evidence.

tartīb al-adilla: arrangement of proofs in order of strength.

taṣarruf: free disposal, personal initiative, discretionary action.

taṣarrufāt fi'līya: torts (offences and technical offences).

taṣarrufāt qawlīya: legal transactions (contracts and unilateral transactions).

tawātur: the quality of being *mutawātir*.

ta'wīl: allegorical interpretation.

tawsī'a: flexibility, as *takhfīf.*

ta'yīn: specifying, naming, identifying.

ṭuruq an-naẓar: methods of investigation.

'urf: common acknowledgement, customary practice.

uṣūl: plural of *aṣl*, the basic principles of any source, used in *fiqh*.

uṣūl al-fiqh: Islamic legal theory, legal methodology, theoretical jurisprudence.

uṣūl al-Qānūn: modern jurisprudence.

uṣūli: legal theoretician.

wafā' bi'l-'uhūd: fulfilling contracts or undertakings as in *"Honour My contract and I will honour your contract."* (Qur'ān 2:40).

ẓāhir: apparent, probablistic; a *ẓāhir* text can mean one of two or more things.

ẓawāhir: plural of *ẓāhir*.

Business Terms

abdān: the plural of *badan*, "body", used in *sharika al-abdān*, partnership in physical labour for gain.

'adl: equity; the root of this word refers to the balance obtained when the two pannier-bags on either side of a beast of burden are of equal weight.

ajal: a delay granted to the debtor for repayment of a loan or for the performance of an obligation.

amāna: a trust, a fiduciary relationship, a deposit on trust.

'āmil: the agent who works with the *qirāḍ* investment.

amīn: trustee.

'aqd (plural *'uqūd*)**:** a contract.

'āqid: the contracting party.

'arḍ: merchandise, goods.

'arīya: a kind of sale by which the owner of an *'arīya* is allowed to sell fresh dates while they are still on the palms by means of estimation, in exchange for dried plucked dates.

'āshir: public collector, one who collects tolls from non-Muslim traders entering Muslim territory.

Āyat al-Mudāyana: "the *āyat* of buying and selling," Qur'ān 2:282, which requires witnesses to commercial contracts.

'ayb (plural *'uyūb*)**:** a defect in goods.

'ayn: ready money, cash; a capital asset or object with material value.

bā'i: a buyer.

bāṭil: null and void (a contract).

bay' (plural *buyū'*)**:** sale; there are various types of sale such as *munābadha, mulāmasa, muḥāqala, mukhādara, ḥaṣa*, etc.

biḍā'a (plural *baḍā'i*)**:** goods, merchandise; a share in a business venture.

buyū': sales, the plural of *bay'*.

caravanserai: merchant's inn, from the Persian *kārwān* – company of travellers and *sarāi.* It denotes a large inn which was government owed.

ḍamān: surety, guarantee.

ḍarā'ib: general taxes imposed for public welfare by the government.

darak: default in ownership.

dayn (plural *duyūn*)**:** a debt.

ḍimār: bad debt.

fāsid: irregular, deficient. It is between valid and void. A *bāṭil* contract is unlawful, whereas one which is *fāsid* is lacking some necessary quality, which can sometimes be put right.

faskh: cancellation, invalidation of a contract.

furūq: subtle distinctions.

ghabn: fraud, cheating, swindle; it can also mean "loss" when *ghabn* enters a contract without either of the parties being aware of it.

ghabn fāḥish: a radical discrepancy between the market price of a commodity and the price charged to the customer, determined by custom (*'urf*).

gharar: a sale in which uncertainty is involved. It is forbidden. The sale of futures falls into this category. Any contract in which the availability of goods promised cannot be guaranteed is invalidated through this element of risk.

gharar fāḥish: excessive *gharar.*

gharar yasīr: immaterial *gharar.*

gharīm (plural *ghuramā'*)**:** debtor.

ghayr lāzim: non-binding.

ghayr maṭlūb: not so intended.

ghubn: damage, injury, fraud, lesion. Not much used in Islamic law because of the right of the option to withdraw from the transaction (*ḥaqq al-khiyār*).

ḥabal al-ḥabala: a forbidden business transaction in which a man buys the unborn offspring of a female animal.

ḥajr: limitation of a person's legal competence.

haqq al-khiyār: the option to withdraw from a transaction. There are three kinds (see *khiyār*).

al-ḥaṣa: a type of sale whose outcome is determined by the throwing of a stone. (It involves *gharar* and therefore is forbidden).

ḥawāla: novation, the transference of a debt from one person to another. It is an agreement whereby a debtor is released from a debt by another becoming responsible for it.

ḥirfa (plural *ḥiraf*): profession, trade, guild.

ḥisba: the function of market inspection. The person who undertakes this is called a *muḥtasib*. Under the early khalifs, it was overseen by the khalif or the governor. Under the 'Abbasids, it became a separate department.

ibḍā': type of informal commercial collaboration in which one party entrusts his goods to the care of another, usually to be sold, after which the latter, without any compensation, commission or profit, returns the proceeds of the transaction to the first party.

iflās: bankruptcy.

iḥrāz: original acquisition.

iḥtikār: cornering, hoarding. It is not allowed with essential staple items, such as grain.

ījāb: the offer in contracts. It is followed by the acceptance (*qabūl*).

ijāra: lease or hire, including work for a regular wage.

ijāra wa iqtinā': hire purchase contract, lease-purchase financing, a modern development combining two concepts. The purpose here is not interest which must not play a part, The instalments are paid into an account and are invested in a *muḍāraba*. Capital and profit offset the cost.

ilzām: binding.

imḍā': ratification, signature.

'inān: in Mālikī law, a partnership limited to either a single commodity or a single transaction. For Mālikīs, Ḥanbalīs and Ḥanafīs contributions cannot be credit, and for Shāfi'īs they cannot be chattels or labour. It implies mutual agency but not mutual surety with regard to the work undertaken and salary owed to employees.

'inān sharikat a'māl (or *abdān*)**:** partnership on the basis of labour. The Ḥanafīs, Mālikīs and Ḥanbalīs consider it to be a *mufāwaḍa*.

intifā': transfer of usufruct.

iqāla: termination of a contract by mutual consent.

‘irban: variant of *‘urbūn.*

i‘sār: insolvency.

istidāna: commercial commitment of the *qirāḍ* by the agent in excess of the capital invested.

istiṣnā‘: contract of manufacture.

‘iwaḍ: countervalue.

jahbādh: officially appointed money examiner and money-changer.

jins: genus, things of the same sort which cannot be exchanged with deferment unless it is same for same (e.g. for the Mālikīs, lead and zinc; wheat, barley and rye; maize, millet and rice; pulses; meat of all poultry; all fishes; meat of all quadrupeds.) Things done to them do not alter the genus, e.g. flour is still wheat.

ju‘āl: contract to complete a specific job for a specific reward in a period of time which is not specified.

juzāf: sale where one of the countervalues is roughly determined by mere viewing. For the Mālikīs, it is allowed when the quantity can be determined by weight or measure and is not an individual item. This would involve things like quantities of pelts, hides, etc.

kafāla: bail; the pledge given by someone to a creditor to ensure that the debtor will be present at a certain time and place.

kafīl: a guarantor of bail.

kharāj: taxes imposed on revenue from land. Originally these were only applied to land owned by non-Muslims.

khazzān: wholesaler dealer.

khiyār: option to withdraw from a business transaction. *Ḥaqq al-khiyār* is of three kinds: *khiyār ar-ru’ya*, the purchaser’s right to reject the object after inspection; *khiyār al-waṣf*, the option determined by quality open to either party; and *khiyār al-‘ayb*, the option of dissolving the contract if the goods are defective.

khulṭa: a state where two properties are so mixed in a partnership that they cannot be separated.

kirā’: hire of property.

lāzim: binding.

maḍāmīn: a forbidden form of sale in which the foetus in the womb of a pregnant animal is sold. (cf. *ḥabal al-ḥabala*).

maghārim: unjust non-*Shari'a* taxes, unlawful taxes, fines.

majlis al-'aqd: meeting of the contracting parties.

māl (plural *amwāl*)**:** property, something that exists and can be utilised, *res in commercio.*

māl ḥāḍir: ready cash.

māl mutaqawwam: corporeal or incorporeal property with a lawful market price (like jewellery).

māl ribawī: property susceptible of *ribā.*

malāqiḥ: a forbidden sale, in which the stud properties of an animal are sold.

manīḥa (plural *manā'iḥ*)**:** a sort of gift in the form of a she-camel or a sheep which is given to somebody temporarily so that its milk may be used and then the animal is returned to its owner.

milk tāmm: full ownership.

mithlī: a fungible property (an article which is measurable or weighable or counted by number when alike), e.g. money or grain.

muḍāraba: commenda, co-partnership, *qirāḍ.*

muḍārib: agent manager, managing trustee.

mufallas: bankrupt, insolvent.

mufāwaḍa: in Mālikī law, a parternship in which each partner confers upon his colleague full authority to dispose of their joint capital in any manner intended to benefit their association.

mughārasa: an agreement similar to the *musāqa* (sharecropping), but involving an orchard.

muḥāl 'alayhi: the new debtor in the *ḥawāla.*

muḥāl lahu: creditor assignee.

muḥāqala: a forbidden sale in which, for instance, unharvested wheat was bartered for harvested wheat, or land was rented for wheat, or wheat for seeds.

muḥīl: debtor assignor.

muḥtasib: the public functionary who supervises the market.

mukhādara: the sale of non-mature agricultural products and the sale of dates which have not shown signs of ripeness. It is forbidden.

mukhtār: free agent.

Mukhtaṣar: an abridgement or summary, especially used for juristic manuals composed for mnemonic and teaching purposes.

mukūs: extra-*Sharīʻa* taxes imposed by later Muslim states.

mulāmasa: a forbidden sale, in which the deal is completed if the buyer touches a thing without seeing or checking it properly.

munābadha: a forbidden sale in which the deal is completed when the seller throws things towards the buyer without giving him a chance to see, touch or check them.

muqāraba: a *qirāḍ*.

murābaḥa: partnership between an investor and a borrower in a profit-sharing re-sale of goods, in which the profit is pre-determined and fixed.

musāqa: sharecropping contract; tending to an existing plantation in exchange for a share of the yield.

musāwama: sale of goods at any price mutually agreed upon by the buyer and seller.

mushāraka: partnership.

mushtarī: a seller.

muwaqqat: contingent on a time limit.

muzābana: a forbidden sale in which something whose number, weight, or measure is known is sold for something whose number, weight or measure is not known.

muzāraʻa: farming partnership, in which someone allows his land to be cultivated in exchange for a portion of the produce. (cf. *musāqa*).

muzāyada: auction.

najash: a trick (of offering a very high price) for something without the intention of buying it but just to allure and cheat somebody else who really wants to buy it although it is not worth such a high price.

najsh: bidding up, the practice of making a tender for goods without any intention of buying them with the aim of increasing their price.

namā': productivity.

naqdān: cash, specie, gold and silver.

nasī'a: a sale in which the price is paid later for goods to be delivered at once; ownership in the goods passes at the time the contract is made.

qabūl: acceptance in a contract.

qarḍ: loan of money or something else.

qarḍ ḥasan: interest-free loan.

qayṣariyya: a market for fine goods.

qirāḍ: wealth put by an investor in the trust of an agent for use for commercial purposes, the agent receiving no wage, but taking a desiganted share of the profits after the capital has first been paid back to the investor.

rabb al-māl: investor, beneficial owner, sleeping partner.

rahn: mortgage; a pledge; pawn.

ramā: a form of usury.

raqqād: long-distance trader.

ribā: usury, which is *ḥarām*, whatever forms it takes, since it it involves obtaining something for nothing through exploitation.

ribā al-faḍl: this involves any discrepancy in quantity in an exchange, for example, an exchange of goods of superior quality for more of the same kind of goods of inferior quality, e.g., dates of superior quality for dates of inferior quality in greater amount. This is forbidden.

ribā al-Jāhiliyya: pre-Islamic *ribā*.

ribā jālī: manifest *ribā*.

ribā khafī: hidden *ribā*.

ribā al-nasī'a: this involves a gap in time in an exchange of two quantities, even if they match in quantity and quality, for example, interest on lent money.

ribḥ: profit.

rukhṣa: an allowance for a transaction which would be forbidden if principles were strictly followed. The *'arīya* is an example of this.

ṣaḥīḥ: a valid sale.

ṣakk (plural *ṣukūk* or *ṣikāk*)**:** the original of "cheque", a commercial document.

salam: a sale in which the price is paid at once for goods to be delivered later; ownership in the goods passes at the time the contract is made.

ṣarf: exchange of two currencies; a barter transaction.

shāfi': a holder of the right of pre-emption.

sharika: also *shirka*; partnership.

sharika al-a'māl: (also *sharika al-abdān*), labour partnership, based on the partners' work.

sharika al-'aqd: contractual partnership.

sharika al-māl: finance partnership, based on the partners' contributions in gold or silver.

sharika al-mulk: proprietary partnership.

sharika fī'l-bay': the transfer at cost price of an article from one person to another who in return becomes a partner in the ownership of the article and agrees to sell it for both of them, the profit to be shared.

sharika wujūh: credit partnership.

shirka: see *sharika.*

shuf'a: pre-emption; this includes *shuf'a ash-sharīk*, the right of a co-owner in a property to have the first option of purchasing his partners' shares; *shuf'a al-khalīt*, the right of partner to have the first option; and *shuf'a al-jār*, the right of the neighbour to have the first option of purchasing a neighbouring property.

shurūṭ (plural of *sharṭ*)**:** legal formularies, preconditions.

ṣīgha: wording, the form of a contract.

ṣinf (plural *aṣnāf*)**:** guild. (see *ḥirfa*).

suftaja: bill of exchange. It is defined as a loan of money repayable by the borrower to a person other than the lender in a different place. It is forbidden.

sūq: market.

at-ta'āṭī: sale by "give and take" which is sanctioned by custom.

taḍamūn: joint liability.

taḍmīn: liability.

tafwīḍ: delegation of authority, proxy.

takāfu': principle of proportionality in Mālikī partnership law requiring the distribution of profit and liability to correspond to the distribution of the various components constituting the investment.

takāful: mutual responsibility, mutual guarantee, the Muslim answer to insurance in which money is pooled and invested.

talaqqi as-sila': going outside the town to buy goods before they arrive which leads to artificially high prices. It is forbidden.

talfīs: bankruptcy.

tanfīdh: implementation, execution.

taqsīr: personal fault or negligence.

tawlīya: resale of goods with a discount from the original stated cost.

thaman: price.

thamaniyya: currency.

tijāra: commerce, trade.

ujrat al-mithl: a fair salary.

'uqūd: the plural of *'aqd.*

'urbūn: earnest money, handsel, down payment.

'urf fāsid: disapproved custom, which conflicts with the *Sharī'a* and is therefore rejected.

'urf ṣaḥīḥ: valid or approved custom, which is in harmony with the *Sharī'a* and is therefore accepted.

'urūḍ: chattels; moveable property, (except money and animals).

'ushr: one tenth of the yield of land to be levied for public assistance.

wadī'a: a deposit, something deposited for safekeeping.

wakāla: agency; power of attorney.

wakīl: agent.

warehouses for merchants: see *caravanserai* for public ones. Private ones are *khān* in the East, *funduq* (from Gr. *pandokeiōn* – guest house) in the West. Also *wakāla.*

zuyūf: debased coins

Inheritance Terms

‘amm: paternal uncle.

‘amma: paternal aunt.

‘aqīl: sane and able to reason, and therefore capable of making a valid bequest and inheriting wealth.

‘aql: intellect, the faculty of reason.

‘aṣaba: male relatives on the father’s side who take the remaining estate, if any, after the heirs with fixed shares have received their shares. Sometimes translated as “universal heir”.

aṣḥāb al-farā’iḍ: those entitled to fixed shares of inheritance by the Qur’ān. They are: father, father’s father however old, half-brother by the mother, husband, wife, daughter, son’s daughter, however young, full sister, consanguine sister, uterine sister, mother, and grandmother.

aṣl: the basic estate.

Āyāt al-Mawārith: “the Verses of Inheritance Shares” in the Qur’ān (4:11-12) which lay down the basic rules of inheritance.

‘awl: adjustment, accommodation by reducing inheritance shares when the shares exceed the total estate.

bi’l-ma‘rūf: according to reasonable usage, in a correct and commonly acceptable manner.

bulūgh: the age of puberty, physical sexual maturity.

dayn: debt. Debts are paid first from the estate before it is divided between the heirs.

dhū'r-raḥm (plural *ulū'l-arḥām*)**:** relatives who receive none of the fixed shares of inheritance and are not among the *‘aṣaba*; blood relatives on the mother's side.

farā’iḍ: plural of *farīḍa,* the fixed shares of inheritance as stipulated in the Qur’ān. The shares are: 1/2, 1/4, 1/3, 1/6, 1/8, and 2/3.

farīḍa (plural *farā’iḍ)***:** share of inheritance.

ḥajb: preventing someone else from inheriting. Such exclusion can be total (*ḥajb ḥarmānī*) or partial (*ḥajb nafsānī*).

irth: inheritance, division of the estate.

'ilm al-farā'iḍ: knowledge of the shares of inheritance.

kalāla: someone who dies without heirs.

khāl (plural *akhwāl*)**:** maternal uncle.

khāla: maternal aunt.

mafqūd: missing person. He is considered to be still alive by the principle of *istiṣḥāb*.

maḥjūb: excluded from inheritance by another heir.

māni' (plural *mawāni'*)**:** hindrance, obstacle, preventative cause which prevents inheritance. These can be: homicide, difference of religion, slavery.

maraḍ al-mawt: the sickness of which a person dies. He cannot dispose of two-thirds of his property in such an illness.

ma'trūh: mentally deficient, idiotic, senile; and therefore incapable of making a valid bequest.

mawāni': legal impediments, the plural of *māni'*.

mawārīth: plural of *mīrāth*.

mīrāth (plural *mawārīth*)**:** law of inheritance.

mumayyiz: someone who is able to differentiate between good and evil.

mūrith: person leaving the estate.

mūṣī: the one who makes a will.

radd: the opposite of *'awl*, redistribution of the residue of inheritance when the shares are less than the estate. This is distributed to the heirs according to their shares.

rushd: the state of full intellectual maturity, able to conduct one's own affairs.

taṣḥīḥ: rectification, multiplying the number of shares by the number of heirs to avoid fractions.

taymīz: the age of discretion and understanding, at which a valid bequest can be made.

wārith (plural *waratha*)**:** heir.

waṣāyā: wills or testaments. The plural of *waṣīya*.

waṣī: executor of a will.

waṣīya: will, bequest. It can be made by a Muslim to a non-Muslim or vice versa, but not to one of the obligatory heirs already entitled to a fixed share.

wilāya: guardianship of minor children of the deceased.

Ḥajj Terms

'Arafa: a plain fifteen miles to the east of Makka on which stands the Jabal ar-Raḥma, the Mount of Mercy. One of the essential rites of *ḥajj* is to stand on 'Arafa on the 9th of *Dhū'l-Ḥijja.*

badana (plural *budn*)**:** a camel or a cow or an ox driven to be offered as a sacrifice, by the pilgrims at the sanctuary of Makka. (cf. *hady*).

Baytu'llah: "the House of Allah", the Ka'ba.

Bayt al-Ḥarām: "the Sacred House", the Ka'ba.

Dhāt 'Irq: the *mīqāt* of the people of Iraq. It is a ruined town two stages from Makka.

Dhū'l-Ḥulayfa: the *mīqāt* of the people of Madina, now called Bayar 'Alī.

hady: an animal offered as a sacrifice during the *ḥajj.*

Ḥajar al-Aswad: the Black Stone.

ḥajj-al-asghar: *'umra.*

ḥajj al-ifrād: *ḥajj* by itself, the simplest way to perform *ḥajj.*

ḥajj mabrūr: a *ḥajj* accepted by Allah for being perfectly performed according to the Prophet's *Sunna* and with legally earned money.

ḥajj al-qirān: the joined *ḥajj.*

ḥajj at-tamattu': the interrupted *ḥajj.*

Ḥajjat al-Wadā': the 'Farewell *Ḥajj,*' the final *ḥajj* performed by the Prophet, may Allah bless him and grant him peace.

ḥājj (plural *ḥujaj*)**:** a hadji, a pilgrim, someone who is performing or has performed the *ḥajj.*

Ḥaram: Sacred Precinct, a protected area in which certain behaviour is forbidden and other behaviour necessary. The area around the Ka'ba in Makka is a *Ḥaram*, and the area around the Prophet's Mosque in Madina is a *Ḥaram*. They are referred to together as the *Ḥaramayn*, 'the two *Ḥarams*'.

al-Ḥasb: a place outside Makka where pilgrims go after finishing all the ceremonies of *ḥajj*.

Ḥaṭīm: the Ḥijr of the Ka'ba, or the wall of the Ḥijr over which is the spout (*Mīzāb*). It is called this because it is where people crowd together to make supplications and, in so doing, press against (*ḥaṭama*) one another.

Ḥijr: the unroofed portion of the Ka'ba which at present is in the form of a semi-circular compound towards the north of the Ka'ba.

ḥujaj: pilgrims, the plural of *ḥājj*.

ifāḍa: "overflow", in the *ḥajj* when the pilgrims hasten from 'Arafat to Muzdalifa.

ifrād: a form of *ḥajj* in which *ḥajj* is performed before *'umra*.

iḥrām: a state in which one is prohibited to practise certain deeds that are lawful at other times. The ceremonies of *'umra* and *ḥajj* are performed in this state. When one assumes this state, the first thing one should do is to express mentally and orally one's intention to assume this state for the purpose of performing *ḥajj* or *'umra*. Then *talbīya* is recited. Two sheets of unstitched cloth are the only clothes a man wears: an *izār* worn below one's waist and a *ridā'* worn round the upper part of the body.

istislām: literally submission, particularly greeting the Black Stone and the Yemeni corner of the Ka'ba during *ṭawāf* by kissing, touching or saluting with the outstretched hand.

Jabal ar-Raḥma: the Mount of Mercy at 'Arafa where it is said that Adam was re-united with Ḥawwā' after years of wandering the earth apart following their expulsion from the Garden of 'Adn.

Jam': al-Muzdalifa, a well-known place between 'Arafa and Mina, known as *al-Jam'* either because people gather there or because it is there that Adam rejoined Ḥawwa'. *Yawm Jam'* refers to the day of 'Arafat, while *Yawm al-Jam'* designates the Day of Resurrection when people will be gathered together. The *Ayyām Jam'* (days of *Jam'*) refer to the days of *tashrīq* at Mina.

jamra: lit. a small walled place, but in this usage a stone-built pillar. There are three *jamras* at Mina. One of the rites of *ḥajj* is to stone them.

Jamrat al-'Aqaba: the largest of the three *jamras* at Mina. It is situated at the entrance of Mina from the direction of Makka.

jimār: plural of *jamra.*

Ji'rāna: a place near Makka, where the Messenger of Allah distributed the booty from the Battle of Ḥunayn and from where he went into *iḥrām* to perform *'umra.*

al-Juḥfa: the *mīqāt* of the people of Syria and Europe.

Ka'ba: the cube-shaped building at the centre of the *Ḥaram* in Makka, originally built by the Prophet Ibrāhīm. Also known as the House of Allah. It is towards the Ka'ba that Muslims face when praying.

Khayf: mosque in Mina located at the east end of the valley.

Labbayk: "At your service", the *talbīya* or chant of the pilgrim.

al-Manāsī: a vast plateau on the outskirts of Madina.

manāsik: the rites, i.e. *iḥrām*, *ṭawāf* of the Ka'ba and *sa'y* of Safa and Marwa, the stay at 'Arafa, Muzdalifa and Mina, the stoning of the *jamras*, the slaughtering of a *hady* (animal) and the *Ṭawāf al-Ifāḍa*, etc.

manāsik al-ḥajj: the rites of pilgrimage.

Maqām Ibrāhīm: the place of the stone on which the Prophet Ibrāhīm stood while he and Ismā'īl were building the Ka'ba, which marks the place of the two *rak'āt* prayer following *ṭawāf* of the Ka'ba.

Marwa: a small hill near the Ka'ba. (See *Ṣafā and Marwa*).

mas'a: walking between Ṣafā and Marwa when performing *sa'y* during *ḥajj*.

mash'ar: a place where certain rites are performed.

Mash'ar al-Ḥaram: a venerated place in the valley of Muzdalifa where it is a *sunna* to stop.

Masjid al-Ḥaram: the great mosque in Makka. The Ka'ba is situated in it.

Masjid an-Nabawī: the Prophet's mosque in Madina. The Prophet's tomb is situated in it.

Masjid al-Qiblatayn: "the Mosque of the two *Qiblas*", the mosque in Madina in which the *qibla* was changed from towards Jerusalem towards the Ka'ba in mid-prayer in 2 AH.

Masjid at-Taqwā: "the Mosque of *Taqwā*", the first mosque to be built by the Prophet and his Companions at Qubā'.

mawāqit: plural of *mīqāt.*

mawqif (plural *mawāqif*)**:** lit. a standing or stopping place. There are two places where pilgrims must stop on the *ḥajj*: 'Arafa and Muzdalifa.

Mijanna: a place at Makka.

Mina: a valley five miles on the road to 'Arafa where the three *jamras* stand. It is part of *ḥajj* to spend three or possibly four nights in Mina during the days of *tashrīq*.

mīqāt (plural *mawāqit*)**:** one of the designated places for entering into *iḥrām* for *'umra* or *ḥajj*.

Mīzāb ar-Raḥma: "the Spout of Mercy," the rainspout at the top of the Ka'ba on its northeast side.

Muhaṣṣab: a valley outside Makka sometimes called Khayf Banī Kinana.

Muḥassar: (Wādī Nār), a depression on the way to Mina where the Army of the Elephant of Abraha was turned away. One should hasten through it.

muḥrim: a person in *iḥrām*.

muḥṣar: someone detained from *ḥajj* by an enemy or an illness.

al-Multazam: the area between the Black Stone and the door of the Ka'ba, where it is recommended to make supplication.

muṭawwif: a pilgrim's guide, traditionally a resident of Makka.

Muzdalifa: a place between 'Arafa and Mina where the pilgrims returning from 'Arafa spend a night in the open between the ninth and tenth day of Dhū'l-Ḥijja after performing *Maghrib* and *'Ishā'* there.

Nafr (day of)**:** the 12th or 13th of Dhū'l-Ḥijja when the pilgrims leave Mina after having completed all the ceremonies of *ḥajj* at 'Arafa, Muzdalifa and Mina.

Naḥr (day of)**:** the 10th of Dhū'l-Ḥijja on which the pilgrims slaughter their sacrifices.

Namira: the site of a large mosque just before 'Arafa where the *ḥajjis* stop on their way to 'Arafa.

qārin: a person who performs *ḥajj al-qirān*.

Qarn: the *mīqāt* of the people of Najd between Ṭā'if and Makka.

qilāda (plural *qalā'id*)**:** a garland around the neck of an animal brought for sacrifice during the *ḥajj*.

qirān: combining *ḥajj* and *'umra* simultaneously.

ramī: throwing pebbles at the *jamras* at Mina.

raml: "hastening" in the *ṭawāf*, a way of walking briskly accompanied by movements of the arms and legs to show one's physical strength. This is to be observed in the first three rounds of *ṭawāf*, and is to be done by the men only and not by the women.

Ṣafā and Marwa: two hills close to the Ka'ba. It is part of the rites of *'umra* and *ḥajj* to go seven times between the two hills.

sa'y: the main rite of *'umra* and part of *ḥajj*. It is going between the hills of Ṣafa and Marwa seven times.

talbīya: saying *"Labbayk"* ("At Your service") during the *ḥajj*.

tamattu': a form of *ḥajj* in which *'umra* is done first, and then the *ḥājji* comes out of *iḥrām* before going back into *iḥrām* for the *ḥajj* itself.

Tan'īm: a place towards the north of Makka outside the sanctuary from where Makkans may assume the state of *iḥrām* to perform *'umra* and *ḥajj*.

taqlīd: garlanding sacrificial animals for the *ḥajj*. (Cf. *qilāda*).

tarwīya: "drawing water", the 8th of Dhū'l-Ḥijja, the day before 'Arafa when the pilgrims gather water and stay overnight at Mina.

tashrīq: "drying meat in the sun", the days of the 10th, 11th, 12th and 13th of Dhū'l-Ḥijja when the pilgrims sacrifice their animals and stone the *jamras* at Mina.

ṭawāf: circumambulation of the Ka'ba, done in sets of seven circuits.

Ṭawāf al-Ifāḍa: the *ṭawāf* of the Ka'ba that the pilgrims must perform after coming from Mina to Makka on the 10th of Dhu'l-Ḥijja. It is one of the essential rites of *ḥajj*.

Ṭawāf al-Qudūm: *ṭawāf* of arrival in Makka (*farḍ* among the Mālikīs).

Ṭawāf al-Wadā': the farewell *ṭawāf* done just before the pilgrim leaves Makka.

Ṭawāf az-Ziyāra: "the *ṭawāf* of the visit", another name for the *Ṭawāf al-Ifāḍa*.

wuqūf: stopping at 'Arafa and Muzdalifa. (Cf. *mawqif*).

Yalamlama: the *mīqāt* of the people of Yemen.

Yemeni corner: the corner of the Ka'ba facing south towards the Yemen.

zā'ir: visitor, someone visiting the tomb of the Prophet.

Zamzam: the well in the Ḥaram of Makka.

ziyāra: visit to a tomb or holy places.

Some Important Fuqahā'

The Mālikī Madhhab

Mālik ibn Anas: Abū 'Abdullāh al-Aṣbaḥi al-Ḥimyarī, born in Madina in 93/712, the famous Imām of Madina in *fiqh* and *ḥadīth*. One of the four Imāms. His love of the Prophet was such that he would not mount a horse in Madina. He always walked barefoot in its streets out of his respect for the Prophet. When he was asked something that he did not know, he would simply say, "I do not know." He would not relate a *ḥadīth* without first doing *wuḍū'*. Ash-Shāfi'ī was one of his pupils. He had great knowledge and piety. He wrote the first collection of *ḥadīth* and *fiqh*, *al-Muwaṭṭa'*. He died in Madina in 179/795.

Some Major Mālikī *fuqahā'*:

Ibn 'Abdi'l-Barr: an-Numayrī, Abū 'Umar, *ḥāfiẓ* of the Maghrib and Shaykh al-Islām. He was born in Cordova in 368/978 and died at the age of 95 in Shatiba in 463/1071. A major *ḥadīth* scholar, Mālikī scholar, author, and *mujtahid*, he was nicknamed "the *Ḥadith* Scholar of the West". Ibn Ḥazm said, "There is no one with more knowledge of the *fiqh* of *ḥadīth* than him." He wrote a number of works, the most famous of which is *al-Isti'āb.* He travelled throughout Andalusia and acted as qadi several times. He wrote the earliest major commentary on the *Muwaṭṭa'* entitled *al-Istidhkār*.

Ibn Abī Zayd al-Qayrawānī: Abū Muḥammad 'Abdullāh, Maliki *faqīh*, 310/922 – 386/996. He was known as "Shaykh al-Faqīh" and "little Malik" and was the head of the Mālikī school in Qayrawan.

He wrote several books, including his *Risāla, Mukhtaṣar al-Mudawwana,* an abridgement of the *Mudawwana*, and *an-Nawādir.*

Ibn al-'Arabī: Qāḍī Abū Bakr Muḥammad ibn 'Abdullāh al-Ishbilī al-Ma'afirī (d. 543/1148), author of *Aḥkām al-Qur'ān.* He was born in Seville and went to North Africa after the fall of the 'Abbadid dynasty and travelled to the east. He then returned to Seville which was under the Murābiṭūn and became Qāḍī and taught *fiqh*. He also witnessed the fall of the Murābiṭūn and rise of the Muwaḥḥidūn. He died near Fes while returning from Marrakesh after a visit to the Muwaḥḥid ruler. He wrote over thirty books, including *'Awāṣim min al-Qawāsim* about the first civil war between Muslims.

Ibn Ḥabīb: 'Abd al-Malik as-Sulamī, a Mālikī jurist of Cordoba who studied under Ibn al-Mājishūn. He was the author of *al-Wadīḥa*, one of the major Mālikī texts which was used in Andalusia. It was one of the most comprehensive books of Mālikī *fiqh*. Although it no longer exists, much of it is quoted in *an-Nawādir* of Ibn Abi Zayd al-Qayrawānī. He travelled throughout the world in search of knowledge and verifying what he had. He died in 238/852. He wrote several books. Al-'Utbī was his pupil and hence most of his work comes through him.

Ibn Juzayy: Muḥammad ibn Aḥmad, Abū'l-Qāsim ibn Juzayy al-Kalbī of Granada, born in 693/1294, a Mālikī scholar and Imām in *tafsīr* and *fiqh*. He wrote *al-Qawā'id al-Fiqhīya.* He died in 741/1340.

Ibn al-Mawwāz: Abū 'Abdullāh Muḥammad ibn Ibrāhīm al-Iskandarī, pupil of Ibn al-Mājishūn and Ibn 'Abdu'l-Ḥakam and early systematiser of Mālikī *fiqh.* He also studied under Aṣbagh and Ashhab. He died in Syria as a refugee in 281/894 where he had fled from the Inquisition about the createdness of the Qur'ān (see *Miḥna*). He wrote a famous book known as *al-Mawwāzīya.*

Ibn al-Qāsim: Abū 'Abdullāh 'Abdu'r-Raḥmān ibn al-Qāsim al-'Atakī (or al-'Utaqi) who had both knowledge and asceticism. He was one of the companions of Mālik who had tremendous influence in recording his school, since he was the source for Saḥnūn for the problems of Mālik. In the Mālikī school, he has the same position as Muḥammad ibn al-Ḥasan ash-Shaybānī in the school of Abū Ḥanīfa. Both of them transmitted the school and made free use of *ijtihād.* Ibn al-Qāsim had opinions which differed from those of his shaykh,

Mālik, so that some said that he was dominated by opinion. Ibn 'Abdu'l-Barr said of him, "He was a *faqīh* dominated by opinion. He was a righteous and steadfast man." He met Mālik after Ibn Wahb and kept his company for a long time – about twenty years. He can be considered as the main transmitter of Mālikī *fiqh* as the *Mudawwana*, of which he is the source, is the largest compendium of Mālikī *fiqh*. He would not accept stipends from the ruler and said, "There is no good in proximity to rulers." He had sat with them at first, but then he abandoned them. He used to consider having a large number of close companions to be a form of slavery since that puts a qāḍī in danger of committing injustice and the scholar of wasting his time. He died in 191/806 at the age of 63.

Ibn Rushd: Averroes. Ibn Rushd was a genius with encyclopaedic knowledge. He spent a great part of his fruitful life as a judge and as a physician, yet he was known in the West for being the great commentator on the philosophy of Aristotle. He was born in Cordova, Spain in 520/1128 and died in 595/1198. His book on jurisprudence *Bidāyat al-Mujtahid wa-Nihāyat al-Muqtaṣid* has been held by some as possibly the best book on the Mālikī school of *fiqh*. His grandfather, Abū'l-Walīd was also known as Ibn Rushd and was a Mālikī *faqīh* who wrote *al-Muqaddimāt*.

Ibn Wahb: Abu Muḥammad 'Abdullāh ibn Wahb al-Fihrī al-Misrī, born in 123/740, a *ḥadīth* scholar. He stayed with Mālik for about twenty years, and also studied with many of the companions of az-Zuhrī. He also related from more than four hundred shaykhs of *ḥadīth* in Egypt, the Hijaz and Iraq. Ibn Wahb noticed that some of his *ḥadīths* were weak. He said, "If it had not been that Allah rescued me through Mālik and al-Layth, I would have been lost." He was asked, "How is that?" He replied, "I had a lot of *ḥadīth* and it confused me. I used to present them to Mālik and al-Layth and they would say, 'Take this and leave that.'" Mālik esteemed and loved him. He used to call him "the *faqīh*" when he wrote to him. He had many excellent books, including what he heard from Mālik which was recorded in about thirty books. He wrote down the *Muwaṭṭā'*. He recorded his answers to questions and consulted them. He was asked to accept the post of qāḍī but refused and withdrew, dying in 197/812 at the age of 72

'Iyāḍ, Qāḍī: 'Iyāḍ ibn Mūsa, Abū'l-Faḍl al-Yaḥṣubī, born in Ceuta in 476/1083. The Imām of the western Muslim lands in *ḥadīth* and Arabic, a gifted Mālikī *faqīh* and scholar who wrote a number of books, especially *ash-Shifā'* and the *Tartīb al-Madārik* which consists of biographies of Mālikī *fuqahā'*. He was a qāḍī in Cordoba, then Granada and then Marrakesh and died of poison in 544/1149.

Khalīl: ibn Isḥāq al-Jundī, a Mālikī *muftī* of Cairo and teacher at the Shaykhūniyya, the largest *madrasa* in Cairo at the time. He died in 669/1365 or 676/1374. He wrote the very popular Mālikī compendium, *al-Mukhtaṣar.*

al-Qarafī: Shihāb ad-din Abū'l-'Abbās Aḥmad b. Abī'l-'Alā' Idrīs, an Egyptian Mālikī, but a Berber by origin from Sanhaja, born in 626 /1228. A Mālikī *faqīh* and *muftī,* he grew up in al-Qarafa in Cairo. He was the most important Mālikī scholar of his time in Cairo. He had knowledge of Hebrew, grammar, lexicography, algebra, magic, astronomy, and opthalmology. He wrote *Sharḥ Tanqīh al-Fuṣūl* on legal theory, *al-Furūq* on *qawā'id*, and a six volume opus of Mālikī *fiqh*, *adh-Dhakhīra*, meant to be one of the best books on Mālikī *fiqh*. *At-Tamyīz* was another book by him. He died in 684/1285.

Saḥnūn: Abū Sa'īd 'Abdu's-Salām ibn Sa'īd at-Tanūkhī, the Mālikī *faqih* and *qāḍī* of North Africa. He met Mālik but did not take anything from him. He wrote the sixteen volume *Mudawanna* on Mālikī *fiqh*. He was born in 160/776-7 in Qayrawan, travelled and studied, especially in Tunis and Egypt. He became Qāḍī in 234/848 under the Aghlabid governor, Muḥammad ibn al-Aghlab, and had hundreds of students. He died in 240/854.

ash-Shāṭibī: Abū Isḥāq Ibrāhim ibn Mūsā al-Gharnatī, (d. 790/1388), a Mālikī *faqih* who wrote *al-I'tiṣām* and *al-Muwāfaqāt*. He presented the doctrines of *Maqāṣid ash-Sharī'a* (the purposes of the law).

al-'Utbī: Muḥammad ibn Aḥmad, scholar of Cordova and pupil of Ibn Ḥabīb, who wrote *al-'Utbiyya*. He was one of the first to popularise Mālik's school in Andalusia. He died in 255/869. His compendium was also called *al-Mustakhraja.*

'Uthmān ibn Fūdī: or Usumān dan Fodio or Fodiye, born in Maratta, Northern Nigeria in 1168/1754. He was an Islamic scholar and Qādirī Shaykh. He led the Fulani *jihād* in northern Nigeria with his younger brother 'Abdullāhi and son Muḥammad Bello. He was a *ḥāfiẓ* of Qur'ān, Māliki *faqih*, poet, and scholar. He was worried about the trend to syncretism and so made *hijra* from the lands of the Gobir to the north and west. He fought for four years against the Gobir and Habe peoples and died in Sifawa in 1230/1817. His famous book, *Iḥyā' as-Sunna,* deals with the daily practices of Islam. He wrote numerous books, including the *Kitāb 'Uṣūl ad-Dīn* and *al-Masā'il al-Muhimma.*

al-Wansharīsī: Aḥmad ibn Yaḥyā, a Mālikī *muftī* of Fez, (c. 834/1430 - 914/1508). He has a twelve volume collection of *fatwās* called *al-Mi'yār al-Mughribān Fatāwā 'Ulamā' Ifriqīya wa'l-Andalus wa'l-Maghrib,* "The Standard, expressing the *fatwās* of the scholars of Tunisia, Andalusia, and Morocco", and other works.

Some Important Mālikī Texts

Bidāyat al-Mujtahid: "The Beginning of the *Mujtahid*" by Ibn Rushd, a systematic account of the principles of derivation of judgements in *fiqh.* His scope extends to the other schools of *fiqh.* Some consider it to be the best book written in the Mālikī school.

al-Mawwāzīya: one of the major sources of the Mālikī school which was written by Ibn al-Mawwāz. It is extremely detailed and comprehensive in its discussion of all the sources.

al- Mi'yār: *al-Mi'yār al-Mughribān Fatāwā 'Ulamā' Ifriqīya wa'l-Andalus wa'l-Maghrib,* "The Standard, expressing the *fatwās* of the scholars of Tunisia, Andalusia, and Morocco" by al-Wansharīsī. A comprehensive collection of *fatwās.* One of the areas it covers is *fiqh an-nawāzil.*

al-Mudawwana: the famous Mālikī legal compendium of Saḥnūn. It contains the replies of Ibn al-Qāsim as well as some of those of Ibn Wahb. It is sometimes called *al-Mukhṭalita* (mixed up) because the problems are lumped together in the various chapters.

Mukhtaṣar al-Akhḍarī: a small booklet dealing with purity and the prayer by al-Akhḍarī.

Mukhtaṣar Khalīl: the principal Mālikī legal textbook by Khalīl which is so compressed that it requires commentary of which there are many.

al-Mustakhraja: See *al-'Utbīya.*

al-Muwaṭṭā': Mālik's famous compendium of *fiqh* and *ḥadīth*. Virtually every *ḥadīth* in it was accepted by al-Bukhārī. Ash-Shāfi'ī said of it, "After the Book of Allah, there is no book on earth sounder than that of Mālik." There are two surviving recensions: that of Yaḥya ibn Yaḥyā al-Laythī al-Maṣmūdī and that of Muḥammad ibn al-Ḥasan ash-Shaybānī.

al-Qawā'id al-Fiqhīya: "Rules of Fiqh" by Ibn Juzayy al-Kalbī (d. 741/1340), a single volume on legal judgements according to the Mālikī school accompanied by the differences and agreements with the other schools.

Risāla: by Ibn Abī Zayd al-Qayrawānī, an immensely popular summary of the principal elements of the *Sharī'a.* It is also known as *Bākāra as-Sa'd,* "The Beginning of Happiness", and *Zubda al-Madhhab,* "Cream of the School". Ibn Abī Zayd wrote it at the age of seventeen to counter the influence of the Fāṭimids. It covers everything from dogma to table manners.

al-'Utbiyya: or *al-Mushtakhraja.* A well-known collection of Malik's opinions, written by Muḥammad al-'Utbī. Some contemporaries said that it contained a number of errors. It contains unusual questions and often omits to mention how they were transmitted to him.

The Ḥanafi Madhhab

Abū Ḥanīfa: Abū Ḥanīfa an-Nu'mān ibn Thābit, founder of the Ḥanafī school in Baghdad. He is one of the four Imams and is known for developing *ra'y* (judicial opinion). He shunned sleep and was called the "Peg" because he used to stand for long periods in night prayers. He only slept between *Ẓuhr* and *'Aṣr.* He grew up in Kūfa and the khalif al-Manṣūr asked him to accept the post of qāḍī. He refused and al-Manṣūr imprisoned him and beat him until he died. He would never sit in the shade of someone to whom he had loaned money, saying, "Every loan that brings benefit is usury." He died in 150/767.

Some Major Ḥanafī *fuqahā'*:

Abū Yūsuf: Ya'qūb ibn Ibrāhīm ibn Ḥabīb al-Anṣārī al-Baghdādī, born in Kūfa in 113/731. He was the student of Abū Ḥanīfa and the first to propagate his school, a *ḥadīth* master and brilliant jurist who had an extensive knowledge of *tafsīr*. He acted as qāḍī in Baghdad for al-Mahdī, al-Hadī and Hārūn ar-Rashīd, who made the Ḥanafī school the official state code for the 'Abbasids. He was also the first to write on the principles (*uṣūl*) of Ḥanafi *fiqh*, and was a *mujtahid*. He died in Baghdad in 182/798. He wrote *Kitāb al-Kharāj* on taxation and constitutional questions.

al-Ḥasan ibn Ziyād al-Lu'lu'ī: one of the famous students of Abū Ḥanifa and a *faqīh* of Kūfa. He wrote several practical works on law, including a handbook for *qāḍīs*. He became *qāḍī* of Kufa in 194/810. He died in Kūfa in 204/820.

Ibn 'Abidīn: Muḥammad Amīn ibn 'Umar, born in Damascus in 1198/1784. Originally a Shāfi'ī, he changed and became the Ḥanafi imām of his time. His most famous work is the eight volume *Ḥāshiyya Radd al-Muhtār*, which is considered authoritative in the Ḥanafī school. He wrote on various areas of knowledge and died in 1252/1836.

al-Khaṣṣāf: Abū Bakr Aḥmad b. 'Amr. His *Kitab Adāb al-Qāḍī* has a special place in Ḥanafī literature. He was a court lawyer in Baghdad for the 'Abbasid khalif al-Muhtadī. When al-Muhtadī was murdered in 256/869, his house was sacked as well. He died in 261/874.

al-Marghīnānī: 'Alī ibn Abī Bakr, author of the Ḥanafī *fiqh* book, *al-Hidāya*. He died in 593/1196.

Muḥammad ibn al-Ḥasan: See *ash-Shaybānī*.

an-Nasafī: 'Abdullāh ibn Aḥmad, Abū 'Abdu'r-Raḥmān of Idhaj, a village near Isfahan, one of the great Ḥanafī Imāms of his time, who wrote on *uṣūl*, *fiqh* and *'aqīda*. He wrote a three volume *tafsīr* called *Madārik at-Tanzīl*. He died in Idhaj in 710/1310. [There are three other well-known scholars also called an-Nasafī.]

al-Qudurī: Abū'l-Ḥusayn Aḥmad b. Muḥammad. He has a well-known compendium or *Mukhtaṣar*. He died in 428/1036-7.

as-Sarakhsī: Muḥhammad ibn Aḥmad, Abū Bakr, a great Ḥanafī Imām, *mujtahid*, *qāḍī* and author of the thirty volume encyclopaedic *al-Mabsūt*, dictated to his students while he was imprisoned in an underground cell in Uzjand near Ferghana for advising a local chief about the *dīn*. He wrote a number of books and died in Ferghana in 483/1090.

ash-Shaybānī: Muḥammad ibn Ḥasan, Abū 'Abdullāh, born in Wāsiṭ in 131/748. A *mujtahid* Imam, he was educated by Abū Ḥanīfa, Abū Yūsuf and Mālik. He was raised in Kūfa where he met Abū Ḥanīfa, joined his school and then moved to Baghdad, where the 'Abbasid khalif Hārūn ar-Rashīd made him a *qāḍī*. He transmitted *al-Muwaṭṭā'* of Mālik. He was one of the shaykhs of ash-Shāfi'ī. He wrote many books and died in Rayy in 189/804. He has *Kitāb al-Aṣl* or *al-Mabsūt*, *al-Jāmi' as-Saghīr* and *al-Jāmi' al-Kabīr*.

at-Taḥāwī: Imām Abū Aḥmad ibn Muḥammad al-Miṣrī at-Taḥawī al-Ḥanafī. Taḥā is a village in Egypt. He began as a Shāfi'ī studying with al-Muzanī, who was his uncle. One day al-Muzanī remarked to him, "By Allah, you have achieved nothing." At-Taḥawī became angry and went to Ibn Abī 'Imrān al-Ḥanafī and became a Ḥanafī, so eager to establish that school that he demanded the transmission of reports of history according to his school and used what others considered to be weak arguments, according to al-Bayhaqī. One of his most famous works is the "Commentary on the Meanings of Traditions". He also has a *Mukhtaṣar* of Ḥanafi *fiqh*. He was born in 239/851 and died in 321/932.

Zufar ibn al-Hudhayl: one of the more prominent pupils of Abū Ḥanīfa. He was considered to be the most perceptive in the correct use of analogy in legal reasoning. No books are transmitted from him. He was *qāḍī* in Basra where he died in 158/775 at the age of 84.

Some Ḥanafī Texts

Badā'i' aṣ-Ṣanā'i': by Abū Bakr al-Kāshānī (d. 587/1191), a systematic arrangement of *fiqh*.

Fatāwā 'Alamgīrīya: a collection of *fatwas* made by jurists in the Moghul empire during the 12th/18th century under 'Alamgīr. It was edited by Niẓām ad-Dīn Burhānpūrī and twenty-four other scholars. The sections dealing with worship are classical in pattern, while those dealing with criminal and civil law are more pragmatic. A source for Muslim law in India.

Ḥāshiya Radd al-Muhtār: by Ibn 'Abidīn (d. 1252/1836).

al-Hidāya: by al-Marghīnānī (d. 593/1196) one of the most important texts outlining the Ḥanafī school which formed one of the bases for Ḥanafi *fiqh* in the sub-continent. The *Hidāya* is a commentary on the *Bidāya al-Mubtadā*, a concise work on *fiqh* by the same author. There are many commentaries and summaries written on it. It has been translated into Persian and English.

Kitāb al-Kharāj: by Abū Yusūf (d. 182/798), one of the earliest legal texts which Abū Yūsuf wrote for the 'Abbasid khalif ar-Rashīd. It is a treatise on taxation and constitutional questions. He clarifed the sources of financial revenue for the state and the areas of taxation in great detail, basing himself on the Qur'ān, transmission from the Prophet, and the *fatwās* of the Companions. He quotes *ḥadīths* and deduces their underlying reasons and the action of the Companions.

al-Mabsūṭ: This is the title of two major sources in the Ḥanafī school. One is by ash-Shaybānī (d. 189/804) and is one of the primary texts of the school and is sometimes known as *al-Aṣl*. It is the largest of ash-Shaybānī's books in which he collected questions on which Abū Ḥanīfa gave *fatwā*. Each chapter begins with the traditions they considered sound regarding it and then relevant questions and their answers. It gives a picture of early Iraqi *fiqh*, but not the legal reasoning behind it. The second book with this title is by as-Sarakhsī (d. 483/1090) which is comprehensive and based on an unpublished work by al-Marwazī.

The Shāfi'ī Madhhab

ash-Shāfi'ī: Abū 'Abdullāh Muḥammad ibn Idrīs, the famous scholar who was born in Ghazza in 150/767 and grew up in Makka. He had learned the Qur'ān by heart when he was seven. He knew grammar, poetry and language. He memorised the *Muwaṭṭā'* in a single night. He gave *fatwās* when he was fifteen. He travelled to Yemen and then Baghdad and then settled in Egypt. He was the founder of one of the four *madhhabs*. In fact, he produced two schools: the first, the "old school" which was based on the school of Madina, and then the "new school" which he produced four years after arriving in Cairo. He wrote *al-Umm* and *ar-Risāla*. He was the first to formulate the principles of abrogating and abrogated verses. He died in 204/820.

Some Major Shāfi'ī *fuqahā'*:

Aḥmad ibn an-Naqīb al-Miṣrī: Aḥmad ibn Lu'lu' ar-Rūmī, Shihāb ad-dīn. His father was a Christian convert from Antakya, Turkey, who was originally captured and enslaved by a Muslim prince who educated him and then set him free. Then he served him as a captain (*naqīb*) and later became a Sufi in the Baybariyya of Cairo where Aḥmad was born in 702/1302. Aḥmad memorised the seven *qirā'āt* and studied Shāfi'ī *fiqh*, *tafsīr*, Arabic, and Sufism. He wrote the *'Umdat as-Sālik*. He died of the plague in Ramaḍān in 769/1368 at the age of 67.

Al-Baghawī: Abū Muḥammad al-Ḥusayn ibn Mas'ūd, born in Bagha near Herat, a Shāfi'ī Imām in various fields. His father was a furrier. He was known to his contemporaries as "the Reviver of the *Dīn*". He has a sixteen volume *Sharḥ as-Sunna*, dealing with Shāfi'ī *fiqh* and the basis for it. He has a *tafsīr* entitled *Lubab at-Ta'wīl*. He died in Marw in 510/1117. He produced the *Masābiḥ as-Sunna* which is a collection of *ḥadīths*.

al-Bayhaqī: Aḥmad ibn al-Ḥusayn, Abū Bakr, born in Khasrajand, a village around Bayhaq near Nishapur. He produced nearly 1,000 volumes. Al-Bayhaqī was one of the great Imāms in *ḥadīth* and Shāfi'ī jurisprudence. He wrote some important books, such *as-Sunan al-Kubrā, as-Sunan as-Sughrā, al-Mabsūṭ,* and *al-Asmā' wa'ṣ-Ṣifāt*. He died in Nishapur in 458/1066.

al-Ghazālī: Muḥammad ibn Muḥammad, Abū Ḥamid aṭ-Ṭūsi, the Shāfi'ī Imām and Sufi born in Tabiran, near Ṭūs in 450/1058. He studied *fiqh* with al-Juwaynī. He taught at the Niẓāmiyya Madrasa before he became a Sufi. He is nicknamed "Shāfi'ī the Second". He died in Tabiran in 505/1111. He was the author of many books, especially *Iḥyā' 'Ulūm ad-Dīn*.

Ibn 'Abdu's-Salām: 'Izz ibn 'Abd as-Salām as-Sulamī, "the Sultan of the Scholars", born in Damascus in 577/1181. He was a Shāfi'ī scholar and companion of Imām Abū'l-Ḥasan ash-Shādhilī. His reputation was the stuff of legends. In Damascus as the *khaṭīb*, he refused to wear black, speak in *saj'* or praise the princes. When as-Ṣaliḥ Ismā'īl made concessions to the Crusaders, Ibn 'Abdu's-Salām condemned him from the minbar. He refused to compromise in any way whatsoever. He later resigned and retired to write a number of books on Shāfi'ī *fiqh, tafsīr*, and other legal areas. His masterpiece was *Qawā'id al-Aḥkām fī Maṣālih al-Anām*. He died in 660/1262.

Ibn Ḥajar al-Haytamī: Aḥmad ibn Muḥammad, born in 909/1504 in Abū Haytam, western Egypt, was the Shāfi'ī Imām of his time. He received permission to give *fatwas* when he was barely 20. He died in Makka in 974/1567. He wrote many definitive works on Shāfi'ī *fiqh*, esp. *Tuḥfat al-Muḥtāj,* a commentary on an-Nawawī's *Minhāj aṭ-Ṭālibīn, al-Fatāwā al-Kubrā,* and *az-Zawājir*.

Ibn aṣ-Ṣalāḥ: Abū 'Amr 'Uthmān ibn 'Abdu'r-Raḥmān ash-Shāhrazūrī, known as Ibn aṣ-Ṣalāḥ. An important Shāfi'ī scholar, he was a Kurd born in Sharkhan in 577/1181. He studied in many cities and became a master of *ḥadīth*. One of his teachers was Ibn Qudāma. He was appointed the head of the Dār al-Ḥadīth in Damascus. He wrote a number of books on various topics, including *fiqh*. He has a famous collection of *fatwās* called *Fatāwā Ibn aṣ-Ṣalāḥ*. He died in 643/1245.

al-Juwaynī: Abū'l-Ma'ālī 'Abdu'l-Mālik ibn 'Abdullāh, Imām of the Two Ḥarams, the Imām of the Arabs and non-Arabs, unique in his time, the possessor of virtues and author of excellent books. Niẓām al-Mulk built a *madrasa* for him at Nishapur. He wrote an unrivalled nineteen volume work, *Nihāya al-Maṭlab,* on the Shāfi'ī school. He was the shaykh of al-Ghazālī and died in Nishapur in 478/1085.

al-Māwardī: 'Alī ibn Muḥammad, the Qāḍī, was born in Baṣra in 364/972 and died in Baghdad in 450/1058 when he was 86. His proficiency in *fiqh*, ethics, political science and literature proved useful in securing a respectable career for him. After his initial appointment as *qāḍī*, he was gradually promoted to higher offices, until he became the Chief Qāḍī at Baghdad. The 'Abbasid khalif al-Qā'im bi'amri'llāh appointed him as his roving ambassador and sent him to a number of countries as the head of special missions. He was a great jurist, *muḥaddith*, sociologist and an expert in political science. His book, *al-Ḥāwī*, on the principles of jurisprudence is held in high repute. His contribution in political science and sociology comprises a number of books, the most famous of which is *al-Aḥkām as-Sulṭānīya.*

al-Muzanī: Abū Ibrāhīm ibn Ismā'īl, born in 175/791 in Egypt. Ash-Shāfi'ī said about him, "If he had debated with Shayṭān, he would have defeated him." A Shāfi'ī *mujtahid*, he wrote *al-Mukhtaṣar* about Shāfi'ī *fiqh*. If he missed a *farḍ* prayer, he would pray it twenty-five times alone; and he used to wash the dead without payment hoping for a reward. He died in 264/878.

an-Nawawī: Yaḥyā ibn Sharaf, Abū Zakariyyā, born in the village of Nawa on the Horan Plain of southern Syria in 631/1233. He was the Imām of the later Shāfi'ītes and wrote many books: *Minhāj aṭ-Ṭālibīn, Kitāb al-Adhkār, Riyāḍ aṣ-Ṣāliḥīn* and other books He lived very simply. After twenty-seven years in Damascus, he returned home and died at the age of 44 in 676/1277.

Rabī' ibn Sulaymān al-Murādī: Abū Muḥammad, he was a long-standing student and the main transmitter of ash-Shāfi'ī's books. He was known as "the *mu'adhdhin*" because he gave the *adhān* in the Fusṭāṭ mosque until his death. He died in 270/884.

ar-Rafi'ī: 'Abdu'l-Karīm ibn Muḥammad, Abū'l-Qāsim, born in Qazwin in 557/1162. The Imām of his time in *fiqh* and *tafsīr*, he represents with Imām an-Nawawī the principle reference of the later Shāfi'ī school. His main work is a commentary on al-Ghazālī's, *al-*

Wajīz, entitled *Fatḥ al-'Azīz*. He was a mystic and ascetic. He died in Qazwin in 623/1226.

as-Subkī: Taqi ad-Dīn 'Alī ibn 'Abdu'l-Kāfī, born in Subk, Egypt in 683/1284, a Shāfi'ī scholar and *mujtahid*. He wrote more than 150 books including *at-Takmila*, an eleven volume supplement to an-Nawawī's *Sharḥ al-Muhadhdhab*, *Fatāwā as-Subkī* in two volumes, and *al-Ibhāj fī Sharḥ al-Minhāj*. In 739/1339 he moved to Damascus where he was made a *qāḍī*. Eventually he fell ill and was replaced by his son and returned to Cairo where he died in 756/1355.

Some Shāfi'ī Texts

al-Aḥkām as-Sulṭānīya: "The Laws of Islamic Governance" by Abū'l-Ḥasan al-Māwardī (d. 450/1058). A classical work on the laws of Islamic governance in practice. It deals with the principles of political science, with special reference to the functions and duties of the khalifs, the chief minister and other ministers, the relationships between various elements of the public and the government, and measures to strengthen the government, and ensure victory in war. He is considered as being the author and supporter of the "Doctrine of Necessity" in political science.

Fatḥ al-'Azīz: "The Victory of the Mighty", by ar-Rāfi'ī (d. 623/1226), a commentary on *al-Wajīz* by al-Ghazālī, which in turn provided the basis for the *Minhāj aṭ-Ṭālibīn* of an-Nawawī. It is a main reference of the Shāfi'ī school.

Minhāj aṭ-Ṭālibīn: by Imām an-Nawawī (d. 676/1277), an authoritative reference for the Shāfi'ī school. It is intended as a commentary on *al-Muḥarrar* of ar-Rāfi'ī. He refers back to al-Juwaynī via ar-Rāfi'ī and al-Ghazālī. There are several commentaries on it.

al-Mustaṣfā min 'Ilm al-Uṣūl: a book by al-Ghazālī on the *uṣūl al-fiqh*.

Nihāya al-Maṭlab: by al-Juwaynī (d. 478/1085), a massive fifteen volume collection on the Shāfi'ī school.

Sharḥ as-Sunna: by al-Bayhaqī (d. 458/1066), a sixteen volume work dealing with Shāfi'ī *fiqh* and the basis for it.

at-Tanbīh: by ash-Shīrāzī (d. 470/1083), a standard work on Shāfi'ī doctrine.

Tuḥfat al-Muḥtāj: by Ibn Ḥajar al-Haytami (d. 974/1567), a commentary on the *Minhāj aṭ-Ṭālibīn* by an-Nawawī. It is one of the main authoritative Shāfi'ī texts.

'Umdat as-sālik: by Ibn an-Naqīb (d. 769/1368), a summary of the Shafi'i school which has been translated into English by Nuh Keller as "Reliance of the Traveller".

al-Umm: by ash-Shāfi'ī (d. 204/820) a seven volume collection which contains ash-Shāfi'ī's final school of *fiqh*.

al-Wajīz: by al-Ghazālī (d. 505/1111), a synopsis of the Shāfi'ī school.

The Ḥanbalī Madhhab

Aḥmad ibn Ḥanbal: Abū 'Abdullāh ash-Shaybānī, Imām of the *Ahl as-Sunna*, born in Baghdad in 164/780 and grew up there as an orphan. He was devoted to the *Sunna* so that he became its Imām in his time. He travelled for sixteen years in pursuit of *ḥadīth* and memorised 100,000 *ḥadīths*, 30,000 of which are in his *Musnad*. He was a *ḥāfiẓ* of Qur'ān, memorised *al-Muwaṭṭā'* of Imām Mālik, and learned *fiqh* from ash-Shāfi'ī. He was the founder of the Ḥanbalī *madhhab*. It is said that in his gatherings only the Hereafter was mentioned – nothing of worldly things. He prayed every night and used to recite the entire Qur'ān every day. He was imprisoned and tortured for twenty-eight months under the 'Abbasid khalif al-Mu'taṣim for refusing to state that the Qur'ān was created. He died in 241/855.

Some Major Ḥanbalī *fuqahā'*:

Ibn al-Jawzī: Abū'l Faraj 'Abdu'r-Raḥmān ibn Jawzī, born in Baghdad in 508/1114, a great Ḥanbali scholar of his time in history and *ḥadīth*, famous for his many chronicles of the scholars and saints of the times preceding him. Ibn al-Jawzī's work *Talbīs Iblīs* is one of his best known works. Ibn al-Jawzī opposed all doctrines and practices, regardless of their sources, which were innovations in the rule of *Sharī'a* – i.e. not found in the Qur'ān and *Sunna*, wherever found in the Islamic community, especially in Ibn al-Jawzī's time. He wrote condemning specific innovated practices of many groups, including: philosophers (*mutakallimūn*), theologians, traditionalists (*'ulamā' al-ḥadīth*), jurists (*fuqahā'*), preachers, philologists, poets and false Sufis. He wrote nearly three hundred books on *taṣawwuf, fiqh, 'ilm al-Qur'ān, ḥadīth, tafsīr* and biographies of many of the great men of *taṣawwuf.* Two of his works considered as pillars in the field of *tasawwuf* are *Ṣafwat aṣ-Ṣafa* and *Minhāj al-Qāṣidīn wa Mufīd aṣ-Ṣādiqīn*. In addition, full length biographies in praise of the early Sufis were penned by Ibn al-Jawzī. He is sometimes confused with Ibn al-Qayyim al-Jawziyya. He died in Damascus in 597/1201.

Ibn al-Qayyim: Muḥammad ibn Abī Bakr, Abū 'Abdullāh al-Jawziyya, born in Damascus in 691/1292, a Ḥanbalī *ḥadīth* scholar who wrote *Zād al-Ma'ād.* He also wrote *I'lām al-Muwaqqi'īn* on *uṣūl al-fiqh.* He edited the works of his shaykh, Ibn Taymiyya. He went to prison with him in Damascus and remained with him until Ibn Taymiyya's death in 728/1328. He died in Damascus in 751/1350.

Ibn Qudāma: 'Abdullāh ibn Muḥammad ibn Qudāma, Abū Muḥammad al-Jamā'ilī al-Maqdisī, born in Jamā'il, Palestine, in 541/1146, a Ḥanbalī scholar and Imam educated in Damascus who wrote the nine volume *al-Mughnī* on Ḥanbalī *fiqh.* He died in Damascus in 620/1223.

Ibn Rajab: Abū'l-Faraj 'Abdu'r-Raḥmān b. Aḥmad al-Baghdādī al-Ḥanbalī, who died in 795/1392-3. The author of *adh-Dhayl, al-Istikhrāj* and *al-Qawā'id.* His *Ṭabaqāt al-Ḥanābila* is the most extensive collection of biographies of Ḥanbalīs.

Ibn Taymiyya: Aḥmad ibn 'Abdu'l-Ḥalīm, born in Harran in 661/1263, the famous Ḥanbalī scholar. He was imprisoned for much of his life. He was a copious writer – perhaps too copious. He died in Damascus in 728/1328.

al-Khallāl: Aḥmad ibn Muḥammad ibn Hārūn Abū Bakr, one of the major transitters of Ibn Ḥanbal's *fiqh* who died in 311/933-4. In fact, he is considered the primary collector of Ḥanbali *fiqh*. He travelled extensively to collect the knowledge of Aḥmad ibn Ḥanbal from those who transmitted it from him. After he had assembled his knowledge, he taught a circle of students in the al-Mahdī Mosque in Baghdad from which the Ḥanbali school spread. He collected his texts in the large collection, *al-Jāmi' al-Kabīr*, which was about twenty volumes or more.

al-Khiraqī: Abū'l-Qāsim 'Umar, one of the early Ḥanbalī scholars whose compendium of Ḥanbalī *fiqh* is extant. He left Baghdad for Damascus when the Shi'a gained control there. He died in 334/945-6.

Some Ḥanbalī texts:

al-Ghunya li Ṭālibi Ṭarīq al-Ḥaqq: by 'Abdu'l-Qādir al-Jilānī (d. 561/1166), the famous Sufi and founder of the Qādirī *ṭarīqa*. It contains a summary of Ḥanbalī *fiqh*.

I'lām al-Muwaqqi'īn: by Ibn al-Qayyim al-Jawziyya (d. 751/1350), a major work on *uṣūl al-fiqh*.

al-Mughnī: "The Enricher" by Ibn Qudāma (d. 620/1223), a nine volume work which comments on al-Khiraqī's *al-Mukhtaṣar fī'l-Fiqh*. It is the largest commentary on it. Not content with merely expanding on the text of the *Mukhtaṣar* and explaining the evidence for its positions, he follows that with a comprehensive exposition of the differing views within the Ḥanbalī school and the differences with other schools, even the less well-known schools, and then assesses their relative weaknesses and strengths.

Al-Mukhtaṣar fī'l-Fiqh: al-Khiraqī (d. 334/945-6), one of the most important and most famous Ḥanbali works. Over 300 commentaries have been written on it.

Other Madhhabs

al-Awzā'i: Abū 'Amr 'Abdu'r-Raḥmān, Imām and founder of the *madhhab* followed by the people of the Maghrib before they became Mālikī. He lived in Syria until he died as a *murābiṭ* in the port of Beirut. He was the main Syrian authority on *Sharī'a* in his generation. He placed special emphasis on the "living tradition" of the Muslim community as an authoritative source of law. His *madhhab* spread in North Africa and Spain. His tomb is near Beirut. He died in 157/774.

Jarīrīya: the school founded by Ibn Jarīr aṭ-Ṭabarī which differed so little from the Shāfi'ī school that it soon disappeared.

Ẓāhirīya: a school of *fiqh* which derived its judgements from the literal (*ẓāhir*) text of the Qur'ān and the *Sunna* and rejected *ra'y*, *qiyās*, *iṣtiḥsān*, *taqlīd*, and other legal principles. It was called the Dā'ūdi school after its founder, Dā'ūd ibn Khalaf. The only time it was connected to political power was under the Muwaḥḥid ruler, Ya'qūb al-Manṣūr (580/1184 – 591/1195). The famous Sufi, Muḥyī'd-dīn Ibn 'Arabī was a Ẓāhirī in *fiqh*.

Some notable Ẓāhirīs:

Dā'ūd ibn 'Alī al-Isbahānī: (or Dā'ud ibn Khalaf), the founder of the Ẓahirite *madhhab*, died in 270/884.

Ibn Ḥazm: 'Alī ibn Aḥmad aẓ-Ẓāhirī, born in Cordoba in 384/994. He was the main representative of the Ẓāhirite school after he abandoned the Shāfi'ī school. His contentiousness eventually forced him to withdraw to his family estate where he died in 456/1064.

Imāmīya: the Shi'ite position, also known as the Ja'fariyya after Ja'far aṣ-Ṣādiq (80/699 – 148/765). Abū Ja'far Muḥammad aṭ-Ṭūsī (d. 460/1067-8) is a fundamental source for Imāmī *fiqh*. His books include *al-Mabsūṭ, al-Khilāf, an-Nihāya* and *al-Muḥīt*. Another source is a manual of *fiqh* entitled *Sharā'i' al-Islām* by Ja'far ibn al-Ḥasan al-Ḥillī (d. 676/1277).

Terms used in *Kalām* and Philosophy

'abd: slave, servant of Allah, the creature utterly dependent on its Lord and Creator for its existence and sustenance.

abjad: literally "alphabet", a system of calculation based on the numerical values of the Arabic letters. "Abjad" is the first of a series of eight words which comprise all the letters of the alphabet.

adilla 'aqlīya: logical proofs or evidence.

'adl: justice.

āfāqī: time, from *āfāq*, "horizons". *Āfāqī* time describes time in the created world of human daily life.

Aftaḥīya: Rāfiḍite sect, see *Futḥiyya*.

Ahl al-'adl wa't-tawḥīd: "the people of justice and unity", the title used by the Mu'tazilites for themselves: "justice", because they say that human actions are not predetermined by Allah or it would be unjust for God to reward or punish people; "unity", because they reject the attribution of any physical and human qualities to Allah, saying that Allah is not only unique, but also He has no multiplicity within Him. They hold the view that all anthropomorphic expressions in the Qur'ān must be interpreted as metaphors and images, and must not be understood literally.

Ahl al-Ithbāt: "affirmationists", those who affirmed the *qadar* or Divine omnipotence; blanket term used by the Mu'tazilites for their opponents, from Ḍirar to al-Ash'arī.

Ahl as-Sunna wa'l-Jamā'a: the people of the *Sunna* and the Community: all the people who follow the *Sunna* of the Prophet and who hold together as a community on that basis; the main body of the Muslim Community.

Ajārida: a Kharijite sub-sect, close in belief to the Najdites. They were the followers of 'Abdu'l-Karīm ibn 'Ajrad.

āla: instrument, tool.

'ālam al-ajsām: the world of physical bodies.

'ālam al-amr: the world of dominion, the non-spatial world of the angels and human spirits (also called *'alām al-malakūt*).

'ālam al-arwāḥ: the world of spirits, as distinct from *'ālam al-mithāl* – the world of analogies, which is formal manifestation as a whole.

'ālam al-khalq: the material spatial world (also called *'ālam al-mulk wa shahāda*).

'ālam: other terms involving *'alam* are: *'alām al-lāhūt*, "the world of Divinity"; *'alām al-jabarūt*, "the world of power"; *'alām al-malakūt*; "the world of Dominion"; *'alām an-nāsūt*, "the world of humanity"; and *'alām al-hāhūt*, "the Divine Ipseity".

'ālim (plural *'ulamā'*)**:** a man of knowledge, a scholar, especially in the sciences of Islam.

ālīya: instrumentality.

al-'Amā': the Great Mist: primordial non-spatiality in non-time.

amr: the command (see *Sufism*), the *eidos* of Aristotle, the active pole (Yang) in which the Yin is *ṭabī'a* (nature, or the *hylē* of Aristole).

amthila: examples, plural of *mithāl.*

aniyya: I-ness.

'aqā'id: (plural of *'aqīda)* faith, beliefs.

'aqīda: creed, belief or tenet of faith firmly based on how things are, distinct from the testimony of faith (*shahāda*).

'āqil: intelligent, sane.

'aql: intellect, the faculty of reason.

al-'Aql: the intellect, *al-'Aql al-Awwal*: the first Intellect, analogous to the Pen (*al-Qalam*).

al-'aql al-fā'il: Active Intellect, the *nous* of Plotinus, the *logos*, or "world of ideas" of Plato, a term used by al-Farabī.

'aql gharīzī: inborn intelligence.

al-'aql al-hayūlānī: potential intellect, *intellectus potenta*, latent capacity to acquire external truths, a term used by al-Farabī.

al-'aql al-mustafād: acquired intellect, *intellectus acquisitus*, learned knowledge, a term used by al-Farabī.

'araḍ (plural *a'rāḍ*)**:** an accidental or non-essential, ontic quality. The opposite of *jawhar*. This applies to qualities like colour, heat, cold, motion, rest, etc.

asās: "first principle", an Ismā'īli term.

asbāb: causes, plural of *sabab*.

al-asbāb wa'l-wasā'iṭ: literally causes and means, intermediary causes.

Ash'arites: along with the Māturīdites, articulated the Sunnī position of *kalam*, which is characteristed by rationality while refusing to force it upon matters of faith. The main features of this school are the negation of intermediate cause and effect as everything is caused by Allah and the discontinuity between Allah and His creation. Furthermore, it is asserted, the Divine Attributes are distinct from the Essence, although they cannot be in any way comparable to the attributes of creatures. The Word of Allah, for example, is eternal and uncreated while articulated sounds are created.

al-aṣlaḥ: "the best", the Mu'tazilite doctrine that Allah always chooses the best for his creatures.

asmā' adh-dhāt: the Names of the Essence.

asmā' aṣ-ṣifāt: the Names of the Attributes.

atomism: an Ash'arite position refined by al-Bāqillānī which asserts that atoms are simultaneously both space and time. They are instants in space, but without extension.

al-'ayān ath-thābita: archetypes, fixed essences, source forms.

aysa: term used by al-Kindī for being. Now superseded by *kawn*.

Azāriqa: the Azraqites, the most extreme Khārijite group in Baṣra who followed Nāfi' ibn al-Azraq (d. 65/686), whose position is that anyone who commits a sin or act of disobedience to Allah is an unbeliever and goes to Hell forever. Any Muslim who did not share their opinion in detail was considered a *mushrik*; those who did not emigrate to their camp were considered *mushriks*; and the wives and children of such *mushriks* were considered *mushriks*. Since not joining them was considered a sin they therefore felt justified in fighting, robbing and killing all non-Azraqite Muslims. They utilised the practice of *isti'rāḍ* to ascertain the personal view of a Muslim. If he said, "I am a Muslim," they killed him immediately because there could be no Muslim outside their own camp – but they let non-Muslims live.

badā’: change of mind in relation to Allah’s knowledge. This doctrine was held by some extreme Shi‘ite groups who would forecast certain events, and when what they predicted did not occur would say that Allah had “changed His mind”.

bāṭin: inwardly hidden.

bāṭinī: inward, esoteric.

Bāṭinīya: this usually refers to the Ismā‘īlīs who interpreted religious texts exclusively on the basis of their hidden meanings rather than their literal meanings. This type of interpretation gained currency about the 8th century among certain esoteric sects, especially the Ismā‘īlīs. They believed that beneath every obvious or literal meaning of a sacred text lay a secret, hidden meaning, which could be arrived at through *ta'wil*; thus, every statement, person, or object could be scrutinised in this manner to reveal its true intent. They further stated that Muhammad was only the transmitter of the literal word of God, the Qur’ān, but it was the imām who was empowered to interpret, through *ta’wil*, its true, hidden meaning.

Bayt al-Ḥikma: an academy founded by the ‘Abbasid khalif al-Ma’mūn.

bid‘a: innovation, changing the original teaching of the Prophet, something introduced into Islam after the formative period.

bid‘a ḥaqīqīya: absolute innovation.

bid‘a idāfīya: relative innovation.

bilā kayf: “without asking how”, to avoid conceptualising or specifying or anthropomorphising metaphorical expressions like “Hand of Allah” or “descent”.

burhān: demonstration, demonstrative reasoning, definite proof.

Butrīya: (or Batrīya) a Zaydī sect who said that ‘Alī was best, but that he had entrusted the imamate to Abū Bakr and ‘Umar.

ad-Dahr: unending and everlasting time, not divided into past, present and future. Linear time is called *‘zamān’* in Arabic.

dahrī: materialist or atheist. Probably originally referred to a follower of Zurvanism which is associated with a form of atheistic materialism that asserted the eternity of the material universe.

ḍarūrīyāt: immediately evident propositions.

dawr: arguing in a circle.

Dhāt: Essence.

Druzes: a heterodox sect which developed out of Fāṭimid Ismā'īlism and the 5th/11th century agitation of the Qarmatians. Today there are about half a million Druzes living in Syria, Lebanon, and Palestine who are not considered to be Muslims either by the Shi'ites or the Sunnīs.

fahm: understanding.

falsafa: philosophy, which attempts to form a systematic world-view out of logical and scientific reasoning. (Compare with *kalām*).

fatarāt: Khārijite doctrine of eclipse of belief.

fayḍ: the emanation of created things from Allah. The word is not used in the Qur'ān for creation. Muslim philosophers, such as al-Farabī and Ibn Sīnā, under the influence of Neoplatonism conceived of creation as a gradual unfolding process. Generally, they proposed that the world came into being as the result of God's superabundance. The process of creation begins, they asserted, at the most perfect level and then "descends" to the least perfect: physical matter. All created things yearn for what is more perfect.

faylasūf: philosopher

fikr: reflection.

al-Fiqh al-Akbar: a creed, the most famous is by Abū Ḥanīfa.

Futḥīya: or Aftaḥīya, from al-Aftaḥ ("flat-footed") the nickname of 'Abdullāh, the eldest son of Ja'far aṣ-Ṣādiq. They believed that the Imām passed on the imamate by testament (and so could go from one brother to another).

Ghālīya: same as *Ghulāt*.

gharaḍ: motive, individual interest.

gharīza: instinct.

Ghayb: the Unseen, unmanifest, that which is hidden from the eyes whether or not it is perceived by the heart; or it can be something which is beyond any sort of perception, such as the future.

ghayba: occultation; concealment.

ghayr maḥsūs: not perceived by the senses.

Ghulāt: "Extremists", extreme groups of the Shi'a who claimed that 'Alī was divine. Their most dramatic manifestations were found in the Qarmatians, the Ismā'īlīs, the Druzes, and the 'Alī Ilāhīs.

habā': fine dust, the passive universal substance.

hāhūt: ipseity.

hakīm (plural *ḥukamā'*)**:** sage.

ḥanīf (plural *ḥunafā'*)**:** one who possesses the true religion innately.

Ḥārithīya: a sub-sect of the Ibādites, the followers of al-Ḥārith ibn Mazyad al-Ibādī, who held Mu'tazilite views.

al-Ḥarūrīya: A term used to denote the early Khārijites, from the name of the village which was their centre.

Ḥasbāniya: a group known in the history of philosophy for their doubts, scepticism and sophism.

hawa: passion, desire; also used in the plural (*ahwā'*), meaning opinions which have moved away from the truth.

ḥawādith: originated things, things which exist within the confines of time-span and place.

haykal: bodily form.

hayūlā: from Greek *hylē*, substance in the sense of *materia prima. Al-habā'* has the same meaning. Ibn 'Arabī also calls it *al-Kitāb al-Masṭūr*: the Inscribed Book.

hidāya: active guidance by Allah.

ḥikma: wisdom.

ḥiss: the faculty of sensation, the domain of the senses.

ḥudūth: located in time, the beginning of the universe in time.

ḥudūth al-ashyā': originated, temporal character of things.

ḥujja: proof or argument.

ḥulūl: incarnation.

Ibāḍīya: the followers of 'Abdullāh ibn Ibād. They are the most balanced of the Khārijites and the closest to the Muslims in opinon and thought. They maintain the distinction between *kufr ni'ma* and *kufr shirk*. They assert that every sin is *kufr ni'ma* and that grave sinners will be in the Fire forever.

ifhām: intelligibility.

ihtidā': the quality of being guided.

ījād: bestowing of existence; bringing into existence.

ijbār: determinism.

ikhtiyār: free choice.

Ikhwān aṣ-Ṣafā: "the Brethren of Purity", a secret philosophico-religious society which arose in Baṣra in the fourth/tenth century among some of the Ismā'ilīs.

iktisāb: the same as *kasb*, acquisition.

ilḥād: heresy, deviation.

'illa (plural *'ilal*)**:** underlying reason, effective cause. *Ma'na* and *sabab* are synonyms.

'ilm (plural *'ulūm*)**:** knowledge; science.

'ilm al-ḥurūf: "the science of the letters", a method of interpretation by referring to the numerical equivalents of letters in a word or phrase. For example, the numerical value of the Arabic letters in the phrase *"fatḥ^an^ mubīn^an^"* (Qur'ān 48:1) adds up to 591, the year of the "clear victory" over the Christians by the Muwaḥḥidūn at Alarcos, Spain. They do not, however, add up to all the other years in which there were also clear victories!

'ilm al-jafr: the science of letters.

'ilm an-nujūm: astronomy.

'ilm at-tanjīm: astrology.

īmā': implication, implicit indication.

Imāmī: a term referring to one of the Ithna 'asharite Shi'ites.

īmān: belief, faith, assent, acceptance.

al-Iqtiṣād: "The Just Mean in Belief", a work by al-Ghazālī in which he simplified the work done by al-Juwaynī.

irāda: will, volition, aspirancy. For Māturīdī, there is a difference between *irāda* and *mashī'a*. There is no coercion involved in *mashī'a*, but man's acceptance is involved. Thus *mashī'a* is involved in choosing belief or disbelief. *Irāda* involves coercion.

irjā': suspending or postponing judgement on whether or not someone is a believer.

al-Irshād: a treatise by al-Juwaynī on the Sunnī position in *kalam*.

Ishrāqī: illuminist school of philosophy, an eclectic mystical intellectualism.

ism: name, noun, the Divine Name. Sometimes *al-Ism al-A'ẓam*, the Greatest Name.

'iṣma: infallibility, preservation of the Prophets from wrong action.

istidlāl: deductive reasoning.

Ismā'ilīs: the "Sevener" Shi'a, the followers of Ismā'īl, son of Ja'far aṣ-Ṣādiq (d. 148/765). Many of their doctrines were influenced by those of the Manichaeans. They assert that Ismā'īl completed the cycle of seven imāms after which the era of the hidden imāms began, and these imāms send out emissaries. They believe that if the imām is not manifest (*qā'im*), then his emissary or proof (*ḥujja*) must be manifest.

isti'rāḍ: the practice of the Baṣran Khawārij, killing all non-Khārijites whom they came across. Literally means "questioning" but came to designate the indiscriminate killing of theological opponents. (cf. Azāriqa).

istiṭā'a: the power or capacity to act.

Ithna' 'Asharīya: the Shi'ites who follow twelve Imāms.

i'tiqād: belief, being convinced about the truth of something.

i'tizāl: lit. "withdrawal", the theology of that group which withdrew from the circle of Ḥasan al-Baṣrī and came to be known as the Mu'tazilites.

jabr: predetermination of man's actions by Allah.

jabrīya: pre-determinist, the name given to those who, in opposition to the Qadarīya, deny the freedom of the will, and on this point make no distinction between man and inanimate nature, inasmuch as his actions are subordinate to the compulsion (*jabr*) of God. Thus everything has been pre-determined and man has no responsibility whatsoever for his actions. The most prominent champion of this view was Jahm ibn Ṣafwān, as well as many other small sects.

Ja'farī: the "Twelver" Shi'a, the followers of Ja'far aṣ-Ṣādiq (d. 148/765).

Jahmites: followers of Jahm ibn Ṣafwān (d. 128/745) who taught that Allah has no attributes and that man has no free will of any sort at all.

Jārūdīya: one of the Zaydī Shi'ite groups who believed that there was a *shūrā* of the descendants of Ḥasan and Ḥusayn after the death of Ḥasan. They insisted that the rightful Imām must not remain hidden.

jawhar: lit. "jewel", substance, specifically the essence of intrinsic being of a form.

kabīra (plural *kabā'ir*)**:** major wrong actions which are described in the Qur'ān or *ḥadīth* along with an explicit penalty or threat.

kalām: 'theology' and dogmatics. *Kalām* begins with the revealed tradition and uses rationalistic methods in order to understand and explain it and to resolve apparent contradictions. The name was either derived from the fact that their primary question was the "Word of Allah" or in imitation of philosophers who called "logic" *"kalām"*. (Compare with *falsafa*).

kasb: (or *iktisāb*) acquisition. Among the Ash'arites, the action of a creature is said to be created and originated by Allah and 'acquired' by the creature, meaning it is brought into connection with his power and will without there resulting any effect from him in bringing it into existence. He is simply a locus for it. It also refers to knowledge which is obtained by the voluntary application of secondary causes.

kawn: Being, all phenomena.

kayfīya: modality, quality.

Kaysānīya: Shi'ite group, who maintained that after the death of Ḥusayn, the Imām was another son of 'Alī, Muḥammad ibn al-Ḥanafiyya (d. 81/700).

khalq al-Qur'ān: "the createdness of the Qur'ān", a Mu'tazilite doctrine. The Mu'tazilites denied that the attributes of Allah are eternal. Since the Qur'ān is speech, they argued, and since speech is an attribute, they therefore denied the eternal existence of the Qur'ān. This was the source of the controversy which resulted in the *Miḥna*, or Inquisition.

Kharijites: or *Khawārij*, the earliest sect who separated themselves from the body of the Muslims and declared war on all those who disagreed with them, stating that a wrong action turns a Muslim into an unbeliever.

khaṣla (plural *khiṣāl*)**:** a property, quality, element; also a branch or part of something (e.g. the branches of faith).

khaṭī'a (plural *khaṭayā*)**:** sin, error, includes both *dhanb* and *ithm*.

khāṭima: "the seal", the final act of a person which determines whether he is a believer or an unbeliever.

Khawārij: See *Kharijites.*

al-Kibrīt al-Aḥmar: "Red Sulphur", the Philosopher's Stone.

kufr ni'ma: ingratitude for a blessing, used by certain Khārijites to indicate commission of a minor sin. (See *Ibāḍīya*).

kufr shirk: also *kāfir dīn,* disbelief in Allah by associating something else with Him. (See *Ibāḍīya*).

al-kullīyāt al-khams: the five universals: life, religion, family, sanity and property.

kullīyāt al-wujūd: universals of being.

kumūn: doctrine that substances have their potentialities present but concealed in them (this used to be a Manichaean doctrine).

lā ḥukm illā lillāh: "There is no judgement except that of Allah", the motto of the Khārijites, used to justify whatever judgements they made.

Lafẓīya: view that while the Qur'an is uncreated in its essence, man's "*lafẓ*" or utterance of it is created. Chiefly represented by al-Karābisī (d. 245-48/859-62) and Ibn ath-Thaljī.

lays: al-Kindī's term for "not-being", now superseded by *'adam.*

luṭf: Divine grace.

mabdā' (plural *mabādi'*): principle, basis, starting point. In the plural it means ideology, fundamental concepts.

mādda: matter.

madrasa: a traditional place of study and learning.

maḥall: locus. For example, al-Māturīdī says that the heart is the locus of faith.

māhīya: quiddity, essential nature.

majāzī: metaphorical, figurative.

maktūb: 'written", pre-ordained, already decided.

malāḥida: heretics, apostates. It is the plural of *mulḥid.*

manṭiq: logic (as a discipline).

al-manzila bayna manzilatayn: "the position between the two positions", one of the five principles of the Mu'tazilites. Politically, they took a position between the Shi'a and the Sunnīs. In respect of belief, they said that someone who is a *fāsiq* is neither a believer nor an unbeliever. On the surface, this seems innocuous, but it is really an offshoot of the earlier Manichaean metaphysical teaching.

maqāla: treatise; doctrinal position.

Maqālāt al-Islāmiyyīn: the famous work by al-Ash'arī. It surveys and assesses the various sects, sets forth the basic creed of the Muslim Community, and surveys the different opinions on the themes of *kalām*. It was the first work of its kind.

maqdī: object of decree.

ma'qūl: rational, intelligible.

marātib al-wujūd: "the chain of being": mineral, plant and animal.

mashī'a: choice (see *irāda*).

Mashshā'ī: a Peripatetic, an Aristotelian.

Māturīdite: a follower of al-Māturīdī (d. 333/944), along with the Ash'arites, responsible for the Sunnī articulation of *kalam*. As al-Māturīdī was from Khorasan, his school was more widespread in the east and Central Asia. It is more intuitional and less concerned with rational expression than the Ash'arites. (See *al-Māturīdī.*)

mawjūdāt: existents.

Miḥna: the Inquisition instituted by the 'Abbasid khalif, al-Ma'mūn, which required all important people to publicly state that they believed that the Qur'ān was created, even if they did not.

millat Ibrahim: religion of Ibrahim, the *fiṭra*, primordial religion.

minhāj: lit. "open, plain road", procedure, manner.

mithāl: a model according to which another thing is made or proportioned, a pattern by which a thing is cut or measured, a precedent, an example or parable, a multi-dimensional metaphor capable of conveying more than one meaning simultaneously.

mithl: like.

mūbiqāt: great destructive sins.

mudarris: teacher.

Mufawwiḍa: a Qadarite group who believed that they are entrusted to themselves by Allah so that they act independently and of their own accord thanks to this delegation of power.

al-Muḥakkima: along with "*Ḥarūrīya*", a name used for the earliest Khārijites. They deserted 'Alī's camp when 'Alī accepted arbitration in his war with Mu'āwiya. Their objection was that 'Alī had followed a human *ḥukm* (judgement) rather than Divine *ḥukm*. They thought that this was tantamount to disbelief and hence they declared 'Alī to be a *kāfir*.

muḥaqqiq: verifier, one who establishes the reality for himself; those who have understanding of reality.

muḥāwara: dialogue, debate.

muḥdath: generated, temporal, contingent, located in time.

muḥdathāt: novelties, innovations

mujaddid: renewer, restorer of the *Dīn*; it is said that one comes every hundred years or so.

Mujbira: another name for the Jabrīya.

mulḥid: a heretic, atheist.

mulḥidāt: heresies.

Mulk: the realm of solid forms, the visible realm; also the title of *Sūra* 67 of the Qur'ān.

mumkināt (plural of *mumkin*): possibilities.

Murji'ites: the opponents of the Khārijites. They held that it is faith and not actions which are important and so they suspend judgement on a person guilty of major sins. They had a number of sub-groups.

Musabbib al-asbāb: the Causer of causes, i.e. Allah.

Mushabbiha: anthropomorphists.

mustaḥīlāt: (the plural of *mustaḥīl*), impossible things.

mutakallim: someone who studies the science of *kalām*, the science of investigating and articulating religious belief.

Mu'tazilite: someone who adheres to the school of the Mu'tazila which is rationalist in its approach to existence. The term means "withdrawers" because they "withdrew" to an intermediate position as regards the evaluation of grave and lesser sins, holding to the position that someone who commits a wrong action is neither a believer nor an unbeliever. They also opposed the view that the Qur'ān was eternal and uncreated, believing that this would compromise the uniqueness of Allah. (See also *Ahl al-'adl wa't-tawḥīd*).

muwāfāt: a person's state of faith at the moment of death.

an-nafs an-nāṭiqa: the rational soul which can make its ideas known by means of speech and which also understands speech. It does not die with the body, as it is an essential substance and not an accident.

Najdīya or Najdāt: Najdites, the followers of Najda ibn 'Umaymir al-Ḥanafī (d. 72/693), an extreme Khārijite group in Yamāna who dropped the label *"shirk"* in favour of *"kufr"*. If a Muslim persists in a sin, they asserted, he is an unbeliever and a *mushrik*. They introduced the distinction between *kufr ni'ma* and *kufr dīn* (ingratitude for blessing and unbelief).

Najh al-Balāgha: a collection of sayings and sermons attributed to 'Alī compiled by Sayyid Muḥammad ar-Raḍi (d. 406/1016).

Nāmūs: from *nomos* (Greek for law), an angel who brought revelation, mentioned by Waraqa when Khadīja informed him that the Prophet had received revelation from Jibrīl.

Nāṣibī: one of the Nawāṣib.

Nāsūt: humanity, corporeality.

na't: attribute, quality, that which describes something.

Nawāṣib: a group of people who go to extremes in their dislike of 'Alī or his family; they are the counterpart of the Rāfiḍites.

naẓar: examination, reasoning, intellectual examination, thinking about a thing and trying to understand it.

naẓāra: debate.

nāẓir: philosopher, debater, investigator.

naẓẓār: someone who examines and decides questions of theology and jurisprudence.

qaḍā': the execution of the Divine decree.

qadar: the decree of Allah.

Qadarīya: a sect who said that people have power (*qadar*) over their actions and hence free will.

qadīm: eternal, ancient.

qā'im: one who rises after death; used by the Ismā'īlīs for the seventh imām before the beginning of the new cycle. The Imāmīya say that the twelfth imām is the *qā'im*.

Qarāmiṭa: the Qarmatians.

Qarmatians: sometimes written Carmathians, a revolutionary Ismā'īlite movement which began as a secret society involving initiation and common property. Their artisans were formed into guilds. Their name is taken from their first leader, Hamdān Qarmaṭ. They were particularly successful in the Arabian peninsula where they seized Makka in 317/930 and carried off the Black Stone, which they kept for twenty years. They believed in the emanation of Divine Light through various veils and interpreted the Qur'ān allegorically.

qidam: timeless eternity, eternity which is not affected at all by temporal time.

qudra: power, ability, capacity.

quwwa al-ghādiya: nutritive faculty.

quwwa al-ḥāssa: sensitive faculty, power of perception.

quwwa al-mutakhayyila: faculty of imagination.

quwwa an-nāfiqa: rational faculty, reason.

quwwa an-nuzū'iyya: appetitive faculty.

Rāfiḍites: the *Rawāfiḍ,* a group of the Shi'a known for rejecting Abū Bakr and 'Umar as well as 'Uthmān. It is a nickname, meaning "deserters".

raj'a: 'return', the Shi'ite doctrine that the Imām is hidden and will return.

ramz (plural *rumūz*)**:** a symbol.

Rasā'il: "the Epistles"; fifty-two treatises written by unknown Ismā'īlī writers from the Ikhwān aṣ-Ṣafā in the fourth/tenth century. They deal with the sciences and philosophy and a great deal of numerical symbolism. Their contents are basically a combination of Neo-Pythagoreanism and Neo-Platonism.

Rawāfiḍ: Rāfiḍites.

risāla: message, also a treatise.

sabab: cause, means of obtaining something.

Sabab al-Awwal: the First Cause, i.e. Allah.

sababīya: causality.

Sab'īya: the "Sevener" Shi'a or Ismā'īlis.

ṣaghīra (plural *saghā'ir*)**:** minor wrong action.

salb: negation, to declare Allah free of any attributes which appertain to created beings.

Shabībya: Khārijites who denied that Allah's foreknowledge had a determining effect and explained human responsibility in terms of a concept of delegation (*tafwīḍ*). (Cf. *Mufawwiḍa*).

shakk: doubt.

ṣifa: attribute.

Ṣufrites: a moderate branch of the Khārijites.

taba''uḍ: the concept of divisibility. In relation to belief, it regards belief as a combination of several qualities.

ṭabī'a: nature.

tafāḍul: difference in degrees, thus giving preference to one over another.

ṭafra: "the leap", the view originated from the Mu'tazilite an-Naẓẓām that a body could move from point A to point B without passing by the intermediary point b.

tajriba: empirical experience.

takfīr: to declare that someone is a *kāfir*. A practice introduced by the Khārijites.

takhmīn: speculation, conjecture.

takwīn: bringing into being; causing something to become manifest in existence through the Divine command, "Be!"

tanāsukh: metempsychosis.

tanzīh: transcendence, disconnecting Allah from creation. The opposite of *tashbīh*.

taqīya: concealment of one's views to escape persecution. It was obligatory for the secret agents of some of the more extreme Ismā'īli groups.

tashbīh: anthropomorphism, comparing or connecting Allah to created things or making Allah resemble created things. Opposite of *tanzīh*.

ta'ṭīl: negation, the concept of denying Allah all attributes.

tawallud: the generation of actions, the causal relationship between the action of the doer and the deed, posited by the Mu'tazilites.

tawaqquf: conditionality; also the Shi'ite position of stopping at a particular imām and believing in his concealment and return.

ta'wīl: allegorical interpretation.

tawlīd: "generation", "natural production", for the Mu'tazilites, the process by which correct reasoning produces knowledge. For the philosophers, it is by logical necessity (*ījāb*). For the Māturīdites, knowledge after correct reasoning is due to the custom established by Allah.

thanawīya: dualism.

thubūt: latency (in respect of existence).

ulūhīya: divinity, Divine nature.

'uqūd arba'a: the four principles of al-Māturīdī which denote the four degrees of knowledge: *tawḥīd*, *ma'rifa*, *īmān* and *Islām*.

al-usūl al-khamsa: the five affirmations of the Mu'tazilites: *tawḥīd*; *'adl* (justice); *al-wa'd wa'l-wa'īd* ("the promise and the threat"); *manzila bayna'l-manzilatayn* (the position between two positions); and commanding the correct and forbidding the rejected.

wa'd: promise, particularly the promise of the Garden.

al-wa'd wa'l-wa'īd: "the promise and the threat", the promise of Heaven and the threat of Hell as recompense for actions. A consequence of this, the Mu'tazilites assert, is that a wrongdoer can never come out of the Fire by Divine Mercy.

waḥdānīya: Divine Oneness.

wa'īd: threat, particularly the threat of the Fire.

al-Wa'īdīya: Mu'tazilites who believe that logically Allah must punish the disobedient as He must reward the obedient; therefore, according to them, if a person committed a major sin and died before repenting, then Allah must not forgive him. This doctrine conflicts with the Qur'ān and the *Sunna*.

Wāqifīya: Rāfiḍites who maintained that Mūsā al-Kāẓim, a son of Ja'far aṣ-Ṣādiq, the sixth Shi'ite Imām, would return and put everything to rights, since they believed that the seventh Imām would complete one cycle and begin a new one; also a sect of Khārijites who suspended judgement. (Cf. *Murji'ites*).

wasā'iṭ: secondary causes.

wujūd: existence or being. *Wājib al-wujūd*, "He Whose existence is necessary" applies to Allah, whereas creation is *mumkin al-wujūd*, "that whose existence is possible".

al-wujūd al-muṭlaq: "Absolute Being" which is impossible to conceive. It did not come out of non-existence, but exists absolutely.

wuqūf: suspension of judgement.

zamān: linear time.

zandaqa: heresy. This is an Arabicised Persian word. The term had been used for heterodox groups, especially Manichaeans, in pre-Islamic Persia, and hence it was originally applied to Magians.

ẓann: opinion, supposition, conjecture, speculation.

Zaydites: the "Fiver" Shi'a. They followed Zayd ibn 'Alī, the grandson of al-Ḥusayn. They say that any of the *Ahl al-Bayt* can be the Imām. They are Mu'tazilite in doctrine and rather puritanical. Sufism is forbidden by them.

zindīq: a term used to describe a heretic whose teaching is a danger to the community or state. Originally under the Sasanids it was a free thinker, atheist or dualist. It was particularly applied to those influenced by the doctrines of Manichaeanism, a dualistic syncretism of pagan, gnostic, Magian, Judaeo-Christian and Indian traditions which experienced a revival in Iraq near the end of the Umayyad period.

Some Major Figures in *Kalām* and early Muslim Philosophy

'Abdu'l-Qāhir ibn Ṭāhir al-Baghdādī: Abū Manṣūr, a Shāfi'ī scholar and Ash'arī theologian, specialising in *uṣūl* and heresies. He was born in Baghdad and taken to Nishapur by his father when young and was educated by Sufi scholars. He lectured to his students on seventeen subjects. He wrote on many subjects including mathematics, Sufism and *kalām*. He is known for his book on heresiography, *al-Farq bayna al-Firaq*, on the sects in Islam. His main work on *kalām* was *Kitāb Uṣūl ad-Dīn*, a summary of the major aspects of Islam. He has a famous book on *naskh* called *an-Nāsikh wa'l-Mansūkh*. He died in Isfara'in in 429/1037.

Abū'l-Hudhayl: Muhammad ibn al-Hudhayl al-'Allāf al-'Abdī, born between 132/748 and 137/753 at Baṣra and died between 226/840 and 235/850, a client of 'Abd al-Qays. He was a famous Mu'tazilite known for his skill in argument whom some consider the founder of *kalām*. He argued well against the Magians and it is said that thousands of them became Muslim through him. He took his views from 'Uthman ibn Khālid aṭ-Ṭawīl who had learned them from al-Wāṣil. He denied predestination and the existiential attributes. He held that there was a generation (*tawallud*) or causal relationship between doer and deed. He also appears to have been the founder of the "atomic" school. (See *atomism*).

al-Ash'arī: Abū'l-Ḥasan 'Alī ibn Ismā'īl. He was born in Baṣra in 260/873-4, and was a descendant of Abū Mūsā al-Ash'arī. He was for a time a Mu'tazilite, a follower of al-Jubbā'i, but later left them. He became an unrivalled great scholar, the Imām of the People of the *Sunna* and author of famous books. He wrote about 300 books. In his *Maqālāt al-Islāmiyīn,* the first book of its kind, he goes into detail about the different sects. He and al-Māturīdī are the founders of Sunnī *kalām*. He died in 324 /936.

Averroes: *see Ibn Rushd.*

Avicenna: *see Ibn Sīnā.*

al-Bāqillānī: Muḥammad ibn aṭ-Ṭayyib, the Qāḍī and Imām of the people of the *Sunna*, d. 403/1013. He was born in Baṣra in 338/950 and became one of the foremost scholars in *kalām*. He was a Mālikī *faqīh* and Ash'arite *mutakallim*. He wrote *I'jāz al-Qur'ān*. He was sent by 'Aḍud ad-Dawla as an envoy to the Byzantines in Constantinople where he debated with Christian scholars in the presence of the emperor. In his *Tamhīd* he presents the position of the Ash'arites and played a pioneering role in elaborating its metaphysics. Ibn Khaldūn credits him with introducing atomism, but it would be more accurate to say that he reworked it. *At-Tamhīd* is the first systematic statement of Ash'arite doctrine.

Bishr ibn Ghiyāth al-Marīsi: He was prominent in publicising the idea that the Qur'ān was created. He was connected most of his life with Kūfa and was born not later than 144/760, the son of a Jewish goldsmith. He studied *fiqh* and *ḥadīth* with Abū Yūsuf and *ḥadīth* with Sufyān ibn 'Uyayna. He became outstanding in *kalām* and Ḥammad ibn Zayd called him a *kāfir*. He moved to Baghdad where he had his own group and was executed probably in 218/833 (or 834 or 842).

Ḍirār ibn 'Amr: possible forerunner of the Mu'tazila, lived in the time of Hārūn ar-Rashid in Baṣra and was a contemporary of Wāṣil ibn 'Aṭā'. He rejected atomism and said that the body was an aggregate of accidents which then becomes the bearer of other accidents. He also denied the positive nature of the Divine Attributes, maintaining, for example, that Allah is knowing and powerful in the sense that He is not ignorant or powerless.

al-Farabī: (Latin, Al-Phrarabius), Abū Naṣr Muḥammad Ibn al-Farakh. Al-Farabī was born near Farab in Turkistan. He was a philosopher, leading logician and expositor of Plato and Aristotle, the founder of Islamic neo-Platonism. He contributed to philosophy, logic, sociology, science, and music. He was best known as the "Second Teacher", Aristotle being the first. He is said to have grown up in Damascus. He studied philosophy at night, while working as a gardener in the day. He died in 339/950. He wrote many books on all sorts of topics.

Ghaylān ad-Dimishqī: Abū Marwān Ghaylān ibn Muslim al-Qibṭī. (Qibṭ means either Copt or from the Ḥimyar sub-tribe Qibṭ). He was the second most important Qadarite. His father was a *mawlā* of

'Uthmān and he was a secretary in the administration in Damascus. He left a collection of letters. As well as being a Qadarite, he was also a Murji'ite and Kharijite. He was executed towards the end of the reign of Hishām (c. 116/731).

al-Ghazālī: Muḥammad ibn Muḥammad, Abū Ḥamid aṭ-Ṭūsī, (Latin, Algazel), (450/1058 – 505/1111). He taught at the Niẓāmiyya Madrasa before he became a Sufi. He suffered a spiritual crisis in 490/1095 that resulted in a speech impediment and nervous breakdown; he then gave up the academic life for the ascetic regime of a Sufi. He was the author of many books, especially *Tahāfut al-Falāsifa* ("The Incoherence of the Philosophers") and *Iḥyā' 'Ulūm ad-Dīn*. He attempted to defuse the tensions between philosophy and theology and used syllogism to rebut Neoplatonism and bolster Islamic doctrine. He criticised philosophers for denying the Resurrection and for asserting the eternality of the universe. His critique of causality anticipates Hume's, using the Ash'arite position that Allah is the only real cause, and thus denying the so-called necessity between cause and effect. Simultaneity, he asserted, is illusory.

Ibn Bājja: Abū Bakr Muḥammad ibn Yaḥyā, (Latin, Avempace), an Arabic philosopher. He was born in Saragossa near the end of the 5th/11th century. He led a wandering life for a time. He died in Fez in Ramaḍān 533/1139 of poison. When young, he was a *wazīr* for the Murābiṭ governor, Abū Bakr ibn Tifalwit, and later on in Seville for Yaḥyā ibn Yūsuf ibn Tashfīn. He stated that the philosopher must order his own life as a solitary individual, shun the company of non-philosophers and concentrate on reaching his own final goal of achieving intuitive knowledge through contact with the Active Intelligence.

Ibn Ḥazm: 'Alī ibn Aḥmad aẓ-Ẓāhirī, born in Cordoba in 384/994. He was the main representative of the Ẓahirite school. He had to withdraw to his family estate where he died in 456/1064. His *al-Fiṣāl fi'l-Milal* in which he combats the Mu'tazilite position was written between 418/1027 and 421/1030.

Ibn Rushd: Abū'l-Walīd Muḥammad ibn Aḥmad, (Latin, Averroes). Ibn Rushd was a genius with encyclopaedic knowledge. He spent a great part of his fruitful life as a judge and as a physician. Yet he was known in the West for being the great commentator on the philosophy of Aristotle. He was born in Cordova, Spain in 520/1128. Ibn Rushd said that true happiness for man can surely be achieved through mental and psychological health, and people cannot enjoy psychological health unless they follow ways that lead to happiness in the hereafter, and unless they believe in God and His oneness. His book on jurisprudence *Bidāyat al-Mujtahid wa-Nihāyat al-Muqtaṣid* has been held as possibly the best book on the Mālikī School of *fiqh*. He died in 595/1198.

Ibn Sīnā: Abū 'Alī al-Ḥusayn ibn 'Abdullāh (Latin, Avicenna). He was born around 370/980 near Bukhara (now Uzbekistan) and died in 428/1037 in Hamadan, Persia. Avicenna was the most influential of all Arabic philosopher-scientists. He studied logic and metaphysics under some of the best teachers of his day but then continued his studies on his own. In particular he studied medicine. He work on almost every conceivable topic. In philosophy, he was the champion of Islamic Neo-Platonism, incorporating an illuminist (*Ishrāqī*) tendency which shows Ismā'īlī influence.

Ibn Ṭufayl: Abū Bakr, from Wadi Ash, today Guadix, Spain. He lived from around 494/1100 to 581/1185. A philosopher and physician, his mystical philosophy is presented in a novel, *Ḥayy ibn Yaqẓān*, which develops Neo-Platonic themes.

al-'Ijlī: 'Aḍūd ad-Dīn, 'Abdu'r-Raḥmān ibn Aḥmad, a theologian and philosopher. His principle works were *al-Mawāqif* and a catechism, *al-'Aqā'id al-'Aḍūdiyya*. He was from Ig, a fortress in Persia, and was a *qāḍī* and teacher in Shiraz. He died in 756/1355.

Jahm ibn Ṣafwān: Abū Muḥriz ar-Rāsibī of Samarqand, the founder of the Jahmite school. His doctrines first surfaced in Tirmidh. He denied the Divine Attributes and held that man's actions are purely determined by Allah, that Allah is "everywhere", and that the Qur'ān was created. He also asserted that Heaven and Hell will pass away because eternity is impossible. He was executed in 128/745 by Sālim ibn Aḥwaz in Marw for denying that Allah spoke to the Prophet Mūsā.

al-Jubbā'i: Abū 'Alī Muḥammad ibn 'Abdu'l-Waḥḥāb, one of the early Imāms of the Basran Mu'tazilites who was very proficient in the science of *kalām*. He was born in Jubba in Khuzistan and studied under ash-Shaḥḥām, the head of the Mu'tazilites there. Al-Ash'arī studied with him for a period of forty years and then reversed his position and became the Imām of the people of the *Sunna*. He had excellent debates with him. Al-Jubbā'i died in 303/915. He systematised the position of the Mu'tazilites.

al-Juwaynī: Abū'l-Ma'ālī 'Abdu'l-Mālik ibn 'Abdullāh, Imām of the Two Ḥarams, and the shaykh of al-Ghazālī. He died in Nishapur in 478/1085. He was the outstanding Ash'arite *mutakallim* of his time and introduced al-Ghazālī to *kalām*. His Ash'arite treatise is entitled *al-Irshād*.

Al-Ka'bī: Abū'l-Qāsim 'Abdullāh ibn Maḥmūd al-Ka'bī al-Balkhī, (d. 318/929-31). He was the leader of the Mu'tazilties of Baghdad after al-Khayyāṭ and the foremost representative of the Mu'tazilite atomists. He maintained that accidents do not endure for two moments. He has many similarities to al-Ash'arī, who was interested in his work.

al-Khayyāṭ: Abū'l-Ḥusayn 'Abdu'r-Raḥmān ibn Muḥammad. He was the leader of the Mu'tazilites in Baghdad in the second half of the third/ninth century. He was al-Ka'bi's teacher. He went to extremes in maintaining that the non-existent is a thing because there is information known about it. He wrote a book in defence of Mu'tazilism entitled *Kitāb al-Intiṣār*.

al-Kindī: Abū Yūsuf Ya'qūb ibn Isḥāq, (Latin, Alkindus). He was the first outstanding Islamic philosopher, known as "the philosopher of the Arabs". Al-Kindī was born in about 182/800 of noble Arabic descent in Kūfa where his father was governor. He studied in Baṣra and later moved to Baghdad where he flourished under the khalifs al-Ma'mūn and al-Mu'taṣim. He concerned himself not only with those philosophical questions which had been considered by the Aristotelian Neoplatonists of Alexandria, but also with such miscellaneous subjects as astrology, medicine, Indian arithmetic, the manufacture of swords, and cooking. He is known to have written more than 270 works (mostly short treatises), a considerable number of which are extant, some in Latin translations. He died possibly about 252/868.

al-Majriṭī: Abū'l-Qāsim Maslama (d. c. 398/1008). An Andalusian scientist who was the first to introduce the study of the sciences to the western Islamic world. He was born in Madrid and moved to Cordoba where he established a school. He also produced a summary of the *Epistles* of the Brethren of Purity (Ikhwān aṣ-Ṣafā), a secret Ismā'īlī philosophico-religious society which developed at Baṣra.

al-Māturīdi: Abū Manṣūr Muḥammad ibn Muḥammad. Along with al-Ash'arī, with whom he was contemporary, he represents the mainstream view of *kalām*. Very little is known about his life. He was from Maturid, a small place outside Samarqand. He studied Ḥanafī *fiqh* and *kalām* and took a rational approach to *kalām*. Two of his works survive, *Ta'wīlāt al-Qur'ān* and *Kitāb at-Tawḥīd*. He died in 333/944. Abū Ḥanīfa is considered a Māturīdite in his *kalām*.

There were reckoned to be thirteen differences between al-Māturīdī's ideas and those of al-Ash'arī: six in ideas and seven in expression. For example, a Māturīdite would say, "I am truly a believer", while an Ash'arite would say, "I am a believer if Allah wills." Al-Māturīdī accords human free will the logic of its consequences, i.e. the just are saved on that account, while with al-Ash'arī, since Allah's will is unfathomable it is theoretically possible that the just will go to Hell. However, on this point, the Ash'arites have come around to the Māturīdite position. Indeed, the Māturīdite position has steadily penetrated the Ash'arite position so that the modern Sunni Muslim is usually a Māturīdī-Ash'arite, rather than the other way around. Al-Māturīdī did not mind dogmatic antinomies: depending on how you look at it, man has free will but is predestined, and the Speech of Allah is both created and uncreated.

an-Naẓẓām: Abū Isḥāq Ibrāhīm ibn Sayyā. He was born and educated in Baṣra, and died around 221/836 (or 845) in Baghdad where he had been summoned by al-Ma'mūn in 203/818. He was a very important Mu'tazilite. He accepted predestination and denied the existence of the Divine Attributes. A brilliant poet, philologist and dialectician, he studied under Abū'l-Hudhayl and then founded his own school. He devoted a great deal of time to refuting Manichaeism and the Dahrīs. He was very zealous in his defence of *tawḥīd* and the Message of the Qur'ān. His writings have been lost.

ar-Rāzī: Abū Bakr Muḥammad ibn Zakariyyā ar-Rāzī (248/864 – 316/930) was born at Rayy, Iran. Initially, he was interested in music but later on he learnt medicine, mathematics, astronomy, chemistry and philosophy from a student of Ḥunayn ibn Isḥāq, who was well versed in the ancient Greek, Persian and Indian systems of medicine and other subjects. At an early age he gained eminence as an expert in medicine and alchemy. He was a sage, an alchemist and a philosopher. In medicine, his contribution was so significant that it can only be compared to that of Ibn Sīnā. The basic elements in his philosophical system are: the Creator, spirit, matter, space and time. He discusses their characteristics in detail and his concepts of space and time as constituting a continuum are outstanding. His philosophical views were, however, criticised by a number of other Muslim scholars of the era. He was influenced by Plato and Democritus.

ash-Shahrastānī: Abū'l-Fatḥ Muḥammad ibn 'Abdu'l-Karīm (469/1076 – 548/1153), an historian and Ash'arite *mutakallim* from Khorasan who taught for three years in the Niẓāmīya Madrasa at Baghdad. He wrote one of the most comprehensive heresiographies in Arabic: *Kitāb al-Milal wa'n-Niḥal.* He also wrote a compendium of theology, *Nihāyat al-Qidām,* which is extremely coherent and logical.

as-Suhrawardī: Shihāb ad-Dīn Yaḥyā. He is nicknamed "*al-Maqtūl*" (the murdered) or "*ash-Shahīd*" (the martyr). Basing his ideas on Ibn Sīnā, he equated God with absolute light and non-being as darkness, establishing a hierarcy of lights through a process of emanation. He founded the Ishrāqī or illuminist school of philosophy. The substance of his thought is found in a trilogy: *al-Mashāri', al-Muqāwamāt*, and *Ḥikmat al-Ishrāq*. He was executed by Ṣalaḥ ad-Dīn al-Ayyūbī for heresy in 587/1191.

at-Taftazānī: Mas'ūd ibn 'Umar, (722/1322 – 792/1390), a scholar of Herat in Khurasan who wrote on *kalām*, *uṣūl al-fiqh*, grammar and *bayān* (style). He wrote a commentary on the Hanafī-Māturīdite *'aqīda* of 'Umar an-Nasafī (d. 537/1142) which is entitled *Sharḥ al-'Aqā'id an-Nasafīya* and has been translated by E.E. Elder.

Wāṣil ibn 'Aṭā': Abū Ḥudhayfa al-Ghazzāl, the chief of the Mu'tazilites. He was born in Madina in 80/699-700 where he was a *mawlā*. Four theses are ascribed to him: denial of Allah's eternal attributes, free will (with the Qadarīya); intermediate position of a Muslim being between a Muslim and a *kāfir* when he commits a grave sin; and that one of the parties at Ṣiffin was wrong. He died in 131/748-749.

Terms used in Sufism

abad: after-time, eternity without beginning. The secret of after-time is the negation of lastness.

'abd: slave, servant of Allah, the creature utterly dependent on its Lord and Creator for its existence and sustenance.

abdāl: plural of *badl.*

'ābid: one who performs much *'ibāda* or worship.

adab: correct behaviour, both inward and outward, good deportment. It is the deep courtesy observed in acts of worship as the person is aware that he is constantly dependent on and in the presence of Allah.

'adam: the void, non-existence. For Ibn al-'Arabī, this is the realm of the possible out of which all the forms flood endlessly.

af'āl: the acts, of Allah.

afrād: (plural of *fard*), solitary individuals, people who are outside the jurisidiction of the *Quṭb* and follow a solitary spiritual path.

aḥad: "One", designating Allah's unique oneness, disconnected from others. (See Qur'ān 112:1),

aḥadīya: the transcendent unity which is not the object of any distinctive knowledge and so is not accessible to the creature; the state of unity which admits of no plurality whatsoever, the unity is the sum of all potentialities and as such is not an object of worship.

ahl al-ma'rifa: the people of gnosis, the gnostics.

aḥwāl: plural of *ḥāl.*

'ālam al-ajsām: the world of physical bodies.

'ālam al-amr: the world of dominion, the non-spatial world of the angels and human spirits (also called *'ālm al-malakūt*).

'âlam al-arwāḥ: the world of spirits, as distinct from *'ālam al-mithāl* – the world of analogies, which is formal manifestation as a whole.

'ālam al-khalq: the material spatial world (also called *'ālam al-mulk wa shahāda*).

'ālam al-mithāl: "the world of analogies," the world of forms, both spiritual and physical. Corresponds to the *'ālam al-khayāl*, the world of imagination.

Alastu: Allah's declaration in the Qur'ān (7:172): *"A lastu bi-rabbikum?" – "Am I not your Lord?"* which, when He created Adam, He asked of all the souls of Adam's descendants that would exist until the end of the world. This is the primordial covenant (*mīthāq*) between Allah and mankind.

alif: the first letter of the Arabic alphabet. It is often used as a symbol of Divine Unity.

al-'Amā': the Great Mist: primordial non-spatiality in non-time. The Prophet was asked, "Where was Allah before the creation of the universe?" and he replied, "In the *'Amā'*."

amal: hope, a feeling in the heart that something good will happen.

al-Amāna: the trust or the moral responsibility or honesty, and all the duties which Allah has ordained. (See Qur'ān 33:72).

al-amr: the command, "Be!" (*kun*) which translates possibilities into the manifest (*fa yakūn*).

'aql: intellect, the faculty of reason.

al-'Aql: the intellect, *al-'Aql al-Awwal*: the first Intellect, analogous to the Pen (*al-Qalam*).

'araḍ (plural *a'rāḍ*)**:** an accidental or non-essential, ontic quality. The opposite of *jawhar*.

'ārif (plural *'ārifūn*)**:** gnostic, someone with direct knowledge of Allah.

'āshiq: passionate lover, one who possesses *'ishq*.

awliyā': the plural of *walī*.

Awtād: the plural of *watad*. They are four of the *Abdāl* and are part of the spiritual hierarchy. They have a certain spiritual station which is reflected in north, south, east and west.

'ayn: the essence, the eye, the spring.

'ayn al-baṣīra: the inner eye of the heart.

'ayn al-jam': perfect union.

'ayn al-qalb: the eye of the heart, the organ of intuition.

al-'ayn ath-thābita: archetype of a being, a source form in the *Malakūt*. (The plural is *a'yān*).

'ayn al-yaqīn: certainty itself.

aynīya: whereness.

azal: "pre-time," eternity without end; the negation of firstness, from the one who is described by it.

bāb al-abwāb: "the door of doors", meaning repentance.

badāwa: what comes suddenly upon the heart from the Unseen because of joy or sorrow.

badl (plural *abdāl)***:** a gnostic in constant contemplation of Allah, often seen in more than one place at the same time. *Badl* means "substitute". Ibn al-'Arabī says: "They are seven. Whoever travels from one place and leaves his body in its form so that no one recognises that he has gone, only that one is a *badl*." Some say that they are forty.

bakkā'ūn: "those who weep constantly", a term used in reference to the early Sufis in Baṣra.

balā': affliction, trial, which is a sign of Divine love and necessary for spiritual development.

baqā': going on by Allah, when the Sufi returns to mankind after annihilation (*fanā'*).

baraka: blessing, any good which is bestowed by Allah, and especially that which increases, a subtle beneficient spiritual energy which can flow through things or people.

barzakh: an interspace or dimension between two realities which both separates and yet links them.

baṣīra: insight.

basṭ: expansion, an involuntary state over which a human being has no control. It is the expansion of the heart in the state of unveiling which arises from hope. The opposite of *qabḍ*.

bāṭin: inwardly hidden.

bāṭinī: inward, esoteric.

ba'ya: giving allegiance to the shaykh.

bī shar': a Persian term meaning "without *Sharī'a*", a term applied to those who disregard legal obligations.

budalā': another plural of *badl*. Ibn al-'Arabī says that they are not the same as the *Abdāl*, but are twelve other people.

burūz: exteriorisation, being present at different places at the same time. (See *badl*).

ad-Dahr: unending and everlasting time, not divided into past, present and future. Linear time is called *"zamān"* in Arabic.

darwīsh: dervish, from the Persian *darwesh*, meaning poor person, the equivalent of the Arabic *faqīr*.

dawsa: "trampling", a ceremony which used to be performed by the Sa'dīya in *mawlids* of the Prophet in Cairo. The shaykh would ride over the prone dervishes.

Dhāt: Essence, Quiddity, the Absolute Being stripped of all modes, relations and aspects. Also called *al-Māhiyya*.

dhawq: tasting, experience of direct knowledge, sapience (with the original sense of the Latin *sapere*, to taste). One of the first manifestations on the Path.

dhikr: lit. remembrance, mention. Commonly used, it means invocation of Allah by repetition of His names or particular formulae. Forms include: *dhikr al-lisān*, *dhikr* with the tongue; *dhikr an-nafs*, recollection of the self which is inward and not audible; *dhikr al-qalb*, the contemplation of the heart; *dhikr ar-rūḥ*, *dhikr* with the spirit; *dhikr as-sirr*, *dhikr* of the inner secret; *dhikr al-khafī*, secret recollection; *dhikr akhfā al-khafī*, the most secret remembrance of the secret.

dhikru'llāh: "remembrance or invocation of Allah".

dhilla: lowliness, abasement to Allah.

dīwān: a collection of poems primarily concerned with the declaration of *ḥaqīqa*, a description of the *ṭarīqa*, and confirmation of the *Sharī'a*.

du'ā': supplication to Allah.

dunyā: this world, not as a cosmic phenomenon, but as experienced.

ad-Durr al-Bayḍā': "the White Pearl", a term designating the First Intellect.

faḥwānī: "elocution", a technical term of Ibn al-'Arabī. It means Allah's directly addressing people in visionary encounters in the *'ālam al-mithāl*.

fā'ida: a beneficial piece of knowledge which comes to a person.

al-Falak al-Aṭlas: the Starless Heaven, the *'Arsh.*

fanā': annihilation in Allah, the cessation of attributes, total withdrawal from the sensory. Based on the Qur'ān: *"Everyone on it will pass away."* (55:26).

fanā' fī'llah: annihilation in Allah.

fanā' fī'r-rasūl: "annihilation in the Messenger", deep love of the Prophet, may Allah bless him and grant him peace, which leads to love of Allah and ultimately annihilation in Allah.

fanā' fī'sh-shaykh: "annihilation in the shaykh", annihilation in the spiritual guide which leads to annihilation in the Prophet.

faqīr (plural *fuqarā'*): someone who is needy or poor, used to describe someone following a spiritual tradition since the creature is poor and the Creator rich.

faqīrānī: also a *faqīra* (plural *faqīrāt*), the feminine of *faqīr.*

faqr: voluntary indigence, spiritual poverty, absolute need of Allah on the part of creatures. *"O mankind! You are the poor in need of Allah whereas Allah is the Rich beyond need, the Praiseworthy."* (35:15).

farāgh: leisure. Along with laziness, one of the great dangers for someone on the spiritual path.

fard: (singular of *afrād*), a solitary individual.

fardīya: singularity.

farq: (sometimes *tafriqa*), separation, obscuring structures and creation and separating Allah from creation, awareness of creation by creation. The opposite of *jam'.*

fatā: "noble youth", someone who is generous and faithful, a practitioner of *futuwwa.* Al-Qushayrī says, "He has no enemy and does not care whether he is a walī or an unbeliever."

fatḥ: an opening in the soul which sets someone on the Path to realisation. (Cf. *futūḥ*).

fayḍ: overflowing, emanation, effusion, manifestation.

fikr: reflection, seeking the meaning of things as manifestations of the Divine. Also *tafakkur.*

fiṭra: the first nature, the natural, primal condition of mankind in harmony with nature.

fu'ād: the inner heart. According to an-Nūrī, that part of the heart contented only with gnosis.

fuqarā': plural of *faqīr*.

furqān: discrimination, distinguishing the truth from the false.

futūḥ: "opening", the opening of the expression outwardly and sweetness inwardly, and the opening of disclosing and unveiling.

futuwwa: placing others above one's self, as manifested in generosity, altruism, self-denial, indulgence for people's shortcomings.

ghafla: heedlessness, the enemy of *dhikr*.

al-Ghanī: "the Rich-beyond-need" or "Independent", He who has no need of anything. This describes Allah while the creature is poor (*faqīr*).

Ghawth: "succourer", "nurturer", characterised by enormous generosity, the epithet of the *Quṭb*, the head of the *awliya'*. Some say that he is directly below the *Quṭb*. *Al-Ghawth al-A'ẓam*, "the Greatest Help", is used to refer to Shaykh 'Abdu'l-Qādir al-Jilānī. Shaykh Abū Madyan was considered the *Ghawth* of his age.

Ghayb: the Unseen, unmanifest, that which is hidden from the eyes whether or not it is perceived by the heart; or it can be something which is beyond any sort of perception, such as the future.

al-Ghayb al-Muṭlaq: "the Absolutely Unknowable" in reference to the Essence of Allah.

ghayba: absence, the absence of the heart from all that is other than Allah.

ghayr: "other", what is other-than-Allah.

ghazal: a love poem.

ghina: wealth, meaning having no need of other than Allah.

ghurba: exile, from which the one in exile intensely desires to return to witnessing the Creator.

habā': fine dust, the passive universal substance.

ḥadath: situated in time. The opposite is *qidam*.

ḥāḍir: present, wholly aware and not distracted.

haḍra: presence. *al-haḍra al-ilāhiya*, the Divine Presence, sometimes synonymous with *huḍūr*. Also used to designate *'imāra*, a form of *dhikr* done in a circle.

Hāhūt: Divine ipseity, beyond-being, absoluteness.

hājis: firm thought. According to Ibn al-'Arabī, the first thought is the divine thought and is never wrong. Sahl at-Tustarī called it the first cause and the digging of the thought. When it is realised in the self, it becomes will, and when it is repeated it becomes *himma* and the fourth time it is called resolution. When it is directed to action, it is called aim. When the action is begun, it is called intention.

ḥal (plural *aḥwāl*)**:** state, your transient inward state. (cf. *maqām*).

halqa: a circle, gathering.

ḥaqā'iq: realities, the plural of *ḥaqīqa*.

ḥaqīqa: an essential reality which does not admit of abrogation and remains in equal force from the time of Adam to the end of the world.

ḥaqīqa Muḥammadīya: "the reality of Muḥammad", the archetypal Prophet, the Perfect Man through whom Divine consciousness is manifested to Himself, the light in which all things have their origin.

al-Ḥaqq: the Real, the Absolute Truth, Allah, being the opposite of *khalq*, creation.

al-ḥaqq al-makhlūq bihi: "The Truth through which Creation Occurs", the Breath of the Merciful. (cf. Qur'ān 16:3).

ḥaqq al-yaqīn: real certitude, the reality of certainty which is reached in *fanā'*.

hawā: passion, desire (usually not praiseworthy), inclination to something enjoyed by animal appetites; also used in the plural (*ahwā'*), meaning opinions which, swayed by passion, have moved away from the truth.

hawājim: "assaults", impulses or thoughts which involuntarily enter the heart.

hayāmān: passionate love and ecstatic bewilderment.

hayā': shame, modesty, which demands awareness of Allah's presence and behaving accordingly.

hayba: awe, reverential fear, a state in which contemplation of Allah's majesty predominates. The opposite of *uns*.

ḥayra: bewilderment, confusion, continual amazement, perplexity, in which every intellectual channel is blocked; this results in an intensity which allows for illumination, because only finite things can be expressed in words and there is no way to articulate the infinite and ineffable, either mentally or vocally. Ash-Shiblī said, "Real gnosis is the inability to achieve gnosis." How can the temporal grasp the Timeless, the finite the Infinite, the limited the Limitless? Out of confusion comes fusion.

al-Hayūlā al-Kull: the Primal Whole which contains the entire universe by potentiality and by competence.

ḥijāb: "veiling", in Sufism, meaning the impression produced on the heart by phenomena which prevent it from seeing the truth. This is inevitable in this world. (See Qur'an 42:51).

hijāb al-ma'rifa: the veil of gnosis, mentioned by an-Niffarī which in itself is a barrier between man and Allah. "Knowledge is the greatest veil."

ḥijjīr: chant, constant refrain.

ḥikma: wisdom.

himma: spiritual aspiration, yearning to be free of illusion; highest energy impulse in a human to reconnect with reality. There are two types: *jibilla*, inborn, and acquired.

ḥirṣ: greed, avarice.

ḥiss: the faculty of sensation, the domain of the sense perception, the opposite of *ma'nā*.

ḥizb: litany, special prayer formula.

ḥubb: love.

ḥuḍūr: the presence of the heart with Allah.

ḥuḍūr wa ghayba: presence near Allah and absence from oneself.

ḥudūth: located in time.

ḥujjat al-Ḥaqq 'ala'l-khalq: "the demonstrative proof of the Real for the creation," meaning the Perfect Man who was the proof demonstrated to the angels when Ādam informed them of the names of things, a knowledge which they had not been given previously.

hujūm: what comes forcefully into the heart from the moment without any action on your part.

ḥulūl: "indwelling", incarnation, a heretical doctrine.

ḥurrīya: freedom, carrying out the rights owed being a slave of Allah which renders a person free from other than Allah and free from being enslaved to events through awareness of the Creator.

ḥusn aẓ-ẓann: "good opinion", to think well of Allah and the slaves of Allah. This implies complete trust in Allah since Allah says in a *ḥadīth qudsī*, "I am in My servant's opinion of Me."

huwa: (or *hū*) "He", Allah.

huwīya: word derived from the pronoun *huwa* (He), meaning He-ness, Divine Ipseity; the Reality in the World of the Unseen.

ḥuzn: sorrow.

'ibāda: act of worship.

ibn al-waqt: "child of the moment," *see waqt.*

idhn: permission, usually either to be a *shaykh*, or to practice *dhikr* given by a shaykh.

iḥsān: absolute sincerity to Allah in oneself: it is to worship Allah as though you were seeing Him because He sees you.

ījād: to give existence to something.

ikhlāṣ: sincerity, pure unadulterated genuineness.

ikhtilāṭ: to muddle things up and misconstrue things.

ikhtiṣāṣ: Allah's singling out a person for a specific blessing or mercy.

ilāhī: a Turkish genre of mystical poems in popular metre sung at gatherings of *dhikr*.

ilhām: inspiration.

'ilm: knowledge.

'ilm ladunī: directly-given and inspired knowledge from Allah.

'ilm al-qulūb: the science of the hearts, the process of which will bring about gnosis.

'ilm al-yaqīn: knowledge of certainty.

'imāra: technical term for the collective *dhikr* also called *ḥaḍra.*

ināba: turning in repentance, returning from minor sins to love. (cf. *tawba*).

inbisāṭ: see *basṭ.*

'indīya: "at-ness".

infirād: solitude.

innīya: "that-ness". When the Divine Reality described by the attribute of disconnection is witnessed, it annihilates every source except it.

inqibāḍ: anguish. (See *qabḍ).*

al-insān al-kabīr: lit. "Great Man", the macrocosm, the universe.

al-insān al-kāmil: the "perfect man" or universal man. Sufi term for one who has realised all levels of being and understanding.

intibāh: "becoming aware", when Allah restrains His servant out of concern for him.

inzi'āj: disturbance, the effect of admonition in the heart of the believer.

īqān: assurance.

irāda: will, volition, aspirancy.

'irfān: gnosis, a term used mostly by the Shi'a.

'Isawians: For Ibn al-'Arabī, this has a special meaning: the 'Isawian is the one who has brought his timeless reality to life.

ishārāt: allusions, hints, indications of meanings too fine to be expressed directly.

'ishq: passionate and unbounded love for Allah.

ishrāq: illumination.

ism: name, noun, the Divine Name. Sometimes *al-Ism al-A'ẓam*, the Greatest Name, Allah. *Al-Ism al-Jāmi'*, "the All-inclusive Name" is Allah.

isqāṭ at-tadbīr: dropping of management and human planning in favour of Allah's planning, a term used by Ibn 'Aṭā'llāh. Similar to *tafwīḍ.*

isti'dād: predisposition, aptitude, preparedness for receiving knowledge or illumination.

istidāra: circularity, which is the nature of things, since Allah is the First and the Last and all things return to Him. (Cf. Qur'ān 11:123, 31:55, etc.).

istidrāj: baiting by degrees, a fall from grace by a hidden chain of events.

istighfār: asking forgiveness of Allah.

iṣṭilāḥāt: technical vocabularies.

istiqāma: being straight, putting into practice the *Sunna* of the Prophet.

īthār: altruism, to prefer others to oneself.

iṭmi'ān: tranquillity, spiritual peace.

ittiḥād: becoming one, human individuality passing away in the Reality, like a grain of salt in the sea.

'iyān: actual direct vision.

Jabarūt: the world of divine power, the Kingdom of Lights, 'between' *Mulk* and *Malakūt*.

jadhb: divine attraction which overpowers a person.

jalāl: the attributes of force, of Divine awe-inspiring majesty.

jalwa: disclosure, the slave emerging from retreat with the attributes of the Real.

jam': gatheredness, combining all into the whole and ignoring structures in existence in an undifferentiated field of awareness by witnessing Allah. Its opposite is *farq*. Its climax is *jam' al-jam'*.

jam' al-jam': "gatheredness of gatherness", perfect union, confirming the reality without the *faqīr*'s being in it being in any way experiential.

jamāl: Divine beauty.

jam'īya: concentration, comprehensiveness.

jawhar: lit. "jewel", substance, specifically the essence of intrinsic being of a form.

jibilla: innate disposition.

al-jihād al-asghar: the lesser *jihād,* meaning physical fighting against the unbelievers.

al-jihād al-akbar: the greater *jihād*, meaning the inner struggle against the self.

jilāla: name in the Arab West for the Qādirīya *ṭarīqa*.

kamāl: perfection of gnosis – being disconnected from attributes and their effects.

karāmāt: marks of honour, miracles. Distinct from *mu'jizāt* – prophetic miracles, things which cannot be imitated. Both are *kharq al-'adāt*, the extraordinary breaking of normal patterns.

ka's: "the cup", the heart of the shaykh from which the "wine" of the knowledge of the Divine is poured into the hearts of his *murīds* in the "tavern" of the *zawīya*.

kashf: unveiling, knowledge which does not require proof as it is a direct perception of the true nature of things.

al-Kathīb: the Slipping Sand-Heap, the heap where all souls will assemble in the Next World, each taking its place according to its spiritual rank.

kathīf: dense, thick, the opposite of *laṭīf* (subtle).

kawn: Being, all phenomena.

khalīfa: "successor", the representative of the shaykh, who is more accomplished than a *muqaddam* or *nā'ib*. The plural is *khulafā'*.

khalq: "creation", both the act of creation or the result of the act, hence the cosmos.

khalwa: spiritual retreat, seclusion, in order to remember Allah.

khamr: the "wine" of direct knowledge of the Divine.

khānqāh: *zawīya*, a place where seekers of Allah live and meet.

kharq al-'adāt: miracle, an extra-ordinary event, literally it means the "breaking of the normal pattern of things".

khashya: fear of Allah.

khāṣṣa: special, elite.

khāṭir (plural *khawāṭir*)**:** a passing thought, which is quickly removed by another. There are three kinds: those which come from Shayṭān, which are a sort of whispering; those from the self, which are niggling and arise from appetites; and those which come from Allah, which come quickly and with a sort of clarity.

khātim: seal, *khāṭim an-nabiyyīn*: the seal of prophethood, the last of the Prophets.

khatm: seal, *khāṭm al-wilāya*: the seal of sainthood, often used of 'Īsā.

khawf: fear, dread of the Creator and Master of the Day of Judgement.

khayāl: imagination. With Ibn al-'Arabī, it has an inner and outer meaning. Its outer meaning is the ordinary meaning of imagination. In its inner meaning, it is the faculty by which we solidify objects which are, in reality, not there inasmuch as the sensory is not real.

khidhlān: abandonment, when Allah leaves man to his own devices.

khidma: service of others.

al-Khiḍr: or al-Khaḍir, the Green one, whose journey with Mūsā is mentioned in the Qur'ān 18:60-82. He may or may not be a Prophet, and appears often to people, usually to test their generosity.

khirqa: a patched robe worn as a sign of poverty and devotion. (cf. *muraqq'a*).

khuḍū': humble submissiveness, yielding before Allah.

al-Kibrīt al-Aḥmar: "Red Sulphur", the Philosopher's Stone; used to describe the transformative action of the shaykh on the disciple.

kullīyāt al-wujūd: universals of being.

kun: 'Be!' the creating command.

kunh: true nature.

Lāhūt: Godhood, Divine Nature.

laṭīfa (plural *laṭā'if*)**:** all pervading energy within an organism (similar to the Taoist *chi'i*); an indication with a very subtle meaning which flashed in the understanding but cannot be verbally expressed.

lawā'iḥ: glimmers, sudden intuitions, the first gleams affirming the object of desire coming, as it were, as flashes in the dark, a sensory sensation, the precursors of *lawāmi'*.

lawāmi': gleams, intuitions of spiritual light to the heart which last two moments. They are glimpses of meaning which are perceived by the *rūḥ*. These are the first genuine lights, the precursors of *ṭawāli'*.

Lawḥ: board, tablet. *Al-Lawḥ al-Maḥfūz* is the Preserved Tablet in the Unseen which is also referred to as the *Umm al-Kitāb*, the place of recording what will be, the repository of destiny.

Layla: "night", also one of the names used to indicate the Beloved.

laylatu'l-fuqarā': "the night of the *fuqarā'*", meaning the gathering of *dhikr* attended by the *fuqarā'* with their shaykh or one of his *muqaddams*, usually on Thursday night.

lisān al-ḥāl: the tongue of the state, where the state gives expression to the inward of the person.

lubb: "core", the central locus of awareness in the human being, the heart of the heart.

luṭf: kindness or grace, Allah's help which permeates things; the all-pervading texture of the Universe that cannot be grasped or defined.

maḥabba: love. Ibn 'Arīf defines it as "a certain emotional subjection of the heart which prevents one from yielding to anything except his Beloved."

maḥall: locus, the place in which Allah's prescencing is experienced: the heart.

maḥw: effacement, the removal of the attributes of normality, or the cause.

maḥyā: vigil, the night recitation of prayers or *dhikr* through Thursday night until Friday. This was first inaugurated by ash-Shūnī in Cairo in 897/1492.

ma'īya: "with-ness".

majdhūb: attracted, someone who is enraptured and bewildered by the effect of Divine attraction.

majmū': "totality", both the Real and creation.

makhāfa: fear, as *khawf*.

Malakūt: the angelic world, the Kingdom of Unseen forms.

malāma: blame, the path of blame taken by some Sufis which involves deliberately provoking people to have a bad opinion of them, so that it is only possible to turn to Allah.

ma'lūh: one in thrall to God.

ma'na: "meaning". In Sufic terms, spiritual perception of the subtleties behind or within sensory forms.

manajāt: prayer as an intimate dialogue between an individual and his personal Lord.

manzil (plural *manāzil*)**:** way station, stage, a term denoting a particular phase in the gnostic development of the seeker. Each stage has certain qualities and knowledges.

maqām (plural *maqāmāt*)**:** a station of spiritual knowledge, more long lasting than a *ḥāl*.

marabout: a French word from *murābiṭ*, a term for a Sufi in North Africa.

marbūb: one who has a lord, a vassal.

ma'rifa: gnosis, direct, experiential knowledge of higher realities, witnessing the lights of the Names and Attributes of Allah in the heart.

mawadda: love, affection.

mawsim: see moussem.

mawṭin: abode, the world or domain in which we dwell.

misbaḥa (plural *masābiḥ*): prayer beads. (Cf. *tasbīḥ*).

mithāl: In Sufism, this has to do with a modality of experiencing reality. In it, an analogue is produced which is somewhat like a hologram, a multi-dimensional metaphor capable of conveying more than one meaning simultaneously, and then this model is grasped intellectually in a non-linear way.

mīthāq: covenant, the primordial covenant between Allah and the creature.

moussem: French word from *mawsim*, a festival of *dhikr* celebrated by a *walī* and his followers.

mudhākara: a discourse or exposition in a meeting of *dhikr*.

muḥāḍara: the presence of the heart when the proof comes again and again. Ibn al-'Arabī mentions that it is the conversation between the Divine Names regarding the realities.

muḥādatha: discussion, when Allah addresses the gnostics from the visible world, as when Mūsā was addressed from the Burning Bush.

muḥaqqiq: verifier, one who has understanding of reality.

muḥāsaba: self-analysis, reviewing oneself, one's actions and thoughts.

muḥibb: lover.

muḥsin: someone who possesses the quality of *iḥsān*.

mujāhada: self-mortification, forcing the self to do things it finds difficult and opposing passions and desires.

mujarrad: "disengaged", divested of all worldly matters.

mukāshafa: unveiling, it is marked by continual amazement with Allah's infinite greatness. (See *kashf)*.

mukhlaṣ: one who has been made sincere.

mukhliṣ: one who is sincere.

Mulk: the visible realm, the kingdom of solid forms.

munājāt: intimate conversations, prayers.

munāzalāt: mutual way-stations, a term used by Ibn al-'Arabī for stations of unveiling which involves effort on the part of the person as well as unveiling coming from Allah.

muqābala: "encounter", the name of the Mevlevī dance.

muqaddam: "one who is promoted," the representative of the shaykh; (also *nā'ib*).

murābiṭ: "one who is garrisoned", originally, in North Africa, someone living in a *ribāṭ*, a fortified stronghold serving both religious and military functions.

murād: the one who is pulled by Allah from his own will. All things are arranged for him so that he passes through the stations without any exertion.

murāqaba: vigilance; recollection; an aspect of reflection (*tafakkur*); waiting on a spiritual presence; permanent state of awareness, not a spiritual exercise.

muraqqa'a: patched cloak worn by Sufis. (Cf. *khirqa*).

murīd: disciple. He is the one who is stripped of his will (*irāda*) and hands himself over to his shaykh, his guide.

murshid: a spiritual guide.

murū'a: (also *muruwwa*) manliness, the sum total of virtuous virile qualities.

musāfir: traveller, one who travels with his intellect through intelligible matters.

musāmara: night talk, when Allah addresses the gnostics from the World of the secrets and the Unseen, as when the angel brings it into the heart. Hence it often cannot be expressed verbally and communicated to others.

mushāhada: witnessing, contemplation, vision within the heart, seeing things as evidence of *tawḥīd*, or grasping an indication; the fruit of *murāqaba*.

mushtāq: one who yearns.

muta'ahhib: "prepared, ready", someone with the right spiritual aptitude following the Sufic Path.

mutabārikūn: "those who want a blessing," people who join in a *ṭarīqa* merely for the blessing and are passive members.

mutaḥayyiz: spatially confined, a property of physical things.

mutamakkin: one who is steadfast and does not waver in his station.

muttaqūn: pious and righteous persons who fear Allah much (and so abstain from all kinds of sins and evil deeds which He has forbidden), and love Allah much (and so perform all kinds of good deeds which He has ordained).

nafas ar-Raḥmān: "breath of the Merciful," the manifestation of possibilities, in which the entire creation is constantly renewed in each moment.

nafs: the self. Usually in reference to the lower self – either the self which commands to evil, or the reproachful self.

an-nafs al-'ammāra: the insinuating self which is wholly evil and totally under the control of passions and bent only on self-gratification. It is totally blind to any higher reality. *"The lower self of man commands to evil acts except where my Lord shows mercy."* (Qur'ān 12:53).

an-nafs al-lawwāma: the self-reproaching self, which is indecisive in choosing between good and evil and is constantly embroiled in an inner struggle. It is unable to overcome the impulses of the lower self while it nonetheless recognises the higher one. *"No, I swear by the self-reproaching self."* (Qur'ān 75:2).

an-nafs al-mulhama: the inspired self, which recognises its faults and strives to correct them. *"By the self and what proportioned it and inspired it with depravity or godliness!"* (Qur'ān 91:7-8).

an-nafs al-muṭma'inna: Finally there is the self at peace, which is illuminated and acts according to the good and is therefore liberated. *"O self at peace, return to your Lord, well-pleased, well-pleasing. Enter among My servants. Enter My Garden."* (Qur'ān 89:27-30).

nafth: literally, spitting, often meaning to cast something into the mind.

nā'ib (plural *nuwwāb*)**:** the representative of the shaykh, synonym of *muqaddam.*

najwā: the private talk between Allah and each of His slaves on the Day of Resurrection. It also means a secret counsel or conference or consultation.

nakira: non-recognition, the opposite of gnosis (*ma'rifa*).

nāsik (plural *nussāk*)**:** a person of great piety, ascetic.

Nāsūt: manhood, human nature.

nisyān: forgetfulness.

nujabā': "the nobles", part of the spiritual hierarchy. They are eight (or forty) men occupied with bearing the burdens of creation who do not act on their own behalf.

nuqabā’: They are twelve (or 300) “chiefs” and are part of the spiritual hierarchy. They know the hidden things of the selves and consciences and are able to cure people of their ignorance.

pīr: Persian for *murshid.*

qabḍ: contraction, an involuntary state over which a human being has no control. It is the contraction of the heart in a state of being veiled. The opposite of *basṭ*, the residue of burned-up hopes.

qadīm: eternal, ancient.

qahr: force, when Allah forcefully annihilates a person’s desires and restrains his lower self.

qalandar: wandering dervish.

qalb (plural *qulūb*)**:** heart; the faculty for directly perceiving spiritual realities which the mind cannot grasp.

qānitun: They are those whom Allah has assigned obedience, and that is obedience to Allah in all that He commands and forbids. This is only after the descent of the *Sharī‘a,* and what is before the descent of *Shari‘a* is not called *qanūt* or obedience, but it is called good and noble character and doing what is proper.

qarār: settledness, the departure of vacillation from a person.

qaṣīda (plural *qaṣā’id*)**:** ode, poem. (See *dīwān*).

Qawm: “people”, “tribe”, meaning the Sufis when so used.

Qawwālī: Sufi singing in Urdu and also in Persian.

qidam: timeless eternity, eternity which is not affected at all by temporal time.

qubba: kubba, a domed shrine.

qulūb: “hearts”, the plural of *qalb.*

qurb: nearness, proximity to Allah, the closest of which is ‘two bow’s lengths’, the nearest a slave could approach a king.

Quṭb: the pole, the axis of the spiritual hierarchy.

Rabb: Lord, master; the particular Divine name which rules a creature.

raghba: desire, longing, the desire of the self for the reward, the desire of the heart for the reality, and the secret of the secret for the Real.

Raḥamūt: sourcehood, the presence of mercy.

rahba: fear, dread. In the outward it comes from the Threat. Inwardly it is about the change of knowledge. The fear of the secret is about the prior Decree.

rajā': hope, hope for the Garden, hope for Allah's pleasure, hope for the vision of the King.

rajul: the singular of *rijāl.*

rams: negation of a substance, together with every trace of it, from the heart.

ramz (plural *rumūz*)**:** a symbol.

raqā'iq: stories which provoke feelings and emotions.

raqīqa: a very fine, invisible filament of light which extends from one thing to another, thus connecting them over great distances.

rayn: a veil of disbelief and error over the heart which can only be removed by faith. It comes from an *āyat* of the Qur'ān: *"No indeed! Rather what they have earned has rusted up their hearts"* (83:14).

ribāṭ: the stronghold traditionally used by the Muslims to prepare for their *jihād* against the enemies of Islam, situated at exposed points of the frontier; later a *ṭarīqa*-based centre of religious instruction.

riḍā: serene and joyful contentment with Allah's Decree, when there is a balance between fear and hope.

Rijāl: "men", meaning the men of gnosis and illumination. This has no gender attached to it in this usage and so it is also applied to women. The singular is *rajūl.*

riyā': showing off, doing actions for the sake of being seen to do them.

riyāḍa: discipline, the discipline of *adab* is to leave the nature of the self. In general, it involves inculcating good character.

rizq: sustenance, both spiritual and physical, which comes from Allah.

rū': heart

rubā'iyāt: quatrains.

rubūbīya: lordship, the quality of being a lord. The opposite is *'ubūdīya.*

rubuṭ: plural of *ribāṭ.*

rūḥ (plural *arwāḥ*)**:** the spirit which gives life.

rūḥānī: spiritual.

rūḥāniyya: pure spirituality, a non-spatial zone.

Rukhkh: the phoenix.

ru‘ūna: ‘levity,’ stopping at the level of nature.

ru’ya: vision, dream.

ṣābirūn: people who are patient and steadfast.

ṣabr: patience, steadfastness, self-control, endurance, both physical and spiritual, self restraint to act by what is commanded and to abandon what is forbidden.

safar: journey, it is the journey of the heart when it begins to turn to Allah by *dhikr*.

saḥq: pulverisation, the disappearance of your inward and outward structure under the weight of divine force.

sahr: sleeplessness.

ṣaḥw: sobriety, acting in accordance with the *Sunna*, thus concealing inward intoxication.

sakīna: an enveloping stillness which Allah sends down on the hearts.

aṣ-ṣalāt ‘alā’n-Nabī: the prayer on the Prophet.

ṣāliḥ (plural *ṣālihūn*)**:** righteous, a spiritually developed person, one who is in the right place at the right time doing the right thing.

sālik: traveller to Allah. The *sālik* is grounded in the necessary wisdom to prevent becoming mad from the intoxication of yearning and thus acts outwardly in accordance with the *Sharī‘a* while being inwardly intoxicated.

samā‘: listening session, listening to songs about Allah, so that the heart may open.

Ṣamad: the Real in its endless effulgence of creative energy, by which the whole universe of endless forms emerge from the possible into the existent. It is the richness whose wealth is every form in creation. Allah is in need of nothing and everything is in need of Him.

satr: covering, veiling, concealing, the manner in which existence conceals Divine Unity. The opposite of *tajallī*.

sayyāḥūn: roving angels who roam the earth looking for gatherings of *dhikr*, from which the scent of musk emanates in the Unseen.

shajarat al-kawn: “the tree of existence”, the entire universe.

shaṭḥiyāt: ecstatic statements.

shawq: the yearning of the heart to meet the Beloved.

shaykh (plural *shuyūkh*)**:** in Sufism, the spiritual teacher who guides you from knowledge of your self to knowledge of your Lord.

Shaykh al-Akbar: "the Greatest Shaykh", a title given to Muḥyi'd-dīn Ibn al-'Arabī.

shirk: the unforgiveable wrong action of worshipping something or someone other than Allah or associating something or someone as a partner with Him.

shuhūd: contemplative vision, inner witnessing.

shukr: gratitude, giving thanks and acknowledgement of blessing. It begins with the tongue, then with the body and then with the heart.

shurb: "drinking", tasting the sweetness of devotion which increases the meaning and decreases the sensory. It is more permanent than "tasting" (*dhawq*).

shurūd: seeking restlessly to escape from the veils of this world, employing every resource to become unveiled.

shuyūkh: plural of *shaykh*.

ṣiddīq: a man of truth, the *ṣiddīq* is the one who believes in Allah and His Messenger by the statement of the one who reports it, not from any proof except the light of belief which he experiences in his heart, and which prevents him from hesitating, or any doubt entering him, about the word of the Messenger who reported.

ṣidq: truthfulness.

ṣifāt: the attributes, of Allah.

silsila: the chain, in Sufism, the continuity of spiritual descent and transmission of wisdom from shaykh to shaykh from the Prophet.

simsima: "sesame seed", a metaphor for gnosis which is too fine to express.

sirr: inmost consciousness, the secret.

subḥa (plural *subuḥāt*)**:** prayer beads. (See *tasbīḥ*).

ṣuḥba: companionship, company.

sukr: intoxication, drunkenness, rapture.

sukūn: stillness, the heart at peace, a serenity born of emptiness.

sulūk: journeying, the progress on the Way to Allah, maintaining outward stability while inwardly attracted to the Divine (*jadhb*).

tabaddul: *"tabaddul al-'ālam ma' al-anfus"*, the transformation of the world with each breath, meaning that at every single moment, the entire universe emerges anew. This is similar to the expression "*tajdīd al-khalq*" or "renewal of creation", in which the universe is created anew in every instant. (See *nafas ar-Raḥmān*).

tafakkur: pondering, reflection.

tafrīd: inward solitude, isolation, the experience of *tawḥīd* rather than simple knowledge of it.

tafriqa: See *farq*.

tafwīḍ: handing over management of one's affairs to Allah, realising that one is not really in charge, similar to *isqāṭ at-tadbīr*.

taḥakkum: a ruling control over some things given to some people through the force of their *himma*.

taḥallī: imitation of praiseworthy people in word and deed.

taḥqīq: realisation, when someone sees the face of Allah in everything and gives everything its rightful due (*ḥaqq*).

Ṭā'ifa (plural *ṭawā'if*)**:** a group of pupils with a shaykh.

tajallī: self-manifestation, prescencing, self-disclosing, the unveiling of a spiritual reality in the realm of vision, a showing forth of the secrets of the One in existence.

tajdīd al-khalq: the renewal of creation at every instant. (See *tabaddul*).

tajrīd: disengagement, outward separation, stripping away, pure detachment from the world, abandoning the desires and things of this world and being unconcerned with the rewards of the Next World.

takhallī: relinquishment, turning away from distractions which prevent a person from reaching his Goal.

takhlīṣ: cleansing one's soul of relations with anything other than Allah.

takiyya: place of religious retreat, sanctuary. In Turkish, it becomes *tekkē* or *durgah*.

talaqqī: receiving and taking what comes to you from Allah.

talbīs: the appearance of a thing when its appearance is contrary to its reality, as in the Qur'ān (6:9). The good can conceal the bad or *vice versa*.

ṭālib: a seeker of Allah.

talwīn: change and turning from one state to another.

tamkīn: fixity, the state of the people of trial. It is the removal of *talwīn*. All that is other than Allah has been removed from his mind and so he does not vacillate.

ṭams: negation of a substance of which some trace is left.

tanazzulāt: descensions, the gradual descent of illumination; instances of "descents" of the One essence into a manifestation within the sensible world. Amazingly this descent both reveals and hides the One essence.

tanzīh: transcendence, disconnecting Allah from creation. The opposite of *tashbīh*. There are three categories of disconnection: the *tanzīh* of the *Sharī'a*, which the common understand as disconnecting partners from divinity; the *tanzīh* of the intellect, which the elite understand is to disconnect the Real from being described by possibility; the *tanzīh* of unveiling which is to contemplate the presence of the absolute Essence.

taqallub: the constant change and transformation of the heart.

taqrīb: drawing near, one of the attributes of things in-time because they accept drawing-near and its opposite. The Real is the "Near".

taqwā: awe or fear of Allah, which inspires a person to be on guard against wrong action and eager for actions which please Him.

taraqqī: rising through states, stations and knowledges.

Ṭarīqa: the Way, the Path.

tark at-tark: "quitting quitting", complete surrender, forgetting everything. The struggle is not to struggle.

taṣarruf: free disposal, personal initiative. Ibn 'Arabī says it is the control exerted by the *himma* to effect changes in the external world.

taṣawwuf: Sufism, the science of the journey to the King.

tasbīḥ: glorification; also prayer beads.

tashbīh: the recognition that although nothing can be associated with Allah, nevertheless Allah participates in the world of forms, e.g. seeing is His and hearing is His.

tawāḍu': humility.

tawajjuhāt: unceasing Divine favours, the fundamental premise that Divine knowledges are renewed constantly, and while the forms appear the same, in fact they are renewed in every instant.

tawājud: simulated ecstasy – to be avoided.

tawakkul: reliance, unshakeable trust in Allah, the final stage of which is to be like the corpse in the hands of the washer. It is trusting absolutely that Allah will be just and merciful and provide for His servants.

ṭawāli‘: the appearance of the splendours of knowledge of *tawḥīd* in the heart which are so intense that they obliterate any other knowledge.

tawaqqu‘: anticipation. What man anticipates has appeared because whenever he anticipates something it has already manifested itself in him inwardly. Whatever appears inwardly manifests in the outward.

tawba: returning to correct action after error, turning away from wrong action to Allah and asking His forgiveness.

tawḥīd: the doctrine of Divine Unity, Unity in its most profound sense.

tawfīq: success given by Allah.

ta'wīl: allegorical interpretation.

tekke: Turkish *zawīya.*

ṭuruq: the plural of *ṭarīqa*.

‘ubūda: sheer devotion, seeing yourself by your Lord.

‘ubūdīya: slavehood, obedience is illuminated by the recognition that one is the slave of the Lord.

‘ūd: aloes wood, often burned for its fragrant scent during gatherings of *dhikr*.

uns: intimacy, a state in which contemplation of Allah's beauty predominates. The opposite of *hayba*.

Uwaysī: one who obtains illumination without being a follower of a spiritual teacher. The name is taken from Uways al-Qaranī, a gnostic and contemporary of the Prophet who did not meet him, although they knew of each other.

‘uzla: withdrawal after *khalwa* to fix the fruits of *khalwa*. It is less strict than *khalwa*. Withdrawal is to withdraw from every blameworthy attribute and every base character in his state. In his heart, he withdraws from connection to any of Allah's creation.

waḥdānīya: Oneness, the Unity of the Divine Names.

waḥdat ash-shuhūd: unity of consciousness, unity of direct witnessing.

waḥdat al-wujūd: unity of being. There is only one Self which is manifested in multiplicity. Allah is One in His *Dhāt*, His *Ṣifāt* and His

Af'āl. There is only One Entity in existence and multiplicity appears through relations between non-essential entities.

wāḥidīya: the unity of multiplicity.

wahm: opinion, conjecture, illusion, fantasies arising in the mind which are substituted for reality.

waḥsha: loneliness, estrangement from created things.

wajd: rapture, trance, the first degree of ecstasy. Ibn al-'Arabī states: "It is what the heart unexpectedly encounters of its unseen states withdrawn from witnessing.

Wajhu'llāh: "the Face of Allah", meaning for the sake of Allah, irrespective of any reward in this life, purely for Allah.

walad: lit. "child", a beginner on the path.

walah: unbounded ecstasy, utter distraction.

walī (plural *awliyā'*)**:** someone who is "friend" of Allah, thus possessing the quality of *wilāya*.

waqfa: being held between two stations.

wāqi'a: visionary experience, a thought which comes and settles and cannot be repelled.

waqt: lit. time, meaning being in the moment and independent of looking to the past or the future. Sometimes the Sufi is described as "*ibn al-waqt*" (the child of the moment) because of this.

wara': scrupulousness, it extends from avoidance of the unlawful and doubtful to avoiding anything that will cast a shadow on the heart. The *faqīr* must also be scrupulous to avoid basking in his scrupulousness.

wārid: "arriving thing"; an overflowing experience which overcomes a person's heart. It is the first oncoming of gatheredness (*jam'*).

wasā'iṭ: secondary causes to which seekers of Allah attach themselves and thereby gain the object of their desire.

waṣl: union.

wasm: a marking or a stamp. In Ibn al-'Arabī's terminology, a quality which continues from before-time on into after-time.

waswas: the whispering of Shayṭān when he tries to make people deviate.

watad: singular of *awtād*.

waẓīfa: specific set of prayers which are recited.

wijdān: the second degree of ecstasy (after *wajd*). Ibn 'Ajība says that it is when the sweetness of witnessing lasts, usually accompanied by drunkenness and bewilderment.

wilāya: friendship, in particular with Allah, referring to the *wali's* station of knowledge of the Real by direct seeing.

wird (plural *awrād*)**:** a regular spiritual exercise involving recitation of a litany of *dhikr*.

wujūd: "existence". *Dhāt al-wujūd* is "existence itself" in its absolute and unqualified purity. In relation to Allah, *Dhāt Allāh* is the Essence of Allah before being described in any manner whatsoever. This is unknowable and unknown (*Ghayb*) and absolutely One. In relation to mystical stations, *wujūd* is the third degree of ecstasy in which awareness dominates the sense of bewilderment and so the one experiencing it seeks to conceal it. Ibn al-'Arabī said, "*Wujūd* (finding) is experiencing the Real in *wajd* (ecstasy)."

wuṣūl: arrival, attainment.

yaqīn: absolute unshakeable certainty and certitude; *'ilm al-yaqīn* (knowledge of certainty) is given by proof or evidence; *'ayn al-yaqīn* (source or eye of certainty) is given by witnessing and unveiling; and *ḥaqq al-yaqīn* (the truth of *yaqīn*) is knowledge obtained according to what the Witnessed so wills.

zāhid: someone whose heart has no inclination or attachment for this world.

zamān: linear time.

ẓann: opinion, supposition.

zawā'id: abundance of lights of spiritual illumination in the heart.

zawīya: a "corner", small mosque, or religious retreat, often where the shaykh teaches.

ziyāra: visit to tomb or holy places.

zuhd: making do with little of this of world and leaving what you do not need.

zuhhād: plural of *zāhid*.

Some major Ṭarīqas

Aḥmadīya: *ṭarīqa* in Egypt from Aḥmad al-Badawī, the famous Egyptian Sufi (d. 675/1276). It is also called the Badawīya. It has numerous branches, but is confined to Egypt. Its members wear a red turban. It was popular among the Mamluks, and has several sub-branches. (Not to be confused with the sect bearing the same name, also known as the Qadianīs, who by declaring their leader, Mirza Ghulām Aḥmad (d. 1326/1908) to be a prophet have been declared *kāfirūn* by the Sunnī *'ulamā'*.)

'Alāwīya: Algerian branch of the Darqāwa since 1919.

Bektashi: Sufi order, popular among Ottoman janissaries, founded by Ḥājji Bektash Walī of Khorasan (d. 739/1338). Somewhat eclectic, with strong Shi'ite tendencies.

Burhānīya: Egyptian *ṭarīqa*, a branch of the Shādhilī *ṭarīqa.*

Chistīya: an Indian Sufi *ṭarīqa* from Shaykh Chistī (d. 632/1236). Chisht is the village in which the founder of the order, Abū Isḥāq of Syria, settled. They utilise songs and music and wear cinnamon coloured garments.

Darqāwa: also Darqāwīya (or Derqāwiya) a branch of the Shādhilī *ṭarīqa* originating with Mulay al-'Arabī ad-Darqāwī (d. 1289/1823), or more properly, with the teachings of his shaykh, Sidi 'Alī al-Jamal (d. 1193-94/1779-80). It concentrates on renunciation of worldly things and a return to the true teachings of *taṣawwuf.* It has various branches, mainly in northwest Africa. They played a political role in opposition to the Turks and later the French.

Halvetiyye: See *Khalwatīya.*

Ḥarrāqīya: Moroccan branch of the Darqāwa since the 19th century, who have kept the old Andalusian tradition of music alive.

'Īsāwīya: a popular *ṭarīqa* who charm snakes and perform prodiguous feats. Based at Meknes in Morocco.

Jarrāhīya: a Turkish *ṭarīqa* founded by Shaykh Nūr ad-Dīn Muḥammad al-Jarrāḥ of Istanbul (d. 1183/1720).

Jazūlīya: Moroccan reformed Shādhilī *ṭarīqa*. It has various branches, including the Darqāwa.

Khalwatīya: a *ṭarīqa* which is known as the Halvetiyye in Turkish. It was founded by Shaykh 'Umar al-Khalwatī (d. 800/1397) and is based on hunger, silence, vigil, seclusion and *dhikr*. It has many branches.

Kubrāwīya: a Khorasanī branch of the the old Junaydīya *ṭarīqa* from Najm Kubrā (d. 619/1221). It has several branches. They developed an elaborate colour-symbolism: white represents Islam, yellow faith, dark blue *iḥsān*, and so forth. They became important in Kashmir.

Mevlevīya: or the Mawlawīya, Sufi order in Turkey founded by Jalāl ad-Dīn Rūmī (d. 672/1273). They are known in the West as the "whirling dervishes" because of their central practice of turning which is done to the accompaniment of music. Their centre is in Qonya, Turkey.

Naqshbandīya: an order founded by Muḥammad Naqshband (d. 791/1389), characterised by silence for recollection and concentration and the *dhikr* of the heart. Aḥmad Sirhindī (d. 1034/1624) was a member of this order. The Naqshbanīya *ṭarīqa* is the only *ṭarīqa* whose *silsila* traces back to the Prophet through the first khalif Abū Bakr. The other *ṭarīqas* all trace back to the Prophet through the fourth khalif 'Alī.

Ni'matullāhīya: a Shi'ite Sufi order founded by Shāh Walī Ni'matullah (d. 840/1431).

Nūrbakhshīya: Khorasan branch of the Kubrāwīya named after Muḥammad ibn Muḥammad called Nūrbakhsh (d. 869/1465).

Qādirīya: the first *ṭarīqa,* founded by 'Abdu'l-Qādir al-Jilānī (d. 561/1166). It is very active and very widespread.

Raḥmānīya: Algerian *ṭarīqa* named after Muḥammad ibn 'Abdu'r-Raḥmān al-Gushtuli al-Jurjurī who died in 1208/1793-94 in Kabylia. It is a branch of the Khalwatīya and was once called the Bakrīya. In some places it is called the 'Azzūzīya.

Rifā'iyya: a *ṭarīqa* which originated from Basra and has several branches. Known in the West as the "howling dervishes". It was an offshoot of the Qādirīya established by Aḥmad ar-Rifā'ī (d. 578/1187). They developed strange and extreme practices, including the *dawsa*.

Sālimīya: *ṭarīqa* named after Ibn Sālim whose shaykh was Sahl at-Tustarī (d. 282/896).

Sanūsīya: political-religious organisation founded in Libya by Sayyid Muḥammad 'Alī as-Sanūsī (d. 1276/1859), who put up strong resistance to the colonialists.

Shādhilīya: order founded by Abū Madyan of Tlemcen (d. 594/1197) and Abū'l-Ḥasan ash-Shādhilī of Tunis (d. 656/1258). Ash-Shādhilī discouraged monasticism and urged his followers to maintain their ordinary lives, a tradition still followed. It manifests the sobriety which al-Junayd espoused. It has many branches, especially in North Africa.

Shaṭṭārīya: an Indonesian *ṭarīqa* from 'Abdullah Shattār (d. 824/1415 or 837/1428).

Suhrawardīya: Baghdadī order founded by 'Abdu'l-Qādir as-Suhrawardī (d. 564/1168), a disciple of Aḥmad al-Ghazālī (the younger brother of Muḥammad al-Ghazālī), and Abū Ḥafs 'Umar as-Suhrawardī (d. 632/1234). It has several branches. The 'Abbasid khalif an-Nāṣir helped in the diffusion of his teaching and his futuwwa order.

Tījānīya: a widespread *ṭarīqa* in the Maghrib founded by Abū'l-'Abbās Aḥmad at-Tījāni (d. 1230/1815) in Fes. He said that he received the command to found the *ṭarīqa* in a vision of the Prophet. They are exclusivist, not allowing people to join any other *ṭarīqa*, and advocate complete submission to the government, whatever it is.

Some Famous Sufi Texts

'Awārif al-Ma'ārif: "the Gifts of Gnoses", by Abū Ḥafs 'Umar as-Suhrawardī (540/1145 – 632/1234), a treatise on Sufic teaching which was widely read and became a standard text in Indian *madrasas*.

Dalā'il al-Khayrāt: "Guides to Good Things", a popular collection of prayers on the Prophet with emphasis on the Divine Names, by al-Jazūlī (d. 870/1465).

Al-Fatḥ ar-Rabbānī: "Sublime Revelation", a series of discourses by Shaykh 'Abdu'l-Qādir al-Jilānī (d. 561/1166).

Fuṣūṣ al-Ḥikam: "The Seals of Wisdom", an extremely important book regarded as the nucleus of Ibn al-'Arabī's teaching and philosophy: it consists of a series of explanations of the mystical meanings of the particular gnoses granted to each of several major Prophets.

Futūḥ al-Ghayb: "Openings of the Unseen", a series of discourses on the Sufic Path by Shaykh 'Abdu'l-Qādir al-Jilānī (d. 561/1166).

Futūḥāt al-Makkīya: "The Makkan Revelations", Ibn 'Arabī's huge major work which consists of 565 chapters. He was inspired to begin it, hence its name.

Ḥikam: "The Wisdoms", by Ibn 'Aṭā'llāh, a Shādhilī and Māliki *faqīh.* It is a collection of 262 aphorisms followed by four short treatises and some supplications.

Ḥilyat al-Awliyā': "The Embellishment of the Saints", a compendium of Sufic doctrine and biographies by Abū Nu'aym al-Isfahānī (d. 430/1038).

Ḥizb al-Baḥr, Ḥizb al-Barr and **Ḥizb an-Naṣr:** the famous collections of prayers of Shaykh ash-Shādhilī (d. 656/1258).

Ihyā' 'Ulūm ad-Dīn: "The Revivification of the Sciences of Religion", a famous book by al-Ghazālī (d. 505/1111), written over a number of years after he left Baghdad in 488/1095 to become a wandering Sufi. In it, he proposes to radically overhaul the current attitude towards religion by putting fear of Allah at the centre of all actions.

al-Insān al-Kāmil: a treatise by al-Jīlī (d. 811-20/1408-17), on the "Universal Man". He attempts to systematise the teachings of Ibn al-'Arabī, but not always agreeing with him. He discusses the different levels of divine manifestations.

Kashf al-Maḥjūb: "The Lifting of the Veil", the oldest Persian treatise on Sufism, translated by R.A. Nicholson. Al-Hujwirī (d. c. 467/1075) wrote it as a reply to certain questions put to him and to set forth a complete overview of Sufism.

Khamriyya: "The Wine Ode" by Ibn al-Fāriḍ (d. 632/1235), a very famous ode in which wine is a symbol of divine knowledge.

Khaṭm al-Awliyā': "The Seal of the Saints", by al-Ḥakīm at-Tirmidhī (d. 320/931), in which he developed the terminology which has been used ever since: the *Quṭb,* the *Ghawth* and the hierarchy of four, seven, forty, and three hundred based upon their relative levels of gnosis.

Kitāb al-Luma': "Book of Lights", by Abū Naṣr as-Sarrāj (d. 378/988), one of the earliest Sufi manuals. He sets forth the principles of Sufism and shows how they agree with the Qur'ān and *Sunna.*

Manṭiq aṭ-Ṭayr: "The Conference of the Birds", a classic epic poem written by 'Aṭṭār (d. 638/1230) which tells of a conference attended by all types of birds, who pose a series of questions to their leader, the hoopoe. It is an allegory of the soul's journey to union with Allah.

Mathnāwī: Rūmi's (d. 672/1273) six volume epic didactic poem and undisputed masterpiece on the teachings of Sufism.

al-Mawāqif wa'l-Mukhāṭabāt: "Spiritual Stagings and Addresses", by an-Niffarī (d. 354/965), a description of various stations through which the *sālik* passes, translated by A.J. Arberry.

Miftāḥ al-Falāḥ: "The Key to Success" by Ibn 'Aṭā'llāh al-Iskandarī (d. 709/1309), a work on *dhikr*, its meanings, techniques, and benefits.

al-Munqidh min aḍ-Ḍalāl: "The Deliverer from Error", a book by al-Ghazālī (d. 505/1111), in which he gives a detailed acount of his intellectual and religious struggles which culminated in his becoming a Sufi.

Nafaḥāt al-Uns: by Jāmī (d. 898/1492), an account of the Sufis of the Naqshbandīya of the fifteenth century and a summary of Sufi thought.

Qūt al-Qulūb: "The Nourishment of Hearts in dealing with the Beloved and the Description of the Seeker's Way to the Station of declaring Oneness", a famous early work on Sufism by Abū Ṭālib al-Makkī (d. 386/998-9). In its style and arrangement, it is a precursor to al-Ghazālī's *Iḥyā' 'Ulūm ad-Dīn.*

Risāla: "The Treatise", by al-Qushayrī (d. 465/1074), basically a collection of sayings, anecdotes and definitions presented in a somewhat formal method. It is one of the early complete manuals of the science of Sufism.

aṣ-Ṣalāt al-Mashīshīya: the poem in praise of the Prophet composed by Ibn Mashīsh (d. c. 625/1228) which is frequently recited.

Ta'arruf: "Defining the School of the People of Self-purification", a book by al-Kalābādhī (d. 390/1000), translated as *Doctrine of the Sufis.* This book played a great role in winning recognition of Sufism within Islam. In this sense, he was a precursor of al-Ghazalī.

Ṭabaqāt aṣ-Ṣūfiyya: "Biographies of the Sufis", 'Abdu'r-Raḥmān as-Sulamī's (d. 412/1021) biographical account of the Sufis.

Tadhkirat al-Awliyā': "Memorial of the Saints", by 'Aṭṭār (d. 638/1230), a collection of the biographies of the saints.

Tarjumān al-Ashwāq: "Translator of Yearnings", a collection of poetry by Ibn al-'Arabī (d. 638/1240).

Some Famous Sufis

'Abdullāh ibn al-Mubarāk: one of the scholars and Imāms. His mother was from Khwarizm and his father was Turkish. He was from Marw and was born in 118/736. He was a man with knowledge of *ḥadīth, fiqh*, literature, grammar, language, and poetry. He was eloquent, ascetic, and scrupulous. He spent the night in prayer and worship, and went on *ḥajj* and military expeditions. He wrote many books and was the first to produce a book on *jihād*. He died in Hit, Iraq, in 181/797 after a battle with the Byzantines.

'Abdu'l-Ghanī ibn Ismā'il an-Nabūlisī: born in Damascus in 1050/1641. A prolific Ḥanafi Imam, *muftī*, poet, Sufi and author of nearly 500 books, especially *Idāḥ al-Maqṣūd min Waḥdat al-Wujūd* (explaining what the Sufis mean by *'waḥdat al-wujūd'* (the oneness of being)). He wrote commentaries on Ibn al-'Arabī and Ibn al-Fāriḍ. He died in 1143/1733.

'Abdu'l-Karīm al-Jīlī: ibn Ibrāhim, the Sufi *Quṭb* of Jilan, (b. 767/1365-6). A great grandson of 'Abdu'l-Qādir al-Jilānī. He was a Sufi, gnostic and scholar who wrote many books, especially *al-Insān al-Kāmil* ("The Universal Man"). He followed the teachings of Ibn al-'Arabī. He died in about 811-20/1408-17.

'Abdu'l-Qādir al-Jilānī: Muḥyi'd-dīn Abū Muḥammad, preacher and Sufi, the founder of the Qādirīya, known as the spiritual pole of his time, *al-Ghawth al-A'ẓam*. He was born in 470/1077-8 in the city of Jilan, in the northwestern province of Persia, and died in 561/1166. At the age of eighteen he went to Baghdad to study the various sciences, including Ḥanbalī and Shāfi'ī *fiqh*. He turned to Sufism through Shaykh al-Mubārak Sa'īd, the shaykh of most of the Sufis of Baghdad. He received the *ijāza* and leadership of the *ṭarīqa* at the age of fifty. His most famous books are: *al-Ghunya li Ṭālibi Ṭarīq al-Ḥaqq* (a summary of the Ḥanbalī school); *al-Fatḥ ar-Rabbānī*; and *Futūḥ al-Ghayb*. He had a *ribāṭ* outside the Ḥalba gate in Baghdad where he taught.

‘Abdu’l-Wāḥid ibn Zayd: mystic, who died in 177/793-4. He knew al-Ḥasan al-Baṣrī and others. He spent forty years praying *Ṣubḥ* with the *wuḍū’* of *‘Ishā’*. He was much attached to solitude. He was partially paralysed, an affliction which left him when he prayed.

Abū ‘Alī ad-Daqqāq: the Imām of the Sufis of his time and the shaykh of Abū’l-Qāsim al-Qushayrī. Originally from Nishapur, he studied there, after which he travelled to Marw, where he studied Shāfi‘ī *fiqh*. He died in 405/1014.

Abū Madyan: Shu‘ayb ibn al-Ḥusayn al-Anṣārī, (520/1126 - 594/1198), an Andalusian who later taught in Bougie. He was born near Seville and is buried in the village of al-‘Ubbad, outside Tlemcen. He was the *Quṭb, al-Ghawth*, of his time. He met ‘Abdu’l-Qādir al-Jilānī while on *ḥajj*. He is credited with the introduction of the Qādirīya into the Maghrib. He is known as Sidi Boumedienne in Algeria.

Abū Sa‘īd al-Kharrāz: Aḥmad ibn ‘Īsā, a Sufi and author of *Kitāb aṣ-Ṣidq*, (d. c. 286/899). Al-Hujwirī says that he was the first to explain the doctrine of *fanā’* (annihilation) and *baqā’* (going on). He was also known for his emphasis on *‘ishq* (passionate love of Allah) and his scrupulous observance of the *Sharī‘a.*

Abū Ṭālib al-Makkī: Abū Muḥammad ibn Alī, Shaykh of the Sufis and people of the *Sunna*. He was born in Iraq between Baghdad and Wāsiṭ. He was a Sufi, Mālikī *faqīh* and scholar. He wrote the *Qūt al-Qulūb*. He died in Baghdad in 386/998-9. He was the leader of the Sālimīya in Basra.

Aḥmad al-Badawī: a famous Sufi, said to be descended from ‘Alī, the fourth khalif. He was born in Fez in the Zuqaq al-Hajar in 596/1199-1200, the youngest of eight children. He went to Makka with his family while still a child. He knew the seven *qirā’āt*. He went to Tanta (Tandita) in Egypt and became very ascetic. The founder of the Aḥmadīya or Badawīya *ṭarīqa*, he died in 675/1276.

Aḥmad Bamba: (1266/1850 – 1345/1927) His actual name was Muḥammad ibn Muḥammad ibn Ḥabībullāh, the son of a Wolof shaykh. Born in M’Backe, Senegal, he was the founder of the Murīdīya *ṭarīqa* in Senegal, a sub-group of the Qādiriyya. Although he was a *zāhid*, he was persecuted by the French as a possible threat because of his popularity. He founded the village of Touba in Baol for his followers, where they cultivated peanuts. In 1895, he was exiled to Gabon for seven years. He was exiled a second time to Mauritania where he remained until 1325/1907.

al-'Alawī: Shaykh Abū'l-'Abbās Aḥmad ibn Muṣṭafā ibn 'Aliwa, born in Mostaghanem, Algeria in 1291/1874, he was also known as Ibn 'Aliwa. He was a cobbler in his youth. He was a Sufi, Mālikī scholar, poet and renewer of the Shādhilīya *ṭarīqa*, founding the 'Alawī-Darqāwī *ṭarīqa*. His shaykh was al-Buzīdī, a Darqāwī shaykh. Although he could neither read nor write, he dictated several remarkable and complex works, including his commentary on *al-Murshid al-Ma'īn* of Ibn al-'Ashīr, and his *Dīwān* which is still widely sung today. He died in 1353/1934. Many think he was a *mujaddid* or renewer.

al-Anṣārī: Abū Ismā'īl 'Abdullāh, (396/1006 – 482/1089), a Sufi scholar and *mutakallim*. He was first a Shāfi'ī and then a Ḥanbalī. In Persian, he is called Pīr-i-Anṣār. He was born near Herat. He wrote *Munājāt*, *Ṭabaqāt aṣ-Ṣufiyya*, *Manāzil as-Sā'irin*, and other books. He wrote in Persian in rhyming prose interspersed with verses.

'Aṭṭār, Farīd ad-Dīn: (d. 638/1230), Persian Sufi, author of *Tadhkirat al-Awliyā'* and *Conference of the Birds*. He was a born storyteller. He died in Nishapur, possibly killed in the Mongol invasion.

Bishr ibn al-Ḥārith: Abū Naṣr ibn al-Ḥārith al-Ḥāfī, born near Marw in about 150/767 and converted from a life of dissipation. He studied *ḥadīth* in Baghdad and then became a mendicant, dying in Baghdad in 227/841. He was much admired by Aḥmad ibn Ḥanbal.

al-Bisṭāmī: Abū Yazīd Ṭayfūr ibn 'Īsā, known as Bayazid al-Bisṭāmī. He was a famous Sufi who was born in Bistam in 188/804. His grandfather was a Zoroastrian. Bayazid made a detailed study of the *Sharī'a* and practiced self-denial (*zuhd*). Throughout his life he was assiduous in the practice of his religious obligations and in observing voluntary worship. Many Muslim scholars both in his time and after his time, said that Bayazid al-Bisṭāmī was the first to spread the reality of annihilation (*fanā'*). He is famous for his ecstatic expressions. He died in in 260/874 at the age of 71, either in Damascus or Bistam, Persia.

al-Būṣīrī: a Berber born in Cairo, (610/1213 – 695/1296). He was a disciple of ash-Shādhilī and al-Mursī. He was suffering from paralysis when he dreamt that the Prophet put his mantle on him and he awoke cured and wrote *al-Burda,* the famous poem in praise of the Prophet.

Chistī: Mu'īn ad-din Muḥammad, founder of the Sufi order, the Chistīya. He was from Sistan and was born in 537/1142 and lived in various towns. After going on *ḥajj* and during his *ziyāra* at Madina, he was asked to establish Islam in India. After a forty day *khalwa* next to al-Hujwirī's tomb in Lahore, he went to Delhi in 589/1193 and then directly to Ajmīr where he died in 632/1236. Also known as *Gharīb Nawāz,* "the friend of the poor", some historical accounts state that forty thousand families accepted Islam at his hand.

ad-Daqqāq: See *Abū 'Alī ad-Daqqāq.*

ad-Dardīr: Abū'l-Barakāt Aḥmad b. Muḥammad al-'Adawī al-Mālikī, who died in 1201/1786-7. He wrote *ash-Sharḥ as-Saghīr 'alā Aqrab al-Masālik.*

ad-Darqāwī: Mulay al-'Arabī, (1150/1737 – 1239/1823), the nineteenth century *mujaddid* or renewer of Sufism in the Maghrib. He was considered to be the *Quṭb*. He was the founder of the Darqāwī branch of the Shādhilīya. His *Letters* to his disciples contain rules of conduct, instructions and core teachings of the *ṭarīqa*, elucidating and simplifying the teachings of his shaykh, Sīdī 'Alī al-Jamal (d. 1193-4/1779-80).

Dasūqī: See *ad-Dusūqī.*

Dhū'n-Nūn al-Misrī: the ascetic and gnostic of Allah, Abū'l-Fayd Thawbān ibn Ibrāhīm, a man of knowledge and virtue. Of Nubian origin, he was born at Akhmin in Upper Egypt, in about 180/796, studied under several teachers and travelled extensively through Arabia and Syria. In 214/829 Al-Mutawakkil accused him of *zandaqa* but having listened to him, released him. He is said to be the first to have given a systematic explanation of the states (*aḥwāl*) and stations (*maqāmāt*) on the spiritual path. He died in Giza in 245/859.

ad-Dusūqī: Shams ad-dīn Muḥammad b. Aḥmad al-Mālikī, (d. 1230/1815). He wrote a gloss (*ḥāshiya*) on Aḥmad ad-Dardīr's work.

Fuḍayl ibn 'Iyād: Abū 'Alī aṭ-Ṭalaqānī, born in Khorasan. He was a highwayman at the beginning of his life. Then he repented and went to Makka and then to Kufa where he resided for many years, dying in 187/803. He had a reputation as an authority in *ḥadīth* which he studied under Sufyān ath-Thawrī and Abū Ḥanīfa and was bold in preaching before Hārūn ar-Rashīd. He likened this world to a madhouse.

al-Ghazālī: (also written al-Ghazzālī) Muḥammad ibn Muḥammad, Abū Ḥamid aṭ-Ṭūsī, the Shāfi'ī Imam and Sufi born in Tabiran, near Ṭūs in 450/1058. He studied *fiqh* with al-Juwaynī. He taught at the Niẓāmiyya Madrasa before he became a Sufi, pointing out that all religious certainty was a result of spiritual experience. He is nicknamed "Shāfi'ī the Second". He died in Tabiran in 505/1111. He was the author of many books, especially *Iḥyā' 'Ulūm ad-Dīn.*

Ḥabīb ibn Muḥammad al-'Ajamī: al-Basrī, a Persian settled in Basra, a *muḥaddith* who transmitted from Ḥasan al-Basrī, Ibn Sīrīn and others. He converted from a life of ease and self-indulgence to a life of self-denial.

Ḥāfiẓ: (c. 720/1320 – 793/1391), Ḥāfiẓ was the poetic *nom-de-plume* of Shams ad-dīn Muḥammad. He was born in Shiraz, Persia. As a theologian he preached tolerance, and as a poet he produced over 700 poems collected in his *Divan*. Ḥāfiẓ's poems are considered the supreme example of the Persian *ghazal*.

al-Ḥakīm at-Tirmidhī: Abū 'Abdullāh Muḥammad ibn 'Alī, originally from Tirmidh, a Sufi and Shāfi'ī scholar. He was exiled from Tirmidh on account of a book he wrote and went to Balkh (now Wazirabad) where he was welcomed. He died there at the age of 90 in around 320/931. His major work was the *Kitāb Khatm al-Awliyā'*. He discusses things like the light of Muḥammad, the Reality of Ādam, the symbolism of the Arabic letters and angels.

al-Ḥallāj: Ḥusayn ibn Manṣūr, Abū'l-Mughīth, born in about 244/858 near al-Bayda' in Fars, but raised in Wasit in Iraq. He left a *Dīwān* and the *Ṭawāsin*. He was executed in Baghdad in 309/922 because his ecstatic outbursts led people to believe that he was a heretic.

al-Ḥārith ibn Asad al-Muḥāsibī: born in 165/781. He was called al-Muḥāsibī because he frequently called himself to account (*muḥāsaba*) and because of his asceticism. He was an excellent scholar, held in high esteem among the people of his time in both outward and inward knowledge, and wrote many books. His father died leaving him a great deal of wealth, but he refused to take any of it because his father had been a Qadarī. He died in 243/857.

al-Ḥasan al-Baṣrī: Abū Sa'īd ibn Abū'l-Ḥasan, one of the most eminent of the *Tābi'ūn* in asceticism and knowledge. He was born in Madina in 21/642, the son of a slave captured in Maysan who became a *mawlā* of the Prophet's secretary, Zayd ibn Thābit. He was brought up in Baṣra. He went for thirty years without laughing. He met many Companions and transmitted many *ḥadīths*. His mother served Umm Salama, the wife of the Prophet. He died in Basra in 110/728 when he was 88.

al-Hujwirī: Abū'l-Ḥasan 'Alī ibn 'Uthmān al-Jullābī, the Sufi, (d. c. 467/1075). Known also as *Data Ganj Bakhsh* ("the Bestower of Treasures"), he was author of *Kashf al-Maḥjūb,* the first Persian treatise on Sufism. He was a native of Ghazna, Afghanistan. He travelled extensively but little of his life is known. He ended his days in Lahore where he is buried.

Ibn 'Abbād ar-Rundī: a famous Shādhilī Sufi, one of al-Maqqārī's disciples, he wrote a commentary on the *Ḥikam* of Ibn 'Aṭā'llāh which made it widely known throughout the western Muslim lands. He was born in Ronda in 734/1332, studied in Tlemcen and Fez and eventually became Imām of the Qarāwiyīn *madrasa* in Fes. He died in 793/1390.

Ibn Abī Dunyā: a Sufi in Baghdad, (d. 281/894). He had a book entitled *Dhamm ad-Dunyā* ("Censuring this world").

Ibn 'Ajība: Aḥmad ibn Muḥammad, born in Morocco in 1160/1747, a Mālikī scholar, Sufi and *mufassir* (*al-Baḥr al-Madīd*), one of the Shādhilīya *ṭarīqa*, which he took from ad-Darqāwī by way of Muḥammad Buzaydī. He wrote seventeen commentaries on the *Ḥikam*. He died in 'Anjara, Morocco in 1224/1809.

Ibn al-'Arabī: Muḥammad ibn 'Alī, Abū Bakr al-Hātimī aṭ-Ṭā'i, born in Murcia in 560/1165, a *mujtahid*, scholar and Sufi. He is known as Muḥyiddīn (the Reviver of the *Dīn*) and the Shaykh al-Akbar (the Greatest Master). He died in Damascus in 638/1240 with a copy of *Iḥyā' 'Ulūm ad-Dīn* on his lap. He wrote over 350 works including the *Futūḥāt al-Makkiyya* and the *Fuṣūṣ al-Ḥikam*.

Ibn al-'Arīf: the author of *Maḥāsin al-Majālis* ("The Attractions of Mystical Sessions"), his full name was Abū'l-'Abbās Aḥmad ibn

Muḥammad. He lived in Almeria, Spain. In this period, under the Murābiṭūn, Almeria was the centre of Sufism for the Spanish Sufis. He founded a *ṭarīqa* and 130 towns recognised him as *Imām*. He was arrested by the jealous *qāḍī* of the city and sent in chains to the Amīr in Marrakesh who promptly set him free. He died a few days later, in 536/1141. He was the first to interpret the *Iḥyā' 'Ulūm ad-Dīn* of al-Ghazālī in the West.

Ibn 'Aṭā': Abū'l-'Abbās Aḥmad ibn Muḥammad ibn Sahl ibn 'Ata' al-Adamī, a Sufi and companion of Junayd, author of poetry. He was put to death in 309/922.

Ibn 'Aṭā'llāh: Aḥmad ibn Muḥammad, Tāju'd-Dīn, Abū Faḍl al-Iskandarī, the Sufi Imām and author of the *Ḥikam*, *Laṭā'if al-Minan*, *Miftāḥ al-Falāḥ*, and other works, thereby providing the Shādhiliyya with their core literature. His shaykh was Abū'l-'Abbās al-Mursī, whose shaykh was ash-Shādhili. From Alexandria, he moved to Cairo where he died in 709/1309 around the age of sixty. He also taught in the al-Azhar and the Manṣūriya Madrasa. There was a famous debate between him and Ibn Taymiyya in 707/1307, in which Ibn 'Aṭā'llāh defended Ibn al-'Arabī.

Ibn Daqīq al-'Īd: Taqīyyuddīn Muḥammad ibn 'Alī, born in Yanbu', a Shāfi'ī, *mujtahid*, made qāḍī in Cairo in 695. He has poems in praise of Madina. He was born in 625/1228 and died in 702/1302.

Ibn al-Fāriḍ: 'Umar ibn 'Alī, the Sufi poet, born in Cairo in 577/1182 and lived in the Muqattam in Cairo. He died in 632/1235. He is known as the "Sultan of the Lovers" and his collection of poems is very famous because of the high quality of the poetry.

Ibn Khafīf: Abū 'Abdullāh Muḥammad ibn Khafīf ibn Isfikshar ash-Shirazi, born in 276/890. The son of a prince, he became an ascetic Sufi. He was also a Shāfi'ī scholar. He went on *ḥajj* at least six times. He died in Shiraz in 371/982 at the age of 95.

Ibn Mashīsh: 'Abdu's-Salām, the master of Abū'l-Ḥasan ash-Shādhilī, (d. c. 625/1228). He was a Berber and the *Quṭb* of his age. He was a recluse who lived on the Jabal 'Alam, a mountain in Morocco. All he left was the *Ṣalāt al-Mashīshīya*.

Ibn al-Mubārak: See *'Abdullah ibn al-Mubārak*.

Ibn al-Qasiy: Abū'l-Qāsim, disciple of Ibn al-'Arīf, a Sufi who organised a religious militia in the Algarve (southern Portugal) based in

Silves and led an uprising against the ruling class and *fuqahā'* in the Algarve in 536/1141. He had military successes against both the Murābiṭūn and the Muwaḥḥidūn and ruled the region for ten years. He wrote *Khal' an-Na'layn*. He was killed in 546/1151.

Ibn Sālim: 'Alī al-Basrī, (d. 297/909-10), a disciple of Sahl at-Tustarī, founder of the Sālimīya and the main teacher of Abū Ṭālib al-Makkī.

Ibrāhīm ibn Adham: Abū Isḥāq at-Tamīmī al-Balkhī, an early Sufi *zāhid* and saint. Born into a wealthy family of Balkh, he gave it all up to seek knowledge through travel, taking on all sorts of menial jobs and fighting in the *jihād* against the Byzantines. While he was in Massisa, a slave brought the news of the death of his father, who had left him a fortune. He was carrying 10,000 dirhams. Ibrāhīm freed him and gave him the dirhams, saying that he had no need of the rest. He fasted all the time. He attended the gatherings of Sufyān ath-Thawrī. He died in 161/778, probably at Sufnan on the Byzantine frontier.

Ibrāhīm al-Khawwās: ibn Aḥmad, (d. 290/903), a Sufi author who taught al-Khuldī. He lived mostly at Rayy although he studied extensively.

Jāmī: Nūr'd-dīn Abdu'r-Raḥmān, (d. 898/1492). He wrote *Nafaḥāt al-Uns* and and *Lawā'iḥ* ("Flashes").

al-Jazūlī: (d. 870/1465). He studied *fiqh* in Fes and went on *ḥajj*, returned to the Sousse and joined the Shādhilīya. He was a *sharif.* He pursued the classical model of *jihād* in which he led the attack against the Portuguese who had subjected the coastal peoples to tribute. His tomb is in Marrakesh. He wrote the *Dalā'il al-Khayrāt.*

al-Jilānī: See *'Abdu'l-Qadir al-Jilānī.*

al-Jīlī: See *'Abdu'l-Karīm al-Jīlī.*

al-Jullābī: See *al-Hujwirī.*

al-Junayd: Abū'l-Qāsim ibn Muḥammad, the shaykh of his time. His family originated from Nihawand and he grew up in Iraq. His *fiqh* was taken from Abū Thawr and Sufyān ath-Thawrī. He took his *ṭarīqa* from as-Sarī as-Saqaṭī, his uncle, and al-Muḥasibī. He died in 297/910. He was one of the Shāfi'ī *fuqahā'* and is buried in Baghdad. He defined Sufism as "isolating the out-of-time (the eternal without beginning or end) from what originates in time", or as *dhawq*.

al-Kalābādhī: Abū Bakr Muḥammad ibn Isḥāq, an authority on early Sufism who died in Bukhara, probably in 390/1000. He is listed as a Ḥanafi *faqīh*. Kalābādh was a district of Bukhara. He wrote *Kitāb at-Ta'arruf* and *Baḥr al-Fawā'id*.

al-Kharrāz: Abū Sa'īd Aḥmad ibn 'Īsā of Baghdad, a cobbler by trade. He met Dhū'n-Nūn al-Miṣrī and associated with Bishr al-Ḥāfī and Sarī as-Saqaṭī. He was the author of several books, and died between 279/892 and 286/899.

Mā' al-'Aynayn al-Qalqamī: Muḥammad Muṣṭafa ibn Muḥammad, Abū'l-Anwār, born near Walata in the Hawd of southeastern Mauritania in 1247/1831. Of Mauritanian and Moroccan descent, he was a Sufi Shaykh of the Qādirī *ṭarīqa*. He was a prolific writer, a well-digger and founder of *zāwiyas*. He built a *zāwiya* at Smara (in the Saqiyat al-Ḥamrā') which had a reputation for Qur'ānic studies and its large library. It was destroyed by the French. He participated in armed resistance against the French during which he lost several sons. He died in Tiznit in southern Morocco in 1328/1910.

al-Maghīlī: Abū 'Abdullāh, Muḥammad ibn 'Abdu'l-Karīm at-Tilimsāni, a Berber Mālikī *faqīh*, (d. 909/1504), involved in the spread of the Qādiriyya in the western Sahara at the end of the fifteenth century and a key figure in the infusion of Islam among the Tuaregs. He joined the Qādirīya in Cairo through as-Suyūṭī. He lived in Tuwat and went to Gao, to the court of Muḥammad Askia and thence to other Muslim areas. He taught in Tagedda, Air, Gao and Hausaland.

al-Makkī: See *Abū Ṭālib al-Makkī.*

Mālik ibn Dīnār: Abū Yaḥya an-Nājī al-Baṣrī, a Persian *mawlā*, the son of a Persian slave from Sijistan or Kabul, a weeper at Baṣra. He was an early Sufi and one of disciples of Ḥasan al-Baṣrī. He was known for piety, self-mortification, *tawakkul* and learning Isra'ilite stories. He was a reliable *muḥaddith* and calligrapher of the Qur'ān. He never ate anything he had not purchased from payment for making copies of the Qur'ān. He died in Baṣra in 131/748.

Ma'rūf al-Karkhī: Abū Maḥfūẓ ibn Fīrūz, a famous Sufi of the Baghdad school. Karkh Bājadda is a town in eastern Iraq. His parents were either Christians or Sabi'ians. He had a great influence on as-Sarī as-Saqaṭī, whose shaykh he was, and taught *ḥadīth* to Ibn Ḥanbal. His tomb is in Baghdad. He died in 200/815-6 or 204/819/20).

al-Muḥāsabī: See *al-Ḥarith ibn Asad al-Muḥāsabī.*

Muzaffer: Shaykh Muzaffer was born in Istanbul in 1334/1916. His father, Ḥajji Mehmed Effendi of Konya, a scholar and teacher at the court of Sultan 'Abdal-Hamid II, died when he was only six. Thereafter he was looked after by Shaykh Seyyid Samiyyi Saruhani, the leader of the Qādirī, Naqshbandī, Ushakī and Halvetiyye *ṭarīqas* at the time. After learning from several shaykhs, he became the leader of the Halvetiyye-Jerrahī *ṭarīqa.* Despite the attempts of Ataturk and his successors to destroy the Sufis and Islam in Turkey, Shaykh Muzaffer continued to teach until his death in 1406/1986.

an-Nabūlisī: See *'Abdu'l-Ghanī ibn Ismā'īl an-Nabūlisī.*

Naqshband: Muḥammad ibn Muḥammad Bahā' ad-Dīn al-Bukharī, (717/1317 – 791/1389). Born in a village some distance from Bukhara.

an-Nawawī: Yaḥya ibn Sharaf, Abū Zakariyyā, born in the village of Nawa on the Horan Plain of southern Syria in 631/1233. Imam of the later Shāfi'ites. He wrote many books, including *Minhāj aṭ-Ṭālibīn, Kitāb al-Adhkār, Riyāḍ aṣ-Ṣāliḥīn.* He lived very simply. After twenty-seven years in Damascus, he returned home and died at the age of 44 in 676/1277.

an-Niffarī: Muḥammad ibn 'Abdu'l-Jabbār, an Iraqi Sufi of the 4th/10th century. Very little is known about his life. He died probably in 354/965. He wrote *al-Mawāqif wa'l-Mukhāṭabāt.*

Niẓāmī: Abū Yūsuf Muḥammad Niẓām ad-dīn (535/1141 – 598/1202), a Persian poet and mystic, born in Ganja (Kirovābād), who wrote *Laylā and Majnūn*, which is part of a collection called the *Khamsa.*

Niẓāmu'd-Dīn Awliyā': one of the greatest Chistī Sufi masters of mediaeval India, born in Bada'un in 636/1238. After studying to become a *qāḍī*, he became the *murīd* and eventually the successor of Farīdu'd-Dīn Gangi Shakar. Among his close followers was Amīr Khusrau, the famous poet who developed and perfected the art of *qawwālī*, and who immediately died on the spot when he learned that his shaykh had died, in 725/1325. They are buried not far apart in Delhi, India.

Nūrbaksh, Muḥammad: (795/1393 – 869/1465), a Sufi in Persia who was called Nūrbaksh (gift of Allah) by his shaykh. He declared himself the Maḥdī and Khalif and tried to seize power. The *ṭarīqa* descending from him became Shi'ite.

an-Nūrī: Abū'l-Ḥusayn Aḥmad ibn Muḥammad, a native of Baghdad of a Khorasani family, a pupil of Sarī as-Saqaṭī and companion of al-Junayd. He wrote some fine poetry and died in 295/908.

al-Qushayrī: Abū'l-Qāsim 'Abdu'l-Karīm ibn Hawāzin, the shaykh of Khurasan in his time in asceticism and knowledge of the *dīn*. He was born in 376/986. He was based at Nishapur and died there in 465/1074. He has various books, the most famous of which are the *Risāla al-Qushayrīya* about *taṣawwuf* and the biographies of the Sufis, and the *Laṭā'if al-Ishārāt* on *tafsīr*. In *kalām* he was the student of the Ash'arite, Abū Bakr ibn Fūrak, and in Sufism the follower of as-Sulamī, and Abū 'Alī ad-Daqqāq whose daughter Fāṭima he married. He battled the Mu'tazilites in Nishapur until he had to flee to Makka to protect his life.

Rābi'a bint Ismā'īl al-'Adawiyya: sold into slavery as a child after the death of her parents, she later settled in Baṣra where she became famous as a saint and preacher. She was born in 95/713-14 and died either in 135/752 or in 185/801. She is the most famous woman Sufi. She emphasized the importance of selfless love and devotion to Allah. She was a contemporary of al-Ḥasan al-Baṣrī.

ar-Rifā'ī: Abū'l-'Abbās Aḥmad ibn 'Alī, the founder of the Rifā'ī *ṭarīqa*. He grew up in the area around Basra and eventually established his *zāwīya* in Umm 'Abīda. He died in 578/1182.

ar-Rūmī: Jalāl ad-Dīn Muḥammad ibn Muḥammad ibn Muḥammad ibn Ḥusayn, the founder of the Mevlevī Sufi order. He was born in Balkh (Afghanistan) in 604/1207-08 to a family of learned theologians. Escaping the Mongol invasion, he and his family travelled extensively in the Muslim lands, performed the pilgrimage to Makka and finally settled in Konya, Anatolia (Turkey), where he succeeded his father in 629/1231 as professor in religious sciences. He was introduced into the mystical path by a wandering dervish, Shamsuddīn of Tabrīz. His love for and his bereavement at the death of Shams found their expression in a surge of music, dance and lyric poems, *Divani Shamsi Tabrīzī*. Rūmī is the author of a huge didactic work, *The Mathnāwi*, and his discourses, *Fīhi ma Fīhi*, written to introduce his disciples to metaphysics. Rūmī died on December 17, 672/1273. Men of five faiths followed his bier. He was a truly universal man.

Sa'dī: Muṣlaḥ ad-Dīn, a famous poet from Shiraz, Persia (580/1184 – 692/1292), his shaykh was Shihāb ad-Dīn as-Suhrawardī. He studied at the Niẓāmīya of Baghdad and travelled widely in the Muslim world before returning to Shiraz when over seventy. His major works are the *Bustān*, the *Gūlistān* ("Rose Garden"), and his *Dīwān*.

Sahl ibn 'Abdullāh: ibn Yūnus at-Tustarī, famous man of right action, unique in knowledge and scrupulousness. He was from Shushtar and was born at Tustar (Ahwaz) in 200/815. A Sufi shaykh and ascetic, he also wrote a short *tafsīr*. He had famous miracles (*karāmāt*) and kept the company of Dhū'n-Nūn al-Miṣrī in Makka. He had to seek refuge in Basra, where he died in 282/896. His pupil Ibn Sālim founded the Sālimīya.

Ṣanā'ī: Abū'l-Majd Majdūd ibn Ādam, born at Ghazna. He was a Sufi poet. Several dates have been given for his death, which was in about 545/1150. He wrote the first mystical epic, *Ḥadīqatu'l-Ḥaqīqa*, a *Dīwān* and other poetical works.

as-Sanūsī: Muḥammad 'Alī, Abū 'Abdullāh as-Sanūsī al-Khaṭṭābī al-Ḥasani al-Idrīsi, born in Mosteghanem, Algeria in 1202/1789. He was the founder of the Sanūsī *ṭarīqa*, a Mālikī scholar and Sufi whose disciples included Shaykh al-'Arabī ad-Darqāwī and Ahmad Tījanī. He produced more than forty books and travelled a lot. His main centre was near al-Bayda in Libya. He worked for fifteen years to spread Islam south to the African interior. He then went to Makka where he remained until 1269/853, and then returned to establish a new centre at Jaghbub. He died in 1275/1859.

Sarī as-Saqaṭī: Abū'l-Ḥasan ibn Mughallis, said to be a pupil of Ma'rūf al-Karkhī, in the Baghdad circle of Sufis. He was the maternal uncle and teacher of al-Junayd and one of the first to present Sufism in an organised form. A dealer in second-hand goods, he died in 253/867 at the age of 98.

as-Sarrāj: Abū Naṣr 'Abdullāh ibn 'Alī, author of *Kitāb al-Luma'*, a classic Sufi text. He died in 378/988.

ash-Shādhilī: Abū'l-Ḥasan 'Alī ibn 'Abdullāh, (593/1196 – 656/1258). He was from Ceuta and a disciple of 'Abdu's-Salām ibn Mashīsh. He fled from Tunisia and established a following in Egypt, dying near the Red Sea on the way to Makka. His successor was Abū'l-'Abbās al-Mursī (d. 686/1287), the shaykh of Ibn 'Aṭā'llāh (d. 709/1309). He wrote *Ḥizb al-Baḥr*, *Ḥizb al-Barr*, *Ḥizb an-Naṣr,* and other litanies.

Shāh Walī'ullāh: Quṭbu'd-Dīn Aḥmad, the great Muslim reformer of India born in 1114/1702, whose father founded the Raḥīmīya *madrasa* in Delhi. He memorised the Qur'ān by the age of five, learned Persian by the age of ten, and was initiated by his father into the Qādirīya, Chistīya, and Naqshbandīya *ṭarīqas*. He succeeded his father as principal of the Raḥīmīya at the age of seventeen, and taught there throughout his life. He believed that *al-Muwaṭṭā'* of Imām Mālik was the key to re-establishing Islam in India. He died in 1176/1762.

Shāmil Muḥammad ad-Daghestanī: a shaykh who established the Naqshbandī *ṭarīqa* throughout the Caucasus and fought *jihād* against Tsarist Russia for 35 years. His shaykh was Mullā Muḥammad al-Ghāzī al-Kamrawī whose career began when Russia declared protection for the Christians in Khurjistan and then formally annexed the region from Safavid Persia in 1215/1800. He recruited thousands of Naqshbandīs and fought until his death in 1248/1832. His successor al-Amīr Ḥamza al-Khanzajī was martyred the same year, when Shāmil took over. There followed twenty-seven years of *jihād* against the Russians with many pitched battles, freeing Daghestan and seizing their cannon. In 1260/1844 Russia sent a larger army who fought for fifteen years until he was captured in 1276/1859. He was banished to Turkey from where he went to Madina and spent the rest of his life worshipping in the Rawḍa. He was buried in al-Baqī'.

Shamsi Tabrīzī: Shamsuddīn of Tabrīz, the shaykh of Jalāl ad-Dīn Rūmī (d. 672/1273), whose shaykh belonged to the Suhrawardī *ṭarīqa*. The *ṭarīqa* of Shamsi Tabrīzī is also known as the Firdawsī *ṭarīqa*.

Shaqīq al-Balkhī: Abū 'Alī ibn Ibrāhīm al-Azdī, a man of wide learning. He began life as a merchant and turned to *zuhd.* He went on *ḥajj* to Makka, and died in *jihād* in 194/810. He was one of the founders of the Khorasānī school of Sufism and the disciple of Ibrāhīm ibn Adham. He was a scholar in the *Sharī'a* and known for his discourses on the imminence of the Last Day and on *tawakkul* (reliance on Allah).

ash-Sha'rānī: 'Abdu'l-Wahhāb ibn Aḥmad (848/1492 – 973/1565), Egyptian scholar and Sufi who founded a *ṭarīqa.* He was the author of the *Ṭabaqāt al-Kubrā.*

ash-Shiblī: Abū Bakr Dulaf ibn Jahdar, Khorasānī of origin, but born in Baghdad or Samarra in 247/861, the son of a court official. He was a Mālikī *faqīh.* Then he joined the circle of Junayd and became noted for his eccentric behaviour which led to his commital to an asylum. He died in 334/946 at the age of 87. He left his "Sayings" (*Ishārāt*). His tomb is in Baghdad.

Sirhindī: Shaykh Aḥmad al-Farūqī, born in about 972/1564 at Sirhind, Patiala, India), Indian Sufi and theologian who was largely responsible for the reassertion and revival in India of orthodox Sunnite Islam as a reaction against the syncretistic religious tendencies prevalent during the reign of the Mughal emperor Akbar. He died in 1034/1625.

as-Suhrawardī: Abū Ḥafs 'Umar. He became Shaykh of Shaykhs in Baghdad and acted as ambassador for the 'Abbasid khalif to the Ayyubids and Seljuks. He helped with the organisation of the *futuwwa* ideals and an-Nāṣir may have organised the movement. He died in 632/1234.

as-Sulamī: Abū 'Abdu'r-Raḥmān Muḥammad ibn al-Ḥusayn, a shaykh of the Sufis and author of a book on their history, ranks and *tafsīr*, the *Ṭabaqāt aṣ-Sūfīya.* He was born in Nishapur in 325/936 and died in 412/1021.

Sulaymān al-Khawwāṣ: (d. before 170/787), a *zāhid* of Palestine who studied law under al-Awzā'ī and was a companion of Ibrāhīm ibn Adham.

at-Tādilī: Abū Ya'qūb Yūsuf ibn Yaḥyā, known as Ibn az-Zayyāt, born in Tadla (Tadila), Morocco. He spent most of his life in Marrakesh and around it. He died in 628-629/1230-31 while *qāḍī* of Ragraga.

He completed *at-Tashawwuf ilā Rijāl at-Taṣawwuf* in 617/1220. It is one of the earliest and most important sources for the religious history of Morocco.

at-Tījānī: Abū'l-'Abbās Aḥmad ibn Muḥammad, founder of the Tījānīya. He was born in 1150/1737 at 'Ayn Madi, a village 72 km west of Laghuat. He died in 1230/1815 and is buried in Fes, Morocco.

at-Tirmidhī: See *al-Ḥakīm at-Tirmidhī.*

'Uthmān ibn Fūdī: or Usuman dan Fodio or Fodiye, born in Maratta, Northern Nigeria, in 1167/1754. An Islamic scholar and Qādirī Shaykh. He led the Fulani *jihād* in northern Nigeria with his younger brother 'Abdullahi and son Muhammad Bello. He was a *ḥāfiẓ* of Qur'ān, Mālikī *faqīh*, poet, and scholar. He was worried about the trend to syncretism and so made *hijra* from the lands of the Gobir to the north and west. He fought for four years against the Gobir and Habe peoples and died in Sifawa in 1232/1817.

'Uways al-Barawī: Uways ibn Muḥammad, born in Brava on the southern Somali coast in 1263/1847. He studied Shāfi'ī *fiqh*, *tafsīr* and Sufism before going to Baghdad, the centre of the Qādirī *ṭarīqa* to which he belonged. He returned home with *ijāza* and spread Islam in Tanganiyka, southern Somalia and eastern Zaire. He founded agricultural settlements at Bilad al-Amin and Biolay, north of Brava, and was assassinated in 1326/1909 at the age of 63.

Qāḍī Wakī' ibn al-Jarrāḥ: Abū Sha'bān, a firm *ḥāfiẓ* and *ḥadīth* scholar of Iraq in his time. He refused the qāḍīship of Kūfa out of scrupulousness when Hārūn ar-Rashīd wanted to appoint him to it. He was born in 131/748-49 and died in 197/812. He wrote a book entitled *Kitāb az-Zuhd.*

al-Wāsiṭī: Abū Bakr ibn Mūsā, Imām and gnostic of Allah, and one of al-Junayd's companions. He was one of the most esteemed scholars and Sufis. He was from the city of Wāsiṭ. He died in Marw in 320/932.

Zarrūq, Aḥmad: Aḥmad ibn Aḥmad, Abū'l-'Abbās Zarrūq al-Burnusī, born in Fez in 846/1442. A Sufi, Mālikī scholar and *muḥaddith* who studied *fiqh* in Fez, Cairo and Madina and then became a Sufi and withdrew from worldly things and took to wandering. He was a renowned Shaykh of the Shādhilīya *ṭarīqa*. He was considered the al-Ghazālī of his time. He wrote about thirty commentaries on the *Ḥikam* of Ibn ʻAṭā'llāh. He died in Takrin, Libya in 899/1493.

Index of Subjects

barzakh: 60, 205
baṣīra: 66, 205
basmala: 5, 73
basṭ: 205
bāṭil: 116, 143
bāṭin: 73, 182, 205
bāṭinī: 73, 182, 205
Bāṭinīya: 182
ba'th: 5, 60
batūl: 5
bay': 143
bay'a: 5, 205
bayān: 73, 132
al-Bayḍā': 36
Bayram: 5
Baytu'llah: 155
Bayt al-Ḥaram: 5, 155
Bayt al-Hikma: 182
Bayt al-Māl: 36
Al-Bayt al-Ma'mūr: 60
Bayt al-Maqdīs: 36
bayyina: 74, 116
bedug: 6
Bektashī: 229
bey: 36
Beylerbey: 37
bid'a: 37, 182
biḍā'a: 143
bilā kayf: 182
bi'l-ma'rūf: 152
Bilqīs: 82
bint labūn: 117
bint makhad: 117
Binyamīn: 82
birdhawn: 37
birr: 66
bismi'llāh ar-Raḥmān ar-Raḥīm: 28, 74
bī shar': 205
Bi'tha: 37
Bu'āth: 37
budalā': 206
bukhl: 66
bulūgh: 117, 152
Burāq: 37
al-Burda: 6
burhān: 182
Burhānīya: 229
al-Burūj: 74
burūz: 206
busr: 6
Butrīya: 182
Buwayhids: 37
buyū': 143
buyūtāt: 37

Calendar: 6
Camel, Battle of: 37
caravanserai: 144
Chistīya: 229

dabba: 60
ḍābiṭ: 97
ḍabṭ: 97
daf' al-ḥaraj: 132
daff: 6
dahā': 66
ad-Dahr: 182, 206
dahrī: 182
dā'ī: 37
ḍā'īf: 97
Dajjāl: 6, 60
dakka: 6
dalāla: 132
dalālāt: 132
dalīl: 132
ḍamān: 117, 144
ḍamma: 6
dāniq: 26
Dār al-Ḥarb: 37
Dār al-Hijra: 37
dār al-imāra: 37
Dār al-Islām: 37
Dār Nidwa: 37
dār ar-rizq: 37
dār aṣ-ṣinā'a: 37
Dār aṣ-Ṣulh: 37
ḍarā'ib: 144
darak: 144
ḍarar: 117
Darqāwa: 229

jumla: 135
Jumu‘a: 11
jund: 12
junub: 121
juz’: 75, 99
juzāf: 146

Ka‘ba: 157
kabīra: 187
kafā’a: 121
kafāla: 146
kafan: 121
kaffāra: 122
kāfir: 12
kafīl: 146
kāhin: 41
kalāla: 135
kalām: 187
kalām Allāh: 75
kalīma: 12
kalimatu’llāh: 84
kalīmu’llah: 84
kamāl: 213
kanz: 122
kapudanpasha: 41
karāha: 122
karam: 68
karāmāt: 213
karrama’llāhu wajhahu: 29
karrūbiyūn: 62
ka’s: 213
kasb: 187
kashf: 213
kasra: 12
al-Kathīb: 62, 214
kātib: 41
kātibūn: 62
kathīf: 214
katm: 12
kawn: 187, 214
Kawthar: 62, 84
kayfīya: 187
Kaysāniyya: 187
khabar: 99, 135
al-Khāḍir: 12
khafī: 75, 135
khāl: 153
khāla: 153
khalif: 12
khalīfa: 12, 214
Khalīl: 84
khalq: 214
khalq al-Qur’ān: 187
khalūq: 12
khalwa: 214
Khalwatīya: 230
khamīṣa: 12
khamr: 214
khānqāh: 214
al-Khandaq: 41
kharāj: 146
Khārijites: 41, 187
kharq al-‘adāt: 214
khaṣla: 187
khasya: 214
khāṣṣ: 76, 135
khāṣṣa: 121, 214
khaṭī’a: 187
khaṭīb: 12
khātim: 214
khaṭima: 188
khāṭir: 214
khatm: 76, 214
Khawārij: 41, 188
khawf: 214
khayāl: 214
Khaybar: 42
Khayf: 157
khāzin: 12
Khazraj: 42
khazzān: 146
khedive: 42
khidhlān: 214
khidma: 214
al-Khiḍr: 12, 214
khil‘a: 12
khilāfa: 12
khimār: 12
khirqa: 215
khitān: 122

marfū‘: 100
māristān: 14
marthiya: 14
ma‘rūf: 14, 100, 152
Mārūt: 61, 82
Marwa: 157
Marwānids: 43
Maryam: 84
marzpān: 43
mas‘a: 157
ma‘s-salāma: 29
mas’ala: 123
maṣāliḥ mursala: 136
masḥ: 123
māshā’llāh: 29
mash‘ar: 157
Mash‘ar al-Ḥaram: 157
mashāyikh: 14
mashhad: 14
mashhūr: 100, 136
mashī’a: 189
mashruba: 14
mashshā’ī: 189
mashūra: 14
al-Masīḥ: 63, 84
al-Masīḥ ad-Dajjāl: 14, 63
masīḥī: 14
masjid: 14
Masjid-al-Aqṣā: 14
Masjid al-Ḥaram: 157
Masjid al-Jamā‘a: 14
Masjid an-Nabawī: 157
Masjid al-Qiblatayn: 157
Masjid at-Taqwā: 158
maskūt ‘anhu: 136
maṣlaḥa: 137
masnūn: 15, 123
ma‘ṣūm: 15
mathal: 76
Mathānī: 76
matn: 100
ma‘trūh: 153
matrūh: 100
matrūk: 100
Māturīdite: 43, 181, 189, 194
ma’ūda: 15
mawadda: 216
mawālī: 123
mawāni‘: 43, 100, 153
mawāqit: 158
mawārith: 153
mawāt: 123
mawāzīn: 63
mawḍū‘: 100
maw‘iẓa: 15
mawjūdāt: 189
mawlā: 43, 123
mawlānā: 29
Mawlawīya: 230
mawlid: 15
mawqif: 63,158
mawqūf: 100
mawsim: 216
mawt: 15
mawṭin: 216
maysir: 15
mayyit: 123
maẓālim: 123
Mevlevīya: 230
Miḥna: 43, 189
miḥrāb: 15
Mihrajān: 15
Mijanna: 158
Mikā’īl: 63, 84
mikhṣara: 15
milk tāmm: 147
milla: 43
millat Ibrāhīm: 189
Mina: 158
minbar: 15
minhāj: 189
mīqāt: 158
mīr: 15
Mi‘rāj: 15
mīrāth: 153
mirbaḍ: 15
misbaḥa: 216
miskīn: 15
miṣr 43
al-Miṣrān: 43

Index of People and Books